C++ For Dummies
6th Edition

KV-192-910

Expressions

Expressions have both a value and a type. Expressions take one of the following forms:

```
objName                     // for a simple object
operator expression         // for unary operators
expr1 operator expr2        // for binary operators
expr1 ? expr2 : expr3       // for the ternary operator
funcName([argument list]);  // for function calls
```

Declarations

Declarations use both intrinsic and user-defined types. The intrinsic types are

```
[<signed | unsigned >]char
[<signed | unsigned >]wchar_t
[<signed | unsigned>] [<short | long | long long>] int
float
[long] double
bool
```

Declarations have one of the following forms:

```
[<extern|static>][const] type var[=expression]; // variable
[<extern|static>][const] type array[size][={list}]; // array
[const] type object[(argument list)];           // object
[const] type object [= {argument list}];        // alternative
[const] type * [const] ptr[=pointer expression];// pointer
type& refName = object;                          // reference
type fnName([argument list]);                    // function
```

A function definition has the following format:

```
// simple function
[<inline|constexpr>] type fnName(argument list) {...}
// member function defined outside of class
[inline] type Class::func(argument list) [const] {...}
// constructor/destructors may also be defined outside of class
Class::Class([argument list]) {...}
Class::~Class() {...}
// constructors/destructor may be deleted or defaulted
// in lieu of definition
Class::Class([argument list]) = <delete|default>;
Class::~Class() = <delete|default>;
```

An overloaded operator looks like a function definition. Most overloaded operators may be written either as member or simple functions. When written as a member function, *this is the assumed first argument to the operator:

```
MyClass& operator+(const MyClass& m1, const MyClass& m2);// simple
MyClass& MyClass::operator+(const MyClass& m2); // member;
```

Users may define and instantiate their own enumerated types:

```
enum [class] Name = {label1[=value], label2[=value]...};
Name variable = Name::label1;  // used in an assignment
```

C++ For Dummies, 6th Edition

Cheat Sheet

Users may also define their own types using the `class` or `struct` keywords:

```
<struct | class> ClassName [ : [virtual] [public] BaseClass]
{
      <public|protected>:
       // constructor
       ClassName([arg list]) <: member(val),...] {...} |;>
       ClassName() [= <delete|default>;]
       // destructor
       [virtual] ~ClassName() <{...} | [=<delete|default>;>
       // public data members
       type dataMemberName;
       // public member functions
       type memberFunctionName([arg list]) [{...}]
       // const member function
       type memberFunctionName([arg list]) const [{...}]
       // virtual member functions
       virtual type memberFunctionName([arg list] [{...}];
       // pure virtual member functions
       virtual type memberFunctionName([arg list]) = 0;
};
```

In addition, a constructor with a single argument may be flagged as `explicit`.

Template declarations have a slightly different format:

```
// type T is provided by the programmer at use
template <class T, {...}> type FunctionName([arg list])
template <class T, {...}> class ClassName { {...} };
```

Operators

	Operator	Cardinality	Associativity
Highest precedence	() [] -> .	unary	left to right
	! ~ + - ++ @md & * (cast) sizeof	unary	left to right
	* / %	binary	left to right
	+ -	binary	left to right
	<< >>	binary	left to right
	< <= > >=	binary	left to right
	== !=	binary	left to right
	&	binary	left to right
	^	binary	left to right
	|	binary	left to right
	&&	binary	left to right
	||	binary	left to right
	?:	ternary	right to left
	= *= /= %= += -= &= ^= |= <<= >>=	binary	right to left
Lowest precedence	,	binary	left to right

For Dummies: Bestselling Book Series for Beginners

C++
FOR
DUMMIES®
6TH EDITION

by Stephen R. Davis

WILEY

Wiley Publishing, Inc.

C++ For Dummies® 6th Edition

Published by
Wiley Publishing, Inc.
111 River Street
Hoboken, NJ 07030-5774

www.wiley.com

Copyright © 2009 by Wiley Publishing, Inc., Indianapolis, Indiana

Published by Wiley Publishing, Inc., Indianapolis, Indiana

Published simultaneously in Canada

For general information on our other products and services, please contact our Customer Care Department within the U.S. at 877-762-2974, outside the U.S. at 317-572-3993, or fax 317-572-4002.

For technical support, please visit www.wiley.com/techsupport.

Wiley also publishes its books in a variety of electronic formats. Some content that appears in print may not be available in electronic books.

Library of Congress Control Number: 2009925038

ISBN: 978-0-470-31726-6

Manufactured in the United States of America

10 9 8 7 6 5 4 3 2 1

WILEY

About the Author

Stephen R. Davis lives with his wife and son near Dallas, Texas. He and his family have written numerous books including *C++ Weekend Crash Course*. Stephen works for L-3 Communications in Homeland Security and is studying for a PhD in Geospatial Information Sciences at the University of Texas at Dallas.

Dedication

To my friends and family, who help me be the best Dummy I can be.

Acknowledgments

I find it very strange that only a single name appears on the cover of any book, but especially a book like this. In reality, many people contribute to the creation of a *For Dummies* book. From the beginning, editorial directors Mary Corder and Katie Feltman and my agent, Claudette Moore, were involved in guiding and molding the book's content. During the development of the six editions of this book, I found myself hip-deep in edits, corrections, and suggestions from a group of project editors, copyeditors, and technical reviewers—this book would have been a poorer work but for their involvement. And nothing would have made it into print without the aid of Suzanne Thomas, who coordinated the first and second editions of the project, Susan Pink, who worked on the third and sixth editions, and Danny Kavel, who did the technical review of this edition. Nevertheless, one name does appear on the cover and that name must take responsibility for any inaccuracies in the text.

Finally, a summary of the animal activity around my house. For those of you who have not read any of my other books, I should warn you that this has become a regular feature of my *For Dummies* books.

My two dogs, Scooter and Trude, have been gone for almost five years now. We moved to the "big city" about three years ago, which meant giving away our dogs Chester and Sadie (both are doing quite well with other families). We tried to keep the two Great Danes, Monty and Bonnie, but they were just too much for the backyard. We were forced to give them away as well.

No sooner did I give away the two Danes than my son showed up with his two smallish Catahoula-mix mutts from the pound, Lolli and Bodie. At least they're housebroken. I am pleased to report that they are doing fine and waiting for their nightly walk even as I type.

If you are having problems getting started, I maintain a FAQ of common problems at www.stephendavis.com. You can e-mail me questions from there if you don't see your problem. I can't write your program (you don't know how often I get asked to do people's homework assignments), but I try to answer most questions.

Publisher's Acknowledgments

We're proud of this book; please send us your comments through our online registration form located at http://dummies.custhelp.com. For other comments, please contact our Customer Care Department within the U.S. at 877-762-2974, outside the U.S. at 317-572-3993, or fax 317-572-4002.

Some of the people who helped bring this book to market include the following:

Acquisitions, Editorial, and Media Development

Project Editor: Susan Pink
(Previous Edition: Linda Morris)

Acquisitions Editor: Katie Feltman

Copy Editor: Susan Pink
(Previous Edition: Melba Hopper)

Technical Editor: Danny Kalev

Editorial Manager: Jodi Jensen

Media Development Project Manager:
Laura Moss-Hollister

Media Development Assistant Project Manager: Jenny Swisher

Media Development Associate Producers:
Angela Denny, Josh Frank, Marilyn Hummel, Shawn Patrick

Editorial Assistant: Amanda Foxworth

Sr. Editorial Assistant: Cherie Case

Cartoons: Rich Tennant
(www.the5thwave.com)

Composition Services

Project Coordinator: Katherine Key

Layout and Graphics: Reuben W. Davis, Christin Swinford, Sarah Philippart

Proofreaders: ConText Editorial Services, Inc., Caitie Copple, Jessica Kramer

Indexer: Becky Hornyak

Publishing and Editorial for Technology Dummies

   Richard Swadley, Vice President and Executive Group Publisher

   Andy Cummings, Vice President and Publisher

   Mary Bednarek, Executive Acquisitions Director

   Mary C. Corder, Editorial Director

Publishing for Consumer Dummies

   Diane Graves Steele, Vice President and Publisher

Composition Services

   Gerry Fahey, Vice President of Production Services

   Debbie Stailey, Director of Composition Services

Contents at a Glance

Table of Contents

Introduction

Welcome to *C++ For Dummies*, 6th Edition. Think of this book as C++: *Reader's Digest Edition*, bringing you everything you need to know to start programming without all the boring stuff.

What's in This Book

C++ For Dummies is an introduction to the C++ language. I start from the beginning (where else?) and work my way from early concepts through more sophisticated techniques. I don't assume that you have any prior knowledge (at least, not of programming).

The book is rife with examples. Every concept is documented in numerous snippets and several complete programs.

Unlike other C++ programming books, *C++ For Dummies* considers the "why" just as important as the "how." The features of C++ are like pieces of a jigsaw puzzle. Rather than just present the features, I think it's important that you understand how they fit together. You can also use the book as a reference: If you want to understand what's going on with all the template stuff, for example, just flip to Chapter 25. Each chapter contains necessary references to other earlier chapters in case you don't read the chapters in sequence.

C++ For Dummies is not operating system–specific. It is just as useful to Unix or Linux programmers as it is to Windows-based developers. The book doesn't cover Windows or .NET programming.

You have to master a powerful programming language, like C++, first even if your plan is to become an accomplished Windows application or .NET programmer. Once you've finished *C++ for Dummies* you will be in position to continue in your area of specialization, whatever it might be.

What's on the CD

The CD-ROM included with *C++ For Dummies* contains the source code for the examples in this book. This can spare you considerable typing.

Your computer can't execute these or any other C++ programs directly. You have to run your C++ programs through a C++ development environment, which spits out an executable program. (Don't worry, this procedure is explained in Chapter 1.)

The programs in *C++ For Dummies* are compatible with any environment that implements the latest C++ standard from the International Standards Organization (ISO) as of this writing, the C++ 2009 standard. Since not every C++ compiler implements the complete 2009 standard, a full-featured C++ environment known as Code::Blocks using the GNU gcc compiler is contained on the enclosed CD-ROM.

The version of gcc (combined with Code::Blocks) on the disk is for any version of Windows 2000, XP, and Vista. Versions of gcc for Ubuntu and Debian Linux and for Macintosh OS X (Version 10.4 and later) can be downloaded at http://www.gnu.org. Make sure you download gcc Version 4.4 or later to maximize compatibility with the programs in the book.

What Is C++?

C++ is an object-oriented, low-level standard programming language. As a low-level language similar to and compatible with its predecessor C, C++ can generate very efficient, very fast programs. It is often used to write games, graphics software, hardware control software, and other applications where performance really counts.

As an object-oriented language, C++ has the power and extensibility to write large-scale programs. C++ is one of the most popular programming languages for all types of programs. Most of the programs you use on your PC every day are written in C++ (or the subset, which is the C language).

C++ has been certified as a 99.9 percent pure standard, which makes it a portable language. A standard C++ compiler exists for every major operating system. Some versions support extensions to the basic language — in particular, Visual C++ Express and Visual C++ .NET from Microsoft implement several extensions that allow their programs to interface better with other .NET languages. Nevertheless, any student is better off learning the standard C++ first. Learning the extensions is easy once you've master the basics demonstrated here.

Conventions Used in This Book

When I describe a message that you see onscreen, it appears like this:

```
Hi mom!
```

In addition, code listings appear as follows:

```
// some program
int main()
{
    ...
}
```

If you're entering these programs by hand, you must enter the text exactly as shown with one exception: The amount of *whitespace* (spaces, tabs and new-lines) is not critical. You can't put a space in the middle of a keyword, but you don't have to worry about entering one too many or too few spaces.

C++ words are usually based on English words with similar meanings. This can make reading a sentence containing both English and C++ difficult to make out without a little assistance. To help out, C++ commands and function names appear in a different font, `like this`. In addition, function names are always followed by open and closed parentheses, such as `myFavorite Function()`. The arguments to the function are left off except when there's a specific need to make them easier to read.

Sometimes, I'll tell you to use menu commands, such as File⇨Open. This notation means to use the keyboard or mouse to open the File menu and then choose the Open option.

Use of gender is always a tricky subject when writing a how-to book. I don't want to appear to be telling gentlemen how ignorant they are while giving the ladies a pass by using *he* and *him* all the time. In this book, I use the pronouns *she* and *her* when referring to the programmer and *he* and *him* when referring to the user of the program. So, she writes a program that he can use.

How This Book Is Organized

Each new feature is introduced by answering the following three questions:

- ✔ *What* is this new feature?
- ✔ *Why* was it introduced into the language?
- ✔ *How* does it work?

Small pieces of code are sprinkled liberally throughout the chapters. Each demonstrates some newly introduced feature or highlights some brilliant point I'm making. These snippets may not be complete and certainly don't do anything meaningful. However, every concept is demonstrated in at least one functional program that you can execute and play with on your own computer.

And There's More

A real-world program can take up lots of pages. However, seeing such a program is an important didactic tool for any reader.

I use one simple example program that I call BUDGET. The program starts life as a simple, functionally oriented BUDGET1. This program maintains a set of simple checking and savings accounts. The reader is encouraged to review this program at the end of Part II. The subsequent version, BUDGET2, adds the object-oriented concepts presented in Part III. The examples work their way using more and more features of the language, culminating with BUDGET5, which you should review after you master all the chapters in the book. The BUDGET programs can be found on the book's CD-ROM. You can download a bonus chapter that describes these programs from www.stephendavis.com.

Part I: Introduction to C++ Programming

Part I starts you on your journey. You begin by examining what it means to write a computer program. From there, you step through the syntax of the language (the meaning of the C++ commands).

Part II: Becoming a Functional C++ Programmer

In Part II, you expand upon your newly gained knowledge of the basic commands of C++ by adding the capability to bundle sections of C++ code into modules and reusing these modules in programs. I also introduce that most dreaded of all topics, the C++ pointer. If you don't know what that means, don't worry — you'll find out soon enough.

Part III: Introduction to Classes

The plot thickens in Part III, which begins the discussion of object-oriented programming. Object-oriented (OO) programming is really the reason for the existence of C++. Take the OO features out of C++, and you're left with its predecessor language, C. I discuss things such as classes, constructors, destructors, and making nachos (I'm not kidding, by the way). Don't worry if you don't know what these concepts are (except for nachos — if you don't know what nachos are, we're in big trouble).

Part IV: Inheritance

Inheritance is where object-oriented programming really comes into its own. Understanding this most important concept is the key to effective C++ programming and the goal of Part IV. There's no going back now — after you've completed this part, you can call yourself an Object-Oriented Programmer, First Class.

Part V: Optional Features

By the time you get to Part V, you have the framework upon which to build. From now on it's a matter of expanding your knowledge of additional language features. Features such as file input/output, error-handling constructs, and templates are left to this part.

Part VI: The Part of Tens

What *For Dummies* book would be complete without The Part of Tens? Chapter 28 shows you the top ten best ways to avoid introducing bugs into your programs, bugs that you would otherwise have to ferret out on your own.

Chapter 29 takes you through some of the more esoteric features of C++ '09. The C++ 2009 standard is more than 1,300 pages of very small, terse writing. Fortunately, many of these features are meant for special subsets of the C++ community. You can safely put off understanding these features until you feel comfortable with the basics of the language.

Icons Used in This Book

This is technical stuff that you can skip on the first reading.

Tips highlight a point that can save you a lot of time and effort.

Remember this. It's important.

Remember this, too. This one can sneak up on you when you least expect it and generate one of those really hard-to-find bugs.

This icon flag some 2009 additions to the language compared to the predecessor standard (which is known as C++ 2003). If you already have some familiarity with C++ and something seems completely new or if something doesn't work with your existing C++ tools, it may be because it's an '09 addition.

Where to Go from Here

Finding out about a programming language is not a spectator sport. I'll try to make it as painless as possible, but you have to power up the ol' PC and get down to some serious programming. Limber up the fingers, break the spine on the book so that it lies flat next to the keyboard (and so that you can't take it back to the bookstore), and dive in.

Part I
Introduction to C++ Programming

The 5th Wave   By Rich Tennant

"We've failed to meet our October 31 launch date for TREAT this year, but we're developing a new more robust version that should be available by the first or second quarter of next year."

In this part . . .

*B*oth the newest, hottest flight simulator and the simplest yet most powerful accounting programs use the same basic building blocks. In this part, you discover the basic features you need to write your killer application.

Chapter 1

Writing Your First C++ Program

· ·

In This Chapter

▶ Finding out about C++

▶ Installing Code::Blocks from the accompanying CD-ROM

▶ Creating your first C++ program

▶ Executing your program

· ·

*O*kay, so here we are: No one here but just you and me. Nothing left to do but get started. Might as well lay out a few fundamental concepts.

A computer is an amazingly fast but incredibly stupid machine. A computer can do anything you tell it (within reason), but it does *exactly* what it's told — nothing more and nothing less.

Perhaps unfortunately for us, computers don't understand any reasonable human language — they don't speak English either. Okay, I know what you're going to say: "I've seen computers that could understand English." What you really saw was a computer executing a *program* that could meaningfully understand English.

Computers understand a language variously known as *computer language* or *machine language*. It's possible but extremely difficult for humans to speak machine language. Therefore, computers and humans have agreed to sort of meet in the middle, using intermediate languages such as C++. Humans can speak C++ (sort of), and C++ can be converted into machine language for the computer to understand.

Grasping C++ Concepts

A C++ program is a text file containing a sequence of C++ commands put together according to the laws of C++ grammar. This text file is known as the *source file* (probably because it's the source of all frustration). A C++ source file normally carries the extension .CPP just as a Microsoft Word file ends in .DOC or an MS-DOS (remember that?) batch file ends in .BAT.

The point of programming in C++ is to write a sequence of commands that can be converted into a machine-language program that actually *does* what we want done. This is called *compiling* and is the job of the compiler. The machine code that you wrote must be combined with some setup and tear-down instructions and some standard library routines in a process known as *linking* or *building*. The resulting *machine-executable* files carry the extension .EXE in Windows.

That sounds easy enough — so what's the big deal? Keep going.

To write a program, you need two specialized computer programs. One (an editor) is what you use to write your code as you build your .CPP source file. The other (a compiler) converts your source file into a machine-executable .EXE file that carries out your real-world commands (open spreadsheet, make rude noises, deflect incoming asteroids, whatever).

Nowadays, tool developers generally combine compiler and editor into a single package — a development *environment*. After you finish entering the commands that make up your program, you need only click a button to create the executable file.

Fortunately, there are public-domain C++ environments. We use one of them in this book — the Code::Blocks environment. This editor will work with a lot of different compilers, but a version of Code::Blocks combined with the GNU gcc compiler for 32-bit versions of Windows is included on the book's CD-ROM. You can download the most recent version of Code::Blocks from www.codeblocks.org or you can download a recent version that's been tested for compatibility with the programs in this book from the author's Web site at www.stephendavis.com.

You can download versions of the gcc compiler for the Mac or Linux from www.gnu.org.

Although Code::Blocks is public domain, you're encouraged to pay some small fee to support its further development. You don't *have* to pay to use Code::Blocks, but you can contribute to the cause if you like. See the Web site for details.

I have tested the programs in this book with Code::Blocks combined with gcc version 4.4; the programs should work with later versions as well. You can check out my Web site for a list of any problems that may arise with future versions of Code::Blocks, gcc, or Windows.

Code::Blocks is a full-fledged editor and development environment front end. Code::Blocks supports a multitude of different compilers including the gcc compiler included on the enclosed CD-ROM.

The Code::Blocks/gcc package generates Windows-compatible 32-bit programs, but it does not easily support creating programs that have the classic Windows look. I strongly recommend that you work through the examples in this book first to learn C++ *before* you tackle Windows development. C++ and Windows programming are two separate things and (for the sake of your sanity) should remain so in your mind.

Follow the steps in the next section to install Code::Blocks and build your first C++ program. This program's task is to convert a temperature value entered by the user from degrees Celsius to degrees Fahrenheit.

Installing Code::Blocks

The CD-ROM that accompanies this book includes the most recent version of the Code::Blocks environment at the time of this writing.

The Code::Blocks environment comes in an easy-to-install, compressed executable file. This executable file is contained in the CodeBlocks directory on the accompanying CD-ROM. Here's the rundown on installing the environment:

1. **Insert the CD into the CD-ROM drive.**

2. **When the CD interface appears with the License Agreement, click Accept.**

3. **Click the Installing Code::Blocks button on the left.**

4. **Click Open Directory.**

5. **Double-click the codeblocks_setup.exe file.**

   You can also choose Start➪Run and type *x*:**\codeblocks\setup** in the window that appears, where *x* is the letter designation for your CD-ROM drive (normally D).

6. **Depending on what version of Windows you're using, you may get the ubiquitous "An unidentified programs wants access to your computer" warning pop-up. If so, click Allow to get the installation ball rolling.**

7. **Click Next after closing all extraneous applications as you are warned in the Welcome dialog to the CodeBlocks Setup Wizard.**

8. **Read the End User Legal Agreement (commonly known as the EULA) and then click I Agree if you can live with its provisions.**

   It's not like you have much choice — the package really won't install itself if you don't accept. Assuming you *do* click OK, Code::Blocks opens a window showing the installation options. The default options are fine.

9. **Click the Next button.**

   The installation program asks where you want it to install Code::Blocks. This dialog box also shows you how much disk space the installation requires (and whether you have enough). The default is okay assuming you have enough disk space (if not, you'll have to delete one of your reruns of the Simpsons).

10. **Click Install.**

    Code::Blocks commences to copying a whole passel of files to your hard disk. Code::Blocks then asks "Do you want to run Code::Blocks now?"

11. **Click Yes to start Code::Blocks.**

    Code::Blocks now asks which compiler you intend to use. The default is GNU GCC Compiler, which is the proper selection.

12. **Click OK to select the GNU GCC compiler and start Code::Blocks.**

    Code::Blocks now wants to know which file associations you want to establish. The default is to allow Code::Blocks to open .CPP files. This option in fine unless you have another C++ compiler that you would rather have as the default.

13. **Select the Yes, Associate C++ Files with Code::Blocks option if you do not have another C++ compiler installed. Otherwise, select the No, Leave Everything as It Is option. Click OK.**

    You now need to make sure that the compiler options are set to enable all warnings and C++ 2009 features.

14. **From within Code::Blocks, choose Settings⇨Compiler and Debugger. In the Compiler Flags tab, make sure that the Enable All Compiler Warnings is selected.**

15. **Select the Enable All Compiler Warnings option, as shown in Figure 1-1.**

    Start Code::Blocks. From within Code::Blocks, choose Settings⇨Compiler and debugger. In the Compiler Flags tab, make sure that the Enable All Compiler Warnings is selected.

16. **Set the options to ensure C++ 2009 compliance.**

    The 2009 extensions are still considered a bit experimental as of this writing, so you need to tell gcc to enable these features. Click the Other Options tab and add the two lines `-std=c++0x` and `-Wc++0x-compat` as shown in Figure 1-2.

17. **Click OK.**

18. **Click Next in the Code::Blocks Setup window and then click Finish to complete the setup program.**

    The setup program exits.

Figure 1-1:
Ensure that
the Enable
All Compiler
Warnings
is set.

Figure 1-2:
Add these
lines to
enable the
C++ 2009
features.

Creating Your First C++ Program

In this section, you create your first C++ program. You enter the C++ code
into a file called CONVERT.CPP and then convert the C++ code into an executable program.

Creating a project

The first step to creating a C++ program is to create what is known as a project. A *project* tells Code::Blocks the names of the .CPP source files to include and what type of program to create. Most of the programs in the book will consist of a single source file and will be command-line style:

1. **Choose Start⇨Programs⇨CodeBlocks⇨CodeBlocks to start up the CodeBlocks tool.**

2. **From within Code::Blocks, choose File⇨New⇨Project.**

3. **Select the Console Application icon and then click Go.**

4. **Select C++ as the language you want to use from the next window. Click Next.**

   Code::Blocks and gcc also support plain ol' C programs.

5. **Select the Console Application icon and then click Go.**

6. **In the Folder to Build Project In field, navigate to the subdirectory where you want your program built.**

   I have divided the programs in this book by chapter, so I created the folder C:\CPP_Programs\Chap01 using Windows Explorer and then selected it from the file menu.

7. **In the Project Title field, type the name of the project, in this case** Conversion.

   The resulting screen is shown in Figure 1-3.

Figure 1-3: I created the project Conversion for the first program.

8. Click Next.

The next window gives you the option of creating an application for testing or the final version. The default is fine.

9. Click Finish to create the Conversion project.

Entering the C++ code

The Conversion project that Code::Blocks creates consists of a single, default main.cpp file that does nothing. The next step is to enter our program:

1. In the Management window on the left, double-click main, which is under Sources, which is under Conversion.

Code::Blocks opens the empty main.cpp program that it created in the code editor, as shown in Figure 1-4. (Figure 1-4 shows all the projects from the entire book as well.)

Figure 1-4:
The Management window displays a directory structure for all available programs.

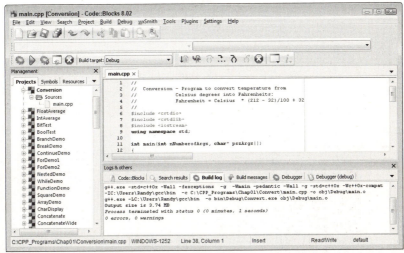

2. Edit main.cpp with the following program exactly as written.

Don't worry too much about indentation or spacing — it isn't critical whether a given line is indented two or three spaces, or whether there are one or two spaces between two words. C++ is case sensitive, however, so you need to make sure everything is lowercase.

You can cheat by using the files contained on the enclosed CD-ROM as described in the next section "Cheating."

```
//
//  Conversion - Program to convert temperature from
//              Celsius degrees into Fahrenheit:
//              Fahrenheit = Celsius  * (212 - 32)/100 + 32
//
#include <cstdio>

#include <cstdlib>
#include <iostream>
using namespace std;

int main(int nNumberofArgs, char* pszArgs[])
{
  // enter the temperature in Celsius
  int celsius;
  cout << "Enter the temperature in Celsius:";
  cin >> celsius;

  // calculate conversion factor for Celsius
  // to Fahrenheit
  int factor;
  factor = 212 - 32;

  // use conversion factor to convert Celsius
  // into Fahrenheit values
  int fahrenheit;
  fahrenheit = factor * celsius/100 + 32;

  // output the results (followed by a NewLine)
  cout << "Fahrenheit value is:";
  cout << fahrenheit << endl;

  // wait until user is ready before terminating program
  // to allow the user to see the program results
  system("PAUSE");
  return 0;
}
```

3. Choose File⇨Save to save the source file.

I know that it may not seem all that exciting, but you've just created your first C++ program!

Cheating

All the programs in the book are included on the enclosed CD-ROM along with the project files to build them. You can use these files in two ways: one way is to go through all the steps to create the program by hand first but copy and paste from the sources on the CD-ROM into your program if you get into trouble (or your fingers start cramping). This is the preferred technique.

Alternatively you can use the following procedure to copy all the programs to your hard disk at once:

1. **Copy all the sources from the CD-ROM to the hard disk.**

   This copies all the source code from the book along with the project files to build those programs.

2. **Double-click `AllPrograms.workspace` in C:\CPP_Programs.**

   A workspace is a single file that references one or more projects. The `AllPrograms.workspace` file contains references to all the projects defined in the book.

3. **Right-click the Conversion project in the Management window on the left. Choose Activate Project from the context-sensitive menu that appears.**

   Code::Blocks turns the Conversion label bold to verify that this is the program you are working with right now.

Building your program

After you've saved your C++ source file to disk, it's time to generate the executable machine instructions.

To build your Conversion program, you choose Build⇨Build from the menu or press Ctrl-F9. Almost immediately, Code::Blocks takes off, compiling your program with gusto. If all goes well, the happy result of *0 errors, 0 warnings* appears in the lower-right window.

Code::Blocks generates a message if it finds any type of error in your C++ program — and coding errors are about as common as ice cubes in Alaska. You'll undoubtedly encounter numerous warnings and error messages, probably even when entering the simple `Conversion.cpp`. To demonstrate the error-reporting process, let's change Line 16 from `cin >> celsius;` to `cin >>> celsius;`.

This seems an innocent enough offense — forgivable to you and me perhaps, but not to C++. Choose Build⇨Build to start the compile and build process. Code::Blocks almost immediately places a red square next to the erroneous line as shown in Figure 1-5. The message in the Build Message tab is a rather cryptic `error: expected primary-expression before '>' token`. To get rid of the message, remove the extra > and recompile.

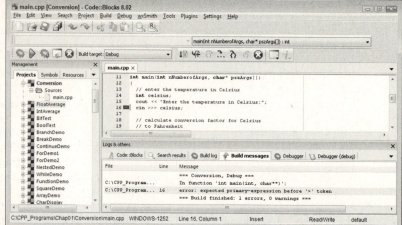

Figure 1-5:
Code::
Blocks flags
the source
of errors
quickly.

You probably consider the error message generated by the example a little cryptic but give it time — you've been programming for only about 30 minutes now. Over time you'll come to understand the error messages generated by Code::Blocks and gcc much better.

Code::Blocks was able to point directly at the error this time but it isn't always that good. Sometimes it doesn't notice the error until the next line or the one after that, so if the line flagged with the error looks okay, start looking at its predecessor to see if the error is there.

Executing Your Program

It's now time to execute your new creation . . . that is, to run your program. You will run the CONVERT.EXE program file and give it input to see how well it works.

To execute the Conversion program, choose Build⇨Build and Run or press F9. This rebuilds the program if anything has changed and executes the program if the build is successful.

A window opens immediately, requesting a temperature in Celsius. Enter a known temperature, such as 100 degrees. After you press Enter, the program returns with the equivalent temperature of 212 degrees Fahrenheit as follows:

```
Enter the temperature in Celsius:100
Fahrenheit value is:212
Press any key to continue . . .
```

The message `Press any key to continue...` gives you the opportunity to read what you've entered before it goes away. Press Enter, and the window (along with its contents) disappears. Congratulations! You just entered, built, and executed your first C++ program.

Notice that Code::Blocks is not truly intended for developing Windows programs. In theory, you can write a Windows application by using Code::Blocks, but it isn't easy. (Building windowed applications is *so* much easier in Visual Studio.NET.)

Windows programs show the user a visually oriented output, all nicely arranged in onscreen windows. Conversion.exe is a 32-bit program that executes *under* Windows, but it's not a Windows program in the visual sense.

If you don't know what *32-bit program* means, don't worry about it. As I said, this book isn't about writing Windows programs. The C++ programs you write in this book have a *command line interface* executing within an MS-DOS box.

Budding Windows programmers shouldn't despair — you didn't waste your money. Learning C++ is a prerequisite to writing Windows programs. I think that they should be mastered separately: C++ first, Windows second.

Reviewing the Annotated Program

Entering data in someone else's program is about as exciting as watching someone else drive a car. You really need to get behind the wheel itself. Programs are a bit like cars as well. All cars are basically the same with small differences and additions — okay, French cars are a lot different than other cars, but the point is still valid. Cars follow the same basic pattern — steering wheel in front of you, seat below you, roof above you, and stuff like that.

Similarly, all C++ programs follow a common pattern. This pattern is already present in this very first program. We can review the Conversion program by looking for the elements that are common to all programs.

Examining the framework for all C++ programs

Every C++ program you write for this book uses the same basic framework, which looks a lot like this:

```
//
//  Template - provides a template to be used as the
//              starting point
//
// the following include files define the majority of
// functions that any given program will need
#include <cstdio>
#include <cstdlib>
#include <iostream>
using namespace std;

int main(int nNumberofArgs, char* pszArgs[])
{
    // your C++ code starts here

    // wait until user is ready before terminating program
    // to allow the user to see the program results
    system("PAUSE");
    return 0;
}
```

Without going into all the boring details, execution begins with the code contained in the open and closed braces immediately following the line beginning `main()`.

I've copied this code into a file called `Template.cpp` located in the main `CPP_Programs` folder on the enclosed CD-ROM.

Clarifying source code with comments

The first few lines in the Conversion program appear to be freeform text. Either this code was meant for human eyes or C++ is a lot smarter than I give it credit for. These first six lines are known as comments. *Comments* are the programmer's explanation of what she is doing or thinking when writing a particular code segment. The compiler ignores comments. Programmers (*good* programmers, anyway) don't.

A C++ comment begins with a double slash (//) and ends with a newline. You can put any character you want in a comment. A comment may be as long as you want, but it's customary to keep comment lines to no more than 80 characters across. Back in the old days — "old" is relative here — screens were limited to 80 characters in width. Some printers still default to 80 characters across when printing text. These days, keeping a single line to fewer than 80 characters is just a good practical idea (easier to read; less likely to cause eyestrain; the usual).

A newline was known as a *carriage return* back in the days of typewriters —
when the act of entering characters into a machine was called *typing* and not
keyboarding. A *newline* is the character that terminates a command line.

C++ allows a second form of comment in which everything appearing after a
/* and before a */ is ignored; however, this form of comment isn't normally
used in C++ anymore. (Later in this book, I describe the one case in which this
type of comment is applied.)

It may seem odd to have a command in C++ (or any other programming language) that's specifically ignored by the computer. However, all computer
languages have some version of the comment. It's critical that the programmer explain what was going through her mind when she wrote the code. A
programmer's thoughts may not be obvious to the next colleague who tries
to use or modify her program. In fact, the programmer herself may forget
what her program meant if she looks at it months after writing the original
code and has left no clue.

Basing programs on C++ statements

All C++ programs are based on what are known as C++ statements. This section reviews the statements that make up the program framework used by
the Conversion program.

A statement is a single set of commands. Almost all C++ statements other
than comments end in a semicolon. (You see one other exception in Chapter
10). Program execution begins with the first C++ statement after the open
brace and continues through the listing, one statement at a time.

As you look through the program, you can see that spaces, tabs, and newlines appear throughout the program. In fact, I place a newline after every
statement in this program. These characters are collectively known as
whitespace because you can't see them on the monitor.

You may add whitespace anywhere you like in your program to enhance
readability — except in the middle of a word:

```
See wha

t I mean?
```

Although C++ may ignore whitespace, it doesn't ignore case. In fact, C++ is
case sensitive to the point of obsession. The variable fullspeed and the
variable FullSpeed have nothing to do with each other. The command int
is completely understandable, but C++ has no idea what INT means. See what
I mean about fast but stupid compilers?

Writing declarations

The line `int nCelsius;` is a declaration statement. A *declaration* is a statement that defines a variable. A *variable* is a "holding tank" for a value of some type. A variable contains a *value,* such as a number or a character.

The term *variable* stems from algebra formulas of the following type:

```
x = 10
y = 3 * x
```

In the second expression, y is set equal to 3 times x, but what is x? The variable x acts as a holding tank for a value. In this case, the value of x is 10, but we could have just as well set the value of x to 20 or 30 or –1. The second formula makes sense no matter what the value of x is.

In algebra, you're allowed but not required to begin with a statement such as x = 10. In C++, the programmer must define the variable x before she can use it.

In C++, a variable has a type and a name. The variable defined on line 11 is called `celsius` and declared to hold an integer. (Why they couldn't have just said *integer* instead of *int,* I'll never know. It's just one of those things you learn to live with.)

The name of a variable has no particular significance to C++. A variable must begin with the letters *A* through *Z,* the letters *a* through *z,* or an underscore (_). All subsequent characters must be a letter, a digit 0 through 9, or an underscore. Variable names can be as long as you want to make them.

It's convention that variable names begin with a lowercase letter. Each new word *within* a variable begins with a capital letter, as in `myVariable`.

Try to make variable names short but descriptive. Avoid names such as x because x has no particular meaning. A variable name such as `lengthOf LineSegment` is much more descriptive.

Generating output

The lines beginning with `cout` and `cin` are known as input/output statements, often contracted to I/O statements. (Like all engineers, programmers love contractions and acronyms.)

The first I/O statement says "Output the phrase *Enter the temperature in Celsius* to *cout*" (pronounced "see-out"). cout is the name of the standard C++ output device. In this case, the standard C++ output device is your monitor.

The next line is exactly the opposite. It says, in effect, "Extract a value from the C++ input device and store it in the integer variable celsius." The C++ input device is normally the keyboard. What we have here is the C++ analog to the algebra formula $x = 10$ just mentioned. For the remainder of the program, the value of celsius is whatever the user enters there.

Calculating Expressions

All but the most basic programs perform calculations of one type or another. In C++, an *expression* is a statement that performs a calculation. Said another way, an expression is a statement that *has a value*. An *operator* is a command that generates a value.

For example, in the Conversion example program — specifically in the two lines marked as a calculation expression — the program declares a variable *factor* and then assigns it the value resulting from a calculation. This particular command calculates the difference of 212 and 32; the operator is the minus sign (–), and the expression is 212-32.

Storing the results of an expression

The spoken language can be very ambiguous. The term *equals* is one of those ambiguities. The word *equals* can mean that two things have the same value as in "a dollar equals one hundred cents." Equals can also imply assignment, as in math when you say that "y equals 3 times x."

To avoid ambiguity, C++ programmers call = the *assignment operator,* which says (in effect), "Store the results of the expression to the right of the equal sign in the variable to the left." Programmers say that "factor is assigned the value 212 minus 32." For short, you can say "factor gets 212 minus 32."

Never say "factor is *equal to* 212 minus 32." You'll hear this from some lazy types, but you and I know better.

Examining the remainder of Conversion

The second expression in the Conversion program presents a slightly more complicated expression than the first. This expression uses the same mathematical symbols: * for multiplication, / for division, and + for addition. In this case, however, the calculation is performed on variables and not simply on constants.

The value contained in the variable called `factor` (which was calculated as the results of 212 – 32, by the way) is multiplied by the value contained in `celsius` (which was input from the keyboard). The result is divided by 100 and summed with 32. The result of the total expression is assigned to the integer variable `fahrenheit`.

The final two commands output the string `Fahrenheit value is:` to the display, followed by the value of `fahrenheit` — and all so fast that the user scarcely knows it's going on.

Chapter 2

Declaring Variables Constantly

The most fundamental of all concepts in C++ is the *variable* — a variable is like a small box. You can store things in the box for later use, particularly numbers. The concept of a variable is borrowed from mathematics. A statement such as

```
x = 1
```

stores the value 1 in the variable x. From that point forward, the mathematician can use the variable x in place of the constant 1 — until he changes the value of x to something else.

Variables work the same way in C++. You can make the assignment

```
x = 1;
```

From that point forward in the execution of the program, until the value of x is changed, the *value of* x is 1. References to x are replaced by the value 1. In this chapter, you will find out how to declare and initialize variables in C++ programs. You will also see the different types of variables that C++ defines and when to use each.

Declaring Variables

A mathematician might write something like the following:

```
(x + 2) = y / 2
x + 4 = y
solve for x and y
```

Any reader who's had algebra realizes right off that the mathematician has introduced the variables x and y. But C++ isn't that smart. (Computers may be fast, but they're stupid.)

You have to announce each variable to C++ before you can use it. You have to say something soothing like this:

```
int x;
x = 10;

int y;
y = 5;
```

These lines of code *declare* that a variable x exists, is of type int, and has the value 10; and that a variable y of type int also exists with the value 5. (The next section discusses variable types.) You can declare variables (almost) anywhere you want in your program — as long as you *declare the variable before you use it.*

Declaring Different Types of Variables

If you're on friendly terms with math (and who isn't?), you probably think of a variable in mathematics as an amorphous box capable of holding whatever you might choose to store in it. You might easily write something like the following:

```
x = 1
x = 2.3
x = "this is a sentence"
```

Alas, C++ is not that flexible. (On the other hand, C++ can do things that people can't do, such as add a billion numbers or so in a second, so let's not get too uppity.) To C++, there are different types of variables just as there are different types of storage bins. Some storage bins are so small that they can handle only a single number. It takes a larger bin to handle a sentence.

Some computer languages try harder to accommodate the programmer by allowing her to place different types of data in the same variable. These languages are called *weakly typed* languages. C++ is a *strongly typed* language — it requires the programmer to specifically declare each variable along with its exact type.

The variable type `int` is the C++ equivalent of an *integer* — a number that has no fractional part. (Integers are also known as *counting numbers* or *whole numbers*.)

Integers are great for most calculations. I made it through most of elementary school with integers. It isn't until I turned 11 or so that my teachers started mucking up the waters with fractions. The same is true in C++: More than 90 percent of all variables in C++ are declared to be of type `int`.

Unfortunately, `int` variables aren't adapted to every problem. For example, if you worked through the temperature-conversion program in Chapter 1, you might have noticed that the program has a potential problem — it can calculate temperatures to the nearest degree. No fractions of a degree are allowed. This integer limitation wouldn't affect daily use because it isn't likely that someone (other than a meteorologist) would get all excited about being off a fraction of a degree. There are plenty of cases, however, where this isn't the case — for example, you wouldn't want to come up a half mile short of the runway on your next airplane trip due to a navigational round-off.

Reviewing the limitations of integers in C++

The `int` variable type is the C++ version of an integer. `int` variables suffer the same limitations as their counting-number integer equivalents in math do.

Integer round-off

Lopping off the fractional part of a number is called *truncation*. Consider the problem of calculating the average of three numbers. Given three `int` variables — `nValue1`, `nValue2`, and `nValue3` — an equation for calculating the average is

```
int nAverage; int nValue1; int nValue2; int nValue3;
nAverage = (nValue1 + nValue2 + nValue3) / 3;
```

Because all three values are integers, the sum is assumed to be an integer. Given the values 1, 2, and 2, the sum is 5. Divide that by 3, and you get 1⅔, or 1.666. C++ uses slightly different rules: Given that all three variables `nValue1`, `nValue2`, and `nValue3` are integers, the sum is also assumed to be an integer. The result of the division of one integer by another integer is also an integer. Thus, the resulting value of `nAverage` is the unreasonable but logical value of 1.

The problem is much worse in the following mathematically equivalent formulation:

```
int nAverage; int nValue1; int nValue2; int nValue3;
nAverage = nValue1/3 + nValue2/3 + nValue3/3;
```

Plugging in the same 1, 2, and 2 values, the resulting value of nAverage is 0 (talk about logical but unreasonable). To see how this can occur, consider that $\frac{1}{3}$ truncates to 0, $\frac{2}{3}$ truncates to 0, and $\frac{2}{3}$ truncates to 0. The sum of 0, 0, and 0 is 0. You can see that integer truncation can be completely unacceptable.

Limited range

A second problem with the int variable type is its limited range. A normal int variable can store a maximum value of 2,147,483,647 and a minimum value of –2,147,483,648 — roughly from positive 2 billion to negative 2 billion, for a total range of about 4 billion.

Two billion is a very large number: plenty big enough for most uses. But it's not large enough for some applications, including computer technology. In fact, your computer probably executes faster than 2 gigahertz, depending on how old your computer is. (*Giga* is the prefix meaning billion.) A single strand of communications fiber — the kind that's been strung back and forth from one end of the country to the other — can handle way more than 2 billion bits per second.

Solving the truncation problem

The limitations of int variables can be unacceptable in some applications. Fortunately, C++ understands decimal numbers that have a fractional part. (Mathematicians also call those *real numbers.*) Decimal numbers avoid many of the limitations of int type integers. To C++ all decimal numbers have a fractional part even if that fractional part is 0. In C++, the number 1.0 is just as much a decimal number as 1.5. The equivalent integer is written simply as 1. Decimal numbers can also be negative, such as –2.3.

When you declare variables in C++ that are decimal numbers, you identify them as floating-point or simply float variables. The term *floating-point* means the decimal point is allowed to float back and forth, identifying as many decimal places as necessary to express the value. Floating-point variables are declared in the same way as int variables:

```
float fValue1;
```

Once declared, you cannot change the type of a variable. `fValue1` is now a `float` and will be a `float` for the remainder of the program. To see how floating-point numbers fix the truncation problem inherent with integers, convert all the `int` variables to `float`. Here's what you get:

```
float fValue;
fValue = 1.0/3.0 + 2.0/3.0 + 2.0/3.0;
```

is equivalent to

```
fValue = 0.333... + 0.666... + 0.666...;
```

which results in the value

```
fValue = 1.666...;
```

I have written the value `1.6666 . . .` as if the number of trailing 6s goes on forever. This is not necessarily the case. A `float` variable has a limit to the number of digits of accuracy, but it's a lot more than I can keep track of.

A constant that has a decimal point is assumed to be a floating-point value. However, the default type for a floating-point constant is something known as a double precision, which in C++ is called simply `double`, as we'll see in the next section.

The programs `IntAverage` and `FloatAverage` are available on the enclosed CD in the `CPP_Programs\Chap02` directory to demonstrate the round-off error inherent in integer variables.

Looking at the limits of floating-point numbers

Although floating-point variables can solve many calculation problems such as truncation, they have some limitations themselves — the reverse of those associated with integer variables. Floating-point variables can't be used to count things, are more difficult for the computer to handle, and also suffer from round-off error (though not nearly to the same degree as `int` variables).

Counting

You cannot use floating-point variables in applications where counting is important. This includes C++ constructs that count. C++ can't verify which whole number value is meant by a given floating-point number.

For example, it's clear to you and me that 1.0 is 1 but not so clear to C++. What about 0.9 or 1.1? Should these also be considered as 1? C++ simply avoids the problem by insisting on using int values when counting is involved.

Calculation speed

Historically, a computer processor can process integer arithmetic quicker than it can floating-point arithmetic. Thus, while a processor can add 1 million integer numbers in a given amount of time, the same processor may be able to perform only 200,000 floating-point calculations during the same period.

Calculation speed is becoming less of a problem as microprocessors get faster. In addition, today's general-purpose microprocessors include special floating-point circuitry on board to increase the performance of these operations. However, arithmetic on integer values is just a heck of a lot easier and faster than performing the same operation on floating-point values.

Loss of accuracy

Floating-point float variables have a precision of about 6 digits, and an extra-economy size, double-strength version of float known as a double can handle about 13 significant digits. This can cause round-off problems as well.

Consider that $\frac{1}{3}$ is expressed as 0.333 . . . in a continuing sequence. The concept of an infinite series makes sense in math but not to a computer because it has a finite accuracy. The FloatAverage program outputs 1.66667 as the average 1, 2, and 2 — that's a lot better than the 0 output by the IntAverage version but not even close to an infinite sequence.

C++ can correct for round-off error in a lot of cases. For example, on output, C++ can sometimes determine that the user really meant 1 instead of 0.999999. In other cases, even C++ cannot correct for round-off error.

Not-so-limited range

Although the double data type has a range much larger than that of an integer, it's still limited. The maximum value for an int is a skosh more than 2 billion. The maximum value of a double variable is roughly 10 to the 38th power. That's 1 followed by 38 zeroes; it eats 2 billion for breakfast. (It's even more than the national debt, at least at the time of this writing.)

Remember, only the first 13 digits or so have any meaning; the remaining 25 digits are noise having succumbed to floating-point round-off error.

Declaring Variable Types

So far in this chapter, I have been trumpeting that variables must be declared and that they must be assigned a type. Fortunately (ta-dah!), C++ provides a number of variable types. See Table 2-1 for a list of variables, their advantages, and limitations.

Table 2-1	Common C++ Variable Types	
Variable	*Defining a Constant*	*What It Is*
`int`	`1`	A simple counting number, either positive or negative.
`short int`	`---`	A potentially smaller version of `int`. It uses less memory but has a smaller range.
`long int`	`10L`	A potentially larger version of `int`. There is no difference between `long` and `int` with gcc.
`long long int`	`10LL`	A potentially even larger version of `int`.
`float`	`1.0F`	A single precision real number. This smaller version takes less memory than a `double` but has less accuracy and a smaller range.
`double`	`1.0`	A standard floating-point variable.
`long double`	`---`	A potentially larger floating-point number. On the PC, `long double` is used for the native size of the 80x86 floating-point processor, which is 80 bits.
`char`	`'c'`	A single `char` variable stores a single alphabetic or digital character. Not suitable for arithmetic.
`wchar_t`	`L'c'`	A larger character capable or storing symbols with larger character sets like Chinese.
`char string`	`"this is a string"`	A string of characters forms a sentence or phrase.
`bool`	`true`	The only other value is false. No, I mean, it's *really* false. Logically false. Not *false* as in fake or ersatz or . . . never mind.

The `long long int` and `long double` were officially introduced with C++ '09.

The integer types come in both signed and unsigned versions. Signed is always the default (for everything except `char` and `wchar_t`). The unsigned version is created by adding the keyword `unsigned` in front of the type in the declaration. The unsigned constants include a *U* or *u* in their type designation. Thus, the following declares an `unsigned int` variable and assigns it the value 10:

```
unsigned int uVariable;
uVariable = 10U;
```

The following statement declares the two variables `lVariable1` and `lVariable2` as type `long int` and sets them equal to the value 1, while `dVariable` is a double set to the value 1.0. Notice in the declaration of `lVariable2` that the `int` is assumed and can be left off:

```
// declare two long int variables and set them to 1
long int lVariable1
long lVariable2;       // int is assumed
lVariable1 = lVariable2 = 1;
// declare a variable of type double and set it to 1.0
double dVariable; dVariable = 1.0;
```

You can declare a variable and initialize it in the same statement:

```
int nVariable = 1;   // declare a variable and
                     // initialize it to 1
```

A `char` variable can hold a single character; a character string (which isn't really a variable type but works like one for most purposes) holds a string of characters. Thus, `'C'` is a `char` that contains the character C, whereas `"C"` is a string with one character in it. A rough analogy is that a `'C'` corresponds to a nail in your hand, whereas `"C"` corresponds to a nail gun with one nail left in the magazine. (Chapter 9 describes strings in detail.)

If an application requires a string, you've gotta provide one, even if the string contains only a single character. Providing nothing but the character just won't do the job.

Types of constants

A *constant value* is an explicit number or character (such as 1, 0.5, or 'c') that doesn't change. As with variables, every constant has a type. In an expression such as n = 1; the constant value 1 is an int. To make 1 a `long` integer, write the statement as n = 1L;. The analogy is as follows: 1 represents a pickup truck with one ball in it, whereas 1L is a dump truck also with one ball. The number of balls is the same in both cases, but the capacity of one of the containers is much larger.

Following the int to long comparison, 1.0 represents the value 1 but in a floating-point container. Notice, however, that the default for floating-point constants is double. Thus, 1.0 is a double number and not a float.

The constant values true and false are of type bool. In keeping with C++'s attention to case, true is a constant but TRUE has no meaning.

A variable can be declared constant when it is created via the keyword const:

```
const double PI = 3.14159; // declare a constant variable
```

A const variable must be initialized with a value when it is declared, and its value cannot be changed by any future statement.

Variables declared const don't have to be named with all capitals, but by convention they often are. This is just a hint to the reader that this so-called variable is, in fact, not.

I admit that it may seem odd to declare a variable and then say that it can't change. Why bother? Largely because carefully named const variables can make a program a lot easier to understand. Consider the following two equivalent expressions:

```
double dC = 6.28318 * dR;   // what does this mean?
double dCircumference = 2 * PI * dRadius; // this is a
                            // lot easier to understand
```

It should be a lot clearer to the reader of this code that the second expression is multiplying the radius of something by 2π to calculate the circumference.

Range of Numeric Types

It may seem odd but the C++ standard doesn't say exactly how big a number each of the data types can accommodate. The standard speaks only to the relative size of each data type. For example, it says that the maximum long int is at least as large as the maximum int.

The authors of C++ weren't trying to be mysterious. They merely wanted to allow the compiler to implement the absolute fastest code possible for the base machine. The standard was designed to work for all different types of processors running different operating systems.

However, it is useful to know the limits for your particular implementation. Table 2-2 shows the size of each number type on a Windows PC using the Code::Blocks/gcc compiler that comes on the enclosed CD-ROM.

Table 2-2		Range of Numeric Types in Code::Block/gcc	
Variable	*Size (bytes)*	*Accuracy*	*Range*
short	2	exact	–32768 to 32767
int	4	exact	–2,147,483,648 to 2,147,483,647
long	4	exact	–2,147,483,648 to 2,147,483,647
long long int	8	exact	–9,223,372,036,854,775,808 to 9,223,372,036,854,775,807
float	4	7 digits	$\pm 3.4028 \times 10^{\pm 38}$
double	8	16 digits	$\pm 1.7977 \times 10^{\pm 308}$
long double	12	19 digits	$\pm 1.1897 \times 10^{\pm 4932}$

Attempting to calculate a number that's beyond the range of its type is known as an *overflow*. The C++ standard generally leaves the results of an overflow as undefined. That's another way that the definers of C++ remained flexible.

On the PC, a floating-point overflow results in an exception, which if not handled will cause your program to crash. (I don't discuss exceptions until Chapter 24.) As bad as that sounds, an integer overflow is worse — C++ silently generates an incorrect value without complaint.

C++ collision with filenames

Windows uses the backslash character to separate folder names in the path to a file. (This is a remnant of MS-DOS that Windows has not been able to shake.) Thus, Root\FolderA\File represents File within FolderA, which is a subdirectory of Root.

Unfortunately, MS-DOS's use of the backslash conflicts with the use of the backslash to indicate an escape character in C++. The character \\ is a backslash in C++. The MS-DOS path Root\FolderA\File is represented in C++ as the string "Root\\FolderA\\File".

Special characters

You can store any printable character you want in a `char` or `string` variable. You can also store a set of nonprintable characters that are used as character constants. See Table 2-3 for a description of these important nonprintable characters.

Table 2-3	Special Characters
Character Constant	*What It Is*
`'\n'`	newline
`'\t'`	tab
`'\040'`	The character whose value is 40 in octal (see Chapter 4 for a discussion of number systems)
`'\x20'`	The character whose value is 20 in hexadecimal (this is the same as `'\040'`)
`'\0'`	null (i.e., the character whose value is 0)
`'\\'`	backslash

You have already seen the newline character at the end of strings. This character breaks a string and puts the parts on separate lines. A newline character may appear anywhere within a string. For example:

```
"This is line 1\nThis is line 2"
```

appears on the output as

```
This is line 1
This is line 2
```

Similarly, the `\t` tab character moves output to the next tab position. (This position can vary, depending on the type of computer you're using to run the program.)

The numerical forms allow you to specify any nonprinting character that you like, but results may vary. The character represented by `0xFB`, for example, depends on the font and the character set (and may not be a legal character at all).

Because the backslash character is used to signify special characters, a character pair for the backslash itself is required. The character pair \\ represents the backslash.

Wide Loads on Char Highway

The standard `char` variable is a scant 1 byte wide and can handle only 255 different characters. This is plenty enough for European languages but not big enough to handle symbol-based languages such as kanji.

Several standards have arisen to extend the character set to handle the demands of these languages. UTF-8 uses a mixture of 8-, 16-, and 32-bit characters to implement almost every kanji or hieroglyph you can think of but still remain compatible with simple 8-bit ASCII. UTF-16 uses a mixture of 16- and 32-bit characters to achieve an expanded character set, and UTF-32 uses 32 bits for all characters.

 UTF stands for Unicode Transformation Format, from which it gets the common nickname Unicode.

 Table 2-4 describes the different character types supported by C++. At first, C++ tried to get by with a vaguely defined wide character type, `wchar_t`. This type was intended to be the wide character type native to the application program's environment. C++ '09 introduced specific types for UTF-16 and UTF-32.

 UTF-16 is the standard encoding for Windows and .NET applications. The `wchar_t` type refers to UTF-16 in the Code::Blocks/gcc compiler included on the CD-ROM.

Table 2-4	The C++ Character Types	
Variable	*Example*	*What It Is*
`char`	`'c'`	ASCII character
`wchar_t`	`L'c'`	Character in wide format
`char_16t`	`u'c'`	UTF-16 character
`char_32t`	`U'c'`	UTF-32 character

Any of the character types in Table 2-4 can be combined into strings as well:

```
wchar_t* wideString = L"this is a wide string";
```

(Ignore the asterisk for now. I have a lot to say about its meaning in Chapter 8.)

Are These Calculations Really Logical?

C++ provides a logical variable called `bool`. The type `bool` comes from *Boole*, the last name of the inventor of the logical calculus. A Boolean variable has two values: `true` and `false`.

There are actually calculations that result in the value `bool`. For example, `"x is equal to y"` is either `true` or `false`.

Mixed Mode Expressions

C++ allows you to mix variable types in a single expression. That is, you are allowed to add an integer with a `double` precision floating-point value. In the following expression, for example, `nValue1` is allowed to be an `int`:

```
// in the following expression the value of nValue1
// is converted into a double before performing the
// assignment
int nValue1 = 1;
nValue1 + 1.0;
```

An expression in which the two operands are not the same type is called a *mixed-mode expression*. Mixed-mode expressions generate a value whose type is equal to the more capable of the two operands. In this case, `nValue1` is converted to a `double` before the calculation proceeds. Similarly, an expression of one type may be assigned to a variable of a different type, as in the following statement:

```
// in the following assignment, the whole
// number part of fVariable is stored into nVariable
double dVariable = 1.0;
int nVariable;
nVariable = dVariable;
```

You can lose precision or range if the variable on the left side of the assignment is smaller. In the preceding example, C++ truncates the value of `dVariable` before storing it in `nVariable`.

Converting a larger value type into a smaller value type is called *demotion*, whereas converting values in the opposite direction is known as *promotion*. Programmers say that the value of `int` variable `nVariable1` is promoted to a `double` in expressions such as the following:

```
int nVariable1 = 1;
double dVariable = nVariable1;
```

Naming conventions

You may have noticed that the name of each of the variables that I create begins with a special character that seems to have nothing to do with the name. These special characters are not special to C++ at all; they are merely meant to jog the reader's memory and indicate the type of the variable. A partial list of these special characters follows. Using this convention, I can immediately recognize dVariable as a variable of type double, for example.

Character	Type
n	int
l	long
f	float
d	double
c	character
sz	string

Religious wars worse than the "Great Palin Debate of 2008" have broken out over whether or not this naming convention clarifies C++ code. It helps me, so I stick with it. Try it for awhile. If after a few months, you don't think it helps, feel free to change your naming convention.

Mixed-mode expressions are not a good idea. Avoid forcing C++ to do your conversions for you.

Automatic Declarations

This entire section works only for C++ '09.

If you are really lazy, you can let C++ determine the types of your variables for you. Consider the following declaration:

```
int nVar = 1;
```

You might ask, "Why can't C++ figure out the type of nVar?" The answer is, as of C++ '09, it will if you ask nicely, as follows:

```
auto var1 = 1;
auto var2 = 2.0;
```

This says, "declare var1 to be a variable of the same type as the constant value 1 (which happens to be an int) and declare var2 to be the same type as 2.0 (which is a double)."

I consider the term auto to be a particularly unfortunate choice for this purpose because prior to C++ '09, the keyword auto had a completely different meaning. However, auto had fallen out of use for at least ten years, so the standards people figured that it would be safe to usurp the term. Just be aware that if you see the keyword auto in some old code, you will need to remove it.

You can also tell C++ that you want a variable to be declared to be of the same type as another variable, whatever that might be, using the keyword decltyple().

```
int var1;
decltype(var1) var2; // declare var2 to be of the
                     // same type as var1
```

C++ replaces the decltype(var1) with the type of var1, again an int.

Chapter 3

Performing Mathematical Operations

. . . .

In This Chapter

▶ Defining mathematical operators in C++

▶ Using the C++ mathematical operators

▶ Identifying expressions

▶ Increasing clarity with special mathematical operators

. . . .

C++ offers all the common arithmetic operations: C++ programs can multiply, add, divide, and so forth. Programs have to be able to perform these operations to get anything done. What good is an insurance program if it can't calculate how much you're supposed to (over) pay?

C++ operations look like the arithmetic operations you would perform on a piece of paper, except you have to declare any variables before you can use them (as detailed in Chapter 2):

```
int var1;
int var2 = 1;
var1 = 2 * var2;
```

This code snippet declares two variables, var1 and var2. It initializes var2 to 1 and then stores the results of multiplying 2 times the value of var2 into var1.

This chapter describes the complete set of C++ mathematical operators.

Performing Simple Binary Arithmetic

A *binary operator* is one that has two arguments. If you can say var1 op var2, op must be a binary operator. The most common binary operators are the simple operations you performed in grade school. The binary operators are flagged in Table 3-1. (This table also includes the unary operators, which I describe a little later in this chapter.)

Table 3-1	Mathematical Operators in Order of Precedence	
Precedence	**Operator**	**What It Is**
1	+ (unary)	Effectively does nothing
1	- (unary)	Returns the negative of its argument
2	++ (unary)	Increment
2	-- (unary)	Decrement
3	* (binary)	Multiplication
3	/ (binary)	Division
3	% (binary)	Modulo
4	+ (binary)	Addition
4	- (binary)	Subtraction
5	=, *=,%=,+=,-= (special)	Assignment types

Multiplication, division, modulus, addition, and subtraction are the operators used to perform arithmetic. In practice, they work just like the familiar arithmetic operations as well. For example, using the binary operator for division with a floating point `double` variable looks like this:

```
double var = 133.0 / 10.0;
```

The expression 133/10 performs integer division, producing the `int` result 13 rather than the floating-point 13.3.

Each of the binary operators has the conventional meaning that you studied in grammar school — with one exception. You may not have encountered modulus in your studies. The *modulus* operator (%) works much like division, except it produces the remainder *after* division instead of the quotient. For example, 4 goes into 15 three times with a remainder of 3. Thus we say 15 modulus 4 is 3:

```
int var = 15 % 4; // var is initialized to 3
```

Modulus is not defined for floating-point variables because it depends on the round-off error inherent in integers. (I discuss round-off errors in Chapter 2.)

Decomposing Expressions

The most common type of statement in C++ is the expression. An *expression* is a C++ statement with a value. Every expression has a type, such as int, double, or char. A statement involving any mathematical operator is an expression since all these operators return a value. For example, 1 + 2 is an expression whose value is 3 and type is int. (Remember that a constant without a decimal point is of type int.)

Expressions can be complex or extremely simple. In fact, the statement 1 is an expression because it has a value (1) and a type (const int). The following statement has five expressions:

```
z = x * y + w;
```

The expressions are

```
x * y + w
x * y
x
y
w
```

Determining the Order of Operations

All operators perform some defined function. In addition, every operator has a *precedence* — a specified place in the order in which the expressions are evaluated. Consider, for example, how precedence affects solving the following problem:

```
int var = 2 * 3 + 1;
```

If the addition is performed before the multiplication, the value of the expression is 2 times 4, or 8. If the multiplication is performed first, the value is 6 plus 1, or 7.

The precedence of the operators determines who goes first. Table 3-1 shows that multiplication has higher precedence than addition, so the result is 7. (The concept of precedence is also present in arithmetic. C++ adheres to the common arithmetic precedence.)

So what happens when two operators of the same precedence appear in the same expression? For example:

```
int var = 8 / 4 / 2;
```

When operators of the same precedence appear in the same expression, they are evaluated from left to right (the same rule applied in arithmetic). Thus, in this code snippet, var is equal to 8 divided by 4 (which is 2) divided by 2 (which is 1).

The expression

```
x / 100 + 32
```

divides x by 100 before adding 32. But what if the programmer wanted to divide x by *100 plus 32?* The programmer can change the precedence by bundling expressions together in parentheses (shades of algebra!), as follows:

```
x /(100 + 32)
```

This expression has the same effect as dividing x by 132. The original expression

```
x / 100 + 32
```

is identical to the expression

```
(x / 100) + 32
```

Performing Unary Operations

Arithmetic binary operators — those operators that take two arguments — are familiar to a lot of us from school days. But consider the *unary operators,* which take a single argument (for example, –a). Many unary operations are not so well known.

The unary mathematical operators are plus, minus, plus-plus, and minus-minus (respectively, +, –, ++, and —). The minus operator changes the sign of its argument. Positive numbers become negative and vice versa. The plus operator does not change the sign of its argument. The plus operator is rarely, if ever, used.

```
int var1 = 10;
int var2 = -var1;   // var2 is now -10
```

The latter expression uses the minus unary operator (–) to calculate the value negative 10.

Why define a separate increment operator?

The authors of C++ noted that programmers add 1 more than any other constant. To provide some convenience, a special add 1 instruction was added to the language. In addition, most present-day computer processors have an increment instruction that is faster than the addition instruction. Back when C++ was created, however — with microprocessors being what they were — saving a few instructions was a big deal.

The ++ and the — operators might be new to you. These operators (respectively) add one to their arguments or subtract one from their arguments, so they're known (also respectively) as the *increment* and *decrement operators*. Because they're dependent upon numbers that can be counted, they're limited to non-floating-point variables. For example, the value of var after executing the following expression is 11:

```
int var = 10;    // initalize var
var++;           // now increment it
                 // value of var is now 11
```

The increment and decrement operators are peculiar in that both come in two flavors: a *prefix* version and a *postfix* version (known as pre-increment and post-increment, respectively). Consider, for example, the increment operator (the decrement works in the same way).

Suppose that the variable n has the value 5. Both ++n and n++ increment n to the value 6. The difference between the two is that the value of ++n in an expression is 6 while the value of n++ is 5. The following example illustrates this difference:

```
// declare three integer variables
int n1, n2, n3;

// the value of both n1 and n2 is 6
n1 = 5;
n2 = ++n1;

// the value of n1 is 6 but the value of n3 is 5
n1 = 5;
n3 = n1++;
```

Thus n2 is given the value of n1 after n1 has been incremented (using the pre-increment operator), whereas n3 gets the value of n1 before it is incremented using the post-increment operator.

Using Assignment Operators

An *assignment operator* is a binary operator that changes the value of its left argument. The equal sign (=), a simple assignment operator, is an absolute necessity in any programming language. This operator puts the value of the right-hand argument into the left-hand argument. The other assignment operators are odd enough that they seem to be someone's whim.

So what about the following:

```
int var1;
int var2 = 2;
var1 = var2 = 1;
```

If we used the left to right rule, `var1` ends up with the value 2 but `var2` with the value 1, which is counterintuitive. To avoid this, multiple assignment operators are evaluated from right to left. Thus, the example snippet assigns the value 1 to `var2` and then copies the same value into `var1`.

The creators of C (from which C++ originated) noticed that assignments often follow the form of

```
variable = variable # constant
```

where # is some binary operator. Thus, to increment an integer operator by 2, the programmer might write

```
nVariable = nVariable + 2;
```

This expression says, "Add 2 to the value of `nVariable` and store the results back into `nVariable`." Doing so changes the value of `nVariable` to 2 more than it was.

Because the same variable appears on both sides of the = sign, the same Fathers of the C Revolution decided to create a version of the assignment operator with a binary operator attached. This says, in effect, "Thou shalt perform whatever operation on a variable and store the results right back into the same variable."

Every binary operator has one of these nifty *assignment versions*. Thus, the assignment just given could have been written this way:

```
nVariable = nVariable + 2;
nVariable += 2;
```

Here the first line says (being very explicit now), "Take the value of nVari-able, add 2, and store the results back into nVariable." The next line says (a bit more abruptly), "Add 2 to the value of nVariable."

Other than assignment itself, these assignment operators are not used all that often. However, as odd as they might look, sometimes they can actually make the resulting program easier to read.

Chapter 4

Performing Logical Operations

. . . .

. . . .

The most common statement in C++ is the expression. Most expressions involve the arithmetic operators, such as addition (+), subtraction (–) and multiplication (*), as demonstrated in Chapter 3.

This chapter describes a whole other class of operators known as the *logical operators*. In comparison with the arithmetic operators, most people don't think nearly as much about this type of operation. It isn't that people don't deal with logical operations such as AND and OR — we compute them constantly. I won't eat cereal unless the bowl contains cereal AND the bowl has milk in it AND the cereal is coated with sugar (lots of sugar). I'll have a Scotch IF it's single-malt AND someone else is paying for it. People use such logical operations all the time but they don't write them down as machine instructions (or think of them in that light).

Logical operators fall into two types. The AND and OR operators are what I will call *simple logical operators*. The second type of logical operator is the *bitwise* operator. People don't use the bitwise operator in their daily business at all; it's unique to the computer world. We'll start with the simple and sneak up on the bitwise in this chapter.

Why Mess with Logical Operations?

C++ programs have to make decisions. A program that can't make decisions is of limited use. The temperature-conversion program laid out in Chapter 1 is about as complex as you can get without *some* type of decision-making. Invariably a computer program gets to the point where it has to figure out situations such as "Do *this* if the *a* variable is less than some value; do that *other* thing if it's not." The ability to make decisions is what makes a computer appear to be intelligent. (By the same token, that same property makes a computer look really stupid when the program makes the wrong decision.) Making decisions, right or wrong, requires the use of logical operators.

Using the Simple Logical Operators

The simple logical operators, shown in Table 4-1, evaluate to `true` or `false`.

Table 4-1	Simple Operators Representing Daily Logic
Operator	**What It Does**
==	Equality; `true` if the left-hand argument has the same value as the right
!=	Inequality; opposite of equality
>, <	Greater than, less than; `true` if the left-hand argument is greater than or less than the right-hand argument
>=, <=	Greater than or equal to, less than or equal to; `true` if either > or == is `true`, OR either < or == is `true`
&&	AND; `true` if both the left-and right-hand arguments are `true`
||	OR; `true` if either the left-or the right-hand argument is `true`
!	NOT; `true` if its argument is `false`; otherwise, `false`

The first six entries in Table 4-1 are comparison operators. The equality operator is used to compare two numbers. For example, the following is `true` if the value of n is 0, and is `false` otherwise:

```
n == 0;
```

Looks can be deceiving. Don't confuse the equality operator (==) with the assignment operator (=). Not only is this a common mistake, but it's a mistake that the C++ compiler generally cannot catch — that makes it more than twice as bad. The following statement does not initialize n to 0; it compares the current value of n with 0 and then does nothing with the results of that comparison:

```
n == 0;    // programmer meant to say n = 0
```

The greater-than (>) and less-than (<) operators are similarly common in everyday life. The following logical comparison is true:

```
int n1 = 1;
int n2 = 2;
n1 < n2;
```

The greater-than-or-equal-to operator (<=) and the less-than-or-equal-to operator (>=) are similar to the less-than and greater-than operators, with one major exception. They include equality; the other operators don't.

The && (AND) and || (OR) work in combination with the other logic operators to build more complex logical expressions, like this:

```
// the following is true if n2 is greater than n1
// AND n2 is smaller than n3
// (this is the most common way determining that n2 is in
// the range of n1 to n3, exclusive)
(n1 < n2) && (n2 < n3);
```

Storing logical values

The result of a logical operation can be assigned to a variable of type `bool`. The term `bool` refers to Boolean algebra, which is the algebra of logic. This was invented by a British mathematician, George Boole, in the nineteenth century.

```
int n1 = 1;
int n2 = 2;
bool b;
b = (n1 == n2);
```

This expression highlights the difference between the assignment operator = and the comparison operator ==. The expression says, "Compare the variables n1 and n2. Store the results of this comparison in the variable b."

The following BoolTest program demonstrates the use of a `bool` variable:

```
// BoolTest - compare variables input from the
//            keyboard and store the results off
//            into a logical variable
#include <cstdio>
#include <cstdlib>
#include <iostream>
using namespace std;
```

```cpp
int main(int nNumberofArgs, char* pszArgs[])
{
    // set output format for bool variables
    // to true and false instead
    // of 1 and 0
    cout.setf(cout.boolalpha);

    // input two values
    int nArg1;
    cout << "Input value 1: ";
    cin >> nArg1;

    int nArg2;
    cout << "Input value 2: ";
    cin >> nArg2;

    // compare them and store the result
    bool b;
    b = nArg1 == nArg2;

    cout << "The statement, " << nArg1
         << " equals "        << nArg2
         << " is "            << b
         << endl;

    // wait until user is ready before terminating program
    // to allow the user to see the program results
    system("PAUSE");
    return 0;
}
```

The first line `cout.setf()` makes sure that our `bool` variable b is output as `"true"` or `"false"`. The next section explains why this is necessary.

The program inputs two values from the keyboard and displays the result of the equality comparison:

```
Input value 1: 5
Input value 2: 5
The statement, 5 equals 5 is true
Press any key to continue . . .
```

The special value `endl` inserts a newline. The difference between the value `endl` and the character `'\n'` as described in Chapter 2 is subtle and explained in Chapter 23.

Using logical int variables

C++ hasn't always had a `bool` type variable. Back in the old days (before that guy on TV kept walking around saying, "Can you hear me now?"), C++ used `int` variables to store logical values. A value of 0 was considered `false` and all other values `true`. By the same token, a logical operator generated a 0 for `false` and a 1 for `true`. (Thus, thus `10 < 5` returned 0 while `10 > 5` returned 1.)

C++ retains a high degree of compatibility between `bool` and `int` to support the older programs. You get completely different output from the `BitTest` program if you remove the line `cout.setf(cout.boolalpha)`:

```
Input value 1: 5
Input value 2: 5
The statement, 5 equals 5 is 1
Press any key to continue . . .
```

Variables of type `int` and `bool` can be mixed in expressions as well. For example, C++ allows the following bizarre statement without batting an eyelid:

```
int n;
n = (nArg1 == nArg2) * 5;
```

This sets n to 5 if `nArg1` and `nArg2` are equal and 0 otherwise.

Be careful performing logical operations on floating-point variables

Round-off errors in floating-point computation can create havoc with logical operations. Consider the following example:

```
float f1 = 10.0;
float f2 = f1 / 3;
bool b1 = (f1 == (f2 * 3.0));   // are these two equal?
```

Even though it's obvious to us that `f1` is equal to `f2` times 3, the resulting value of `b1` is not *necessarily* `true`. A floating-point variable cannot hold an unlimited number of significant digits. Thus, `f2` is not equal to the number we'd call "three-and-a-third," but rather to 3.3333..., stopping after some number of decimal places.

A `float` variable supports about 7 digits of accuracy while a `double` supports a skosh over 16 digits. I say "about" and "skosh" because the computer is likely to generate a number like 3.3333347 due to vagaries in floating-point calculations.

Now, in pure math, the number of 3s after the decimal point is infinite, but no computer built can handle infinity. So, after multiplying 3.3333 by 3, you get 9.9999 instead of the 10 you'd get if you multiplied "three-and-a-third" — in effect, a *round-off error.* Such small differences may be unnoticeable to a person but not to the computer. Equality means exactly that — *exact* equality.

Modern processors are sophisticated in performing such calculations. The processor may, in fact, accommodate the round-off error, but from inside C++, you can't predict exactly what any given processor will do.

The safer comparison follows:

```
float f1 = 10.0;
float f2 = f1 / 3;
float f3 = f2 * 3.0;
float delta = f1 - f3;
bool bEqual = -0.0001 < delta && delta < 0.0001;
```

This comparison is `true` if `f1` and `f3` are within some small delta from each other, which should still be `true` even if you take some small round-off error into account.

Short circuits and C++

The logical AND `&&` and logical OR `||` operators perform what is called *short-circuit evaluation.* Consider the following:

```
condition1 && condition2
```

If `condition1` is *not* `true`, the overall result is *not* `true`, no matter what the value of `condition2`. (For example, `condition2` could be `true` *or* `false` without changing the result.) The same situation occurs in the following:

```
condition1 || condition2
```

If `condition1` is `true`, the result is `true`, no matter what the value of `condition2` is.

To save time, C++ doesn't evaluate `condition2` if it doesn't need to. For example, in the expression `condition1 && condition2`, C++ doesn't evaluate `condition2` if `condition1` is `false`. Likewise, in the expression `condition1 || condition2`, C++ doesn't evaluate `condition2` if `condition1` is `true`. This is known as short-circuit evaluation.

Short-circuit evaluation may mean that `condition2` is not evaluated even if that condition has side effects. Consider the following admittedly contrived code snippet:

```
int nArg1 = 1;
int nArg2 = 2;
int nArg3 = 3;

bool b = (nArg1 > nArg2) && (nArg2++ > nArg3);
```

The variable `nArg2` is never incremented because the comparison `nArg2 > nArg3` is not performed. There's no need because `nArg1 < nArg2` already returned a `false` so the overall expression must be `false`.

Expressing Binary Numbers

C++ variables are stored internally as so-called binary numbers. Binary numbers are stored as a sequence of 1 and 0 values known as *bits*. Most of the time, you don't really need to deal with which particular bits you use to represent numbers. Sometimes, however, it's practical and convenient to tinker with numbers at the bit level — so C++ provides a set of operators for that purpose.

Fortunately, you won't have to deal too often with C++ variables at the bit level, so it's pretty safe to consider the remainder of this chapter a Deep Techie excursion.

The so-called *bitwise* logical operators operate on their arguments at the bit level. To understand how they work, let's first examine how computers store variables.

The decimal number system

The numbers we've been familiar with from the time we could first count on our fingers are known as *decimal numbers* because they're based on the number 10. (If beer by the six-pack had been invented early enough, our number system might well be based on the number 6.) In general, the programmer expresses C++ variables as decimal numbers. Thus you could specify the value of `var` as (say) 123, but consider the implications.

A number such as 123 refers to 1 * 100 + 2 * 10 + 3 * 1. All of these base numbers — 100, 10, and 1 — are powers of 10.

```
123 = 1 * 100 + 2 * 10 + 3 * 1
```

Expressed in a slightly different (but equivalent) way, 123 looks like this:

$$123 = 1 * 10^2 + 2 * 10^1 + 3 * 10^0$$

Remember that *any* number *to the zero power* is 1.

Other number systems

Well, okay, using 10 as the basis (or *base*) of our counting system probably stems from those 10 human fingers, the original counting tools. An alternative base for a counting system could just as easily have been 20 (maybe the inventor of base 10 had shoes on at the time).

If our numbering scheme had been invented by dogs, it might well be based on 8 (one digit of each paw is out of sight on the back part of the leg). Mathematically, such an *octal* system would have worked just as well:

$$123_{10} = 1 * 8^2 + 7 * 8^1 + 3 * 8^0 = 173_8$$

The small 10 and 8 here refer to the numbering system, 10 for decimal (base 10) and 8 for octal (base 8). A counting system may use any positive base.

The binary number system

Computers have essentially two fingers. (Maybe that's why computers are so stupid: without an opposing thumb, they can't grasp anything. And then again, maybe not.) Computers prefer counting using base 2. The number 123_{10} would be expressed this way:

```
123₁₀ = 0*2⁷ + 1*2⁶ + 1*2⁵ + 1*2⁴ + 1*2³ + 0*2² +1*2¹ + 1*2⁰
123₁₀ = 0*128 + 1*64 + 1*32 + 1*16 + 1*8 + 0*4 +1*2 + 1*1
      = 01111011₂
```

Computer convention expresses binary numbers by using 4, 8, 16, 32, or even 64 binary digits, even if the leading digits are 0. This is also because of the way computers are built internally.

Because the term *digit* refers to a multiple of 10, a *binary digit* is called a *bit* (an abbreviation of *binary digit*). A *byte* is made up of 8 bits. (Calling a binary digit a *byte-it* didn't seem like a good idea.) Memory is usually measured in bytes (like rolls are measured in units of baker's dozen).

With such a small base, you have to use a *large* number of bits to express numbers. Human beings don't want the hassle of using an expression such as 01111011_2 to express such a mundane value as 123_{10}. Programmers prefer to express numbers by using an even number of bits. The octal system — which is based on 3 bits — was the default binary system in the early days of C. We see a vestige of this even today — a constant that begins with a 0 is assumed to be octal in C++. Thus, the line:

```
cout << "0173 = " << 0173 << endl;
```

produces the following output:

```
0173 = 123
```

However, octal has been almost completely replaced by the *hexadecimal* system, which is based on 4-bit digits.

Hexadecimal uses the same digits for the numbers 0 through 9. For the digits between 9 and 16, hexadecimal uses the first six letters of the alphabet: A for 10, B for 11, and so on. Thus, 123_{10} becomes $7B_{16}$, like this:

```
123 = 7 * 16¹ + B (i.e. 11) * 16⁰ = 7B₁₆
```

Programmers prefer to express hexadecimal numbers in multiples of 4 hexadecimal digits even when the leading digit in each case is 0.

Finally, who wants to express a hexadecimal number such as $7B_{16}$ by using a subscript? Terminals don't even *support* subscripts. Even on a word processor such as the one I'm using now, it's a drag to change fonts to and from subscript mode just to type two lousy digits. Therefore, programmers (no fools they) use the convention of beginning a hexadecimal number with a 0x. (Why? Well, the reason for such a strange convention goes back to the early days of C, in a galaxy far, far, away . . . never mind.) Thus, 7B becomes 0x7B. Using this convention, the hexadecimal number 0x7B is equal to 123 decimal while 0x123 hexadecimal is equal to 291 decimal. The code snippet:

```
cout << "0x7B  = " << 0x7B  << endl;
cout << "0x123 = " << 0x123 << endl;
```

produces the following output:

```
0x7B  = 123
0x123 = 291
```

You can use all the mathematical operators on hexadecimal numbers in the same way you'd apply them to decimal numbers. (Well, okay, most of us can't perform a multiplication such as 0xC * 0xE in our heads, but that has more to do with the multiplication tables we learned in school than it has to do with any limitation in the number system.)

Performing Bitwise Logical Operations

All C++ numbers can be expressed in binary form. Binary numbers use only the digits 1 and 0 to represent a value. Table 4-2 defines the set of operations that work on numbers *one bit at a time,* hence the term *bitwise* operators.

Table 4-2	Bitwise Operators
Operator	*Function*
~	NOT: Toggle each bit from 1 to 0 and from 0 to 1
&	AND each bit of the left-hand argument with that on the right
|	OR each bit of the left-hand argument with that on the right
^	XOR (exclusive OR) each bit of the left-hand argument with that on the right

Bitwise operations can potentially store a lot of information in a small amount of memory. Many traits in the world have only two possibilities — that are either this way or that way. You are either married or you're not. You are either male or female (at least that's what my driver's license says). In C++, you can store each of these traits in a single bit — in this way, you can pack 32 separate binary properties into a single 32-bit `int`.

In addition, bit operations can be extremely fast. No performance penalty is paid for that 32-to-1 savings.

Even though memory is cheap these days, it's not unlimited. Sometimes, when you're storing large amounts of data, this ability to pack a whole lot of properties into a single word is a big advantage.

The single-bit operators

The bitwise operators — AND (&), OR (|) and NOT (~) — perform logic operations on single bits. If you consider 0 to be `false` and 1 to be `true` (it doesn't *have* to be this way, but it's a common convention), you can say things like the following for the NOT operator:

```
~ 1 (true)  is 0 (false)
~ 0 (false) is 1 (true)
```

The AND operator is defined as following:

```
1 (true) & 1 (true)  is 1 (true)
1 (true) & 0 (false) is 0 (false)
```

It's a similar situation for the OR operator:

```
1 (true)  | 0 (false) is 1 (true)
0 (false) | 0 (false) is 0 (false)
```

The definition of the AND operator appears in Table 4-3.

Table 4-3		Truth Table for the AND Operator
AND	*1*	*0*
1	1	0
0	0	0

You read Table 4-3 as the column corresponding to the value of one of the arguments while the row corresponds to the other. Thus, 1 & 0 is 0. (Column 1 and row 0.) The only combination that returns anything other than 0 is 1 & 1. (This is known as a truth table.)

Similarly, the truth table for the OR operator is shown in Table 4-4.

Table 4-4		Truth Table for the OR Operator
OR	*1*	*0*
1	1	1
0	1	0

One other logical operation that is not so commonly used in day-to-day living is the OR ELSE operator, commonly contracted to XOR. XOR is `true` if either argument is `true` but not if both are `true`. The truth table for XOR is shown in Table 4-5.

Table 4-5		Truth Table for the XOR Operator
XOR	*1*	*0*
1	0	1
0	1	0

Armed with these single-bit operators, we can take on the C++ bitwise logical operations.

Using the bitwise operators

The bitwise operators are used much like any other binary arithmetic operator. The NOT operator is the easiest to understand. To NOT a number is to NOT each bit that makes up that number (and to a programmer, that sentence makes perfect sense — honest). Consider this example:

```
~0110₂ (0x6)
 1001₂ (0x9)
```

Thus we say that ~0x6 equals 0x9 (pronounced "NOT 6 equals 9").

The following calculation demonstrates the & operator:

```
    0110₂
&
    0011₂
    0010₂
```

Beginning with the most significant bit, 0 AND 0 is 0. In the next bit, 1 AND 0 is 0. In bit 3, 1 AND 1 is 1. In the least significant bit, 0 AND 1 is 0. Expressed in hexadecimal, the same expression appears as follows:

```
0x6          0110₂
&            &
0x3          0011₂
0x2          0010₂
```

In shorthand, we say that 0x6 & 0x3 equals 0x2 (pronounced "6 AND 3 equals 2").

A simple test

The following program illustrates the bitwise operators in action. The program initializes two variables and outputs the result of ANDing, ORing, and XORing them:

```
// BitTest - initialize two variables and output the
//           results of applying the ~,& , | and ^
//           operations
#include <cstdio>
#include <cstdlib>
#include <iostream>
using namespace std;
```

```
int main(int nNumberofArgs, char* pszArgs[])
{
    // set output format to hexadecimal
    cout.unsetf(cout.dec);
    cout.setf(cout.hex);

    // initialize two arguments
    int nArg1 = 0x78ABCDEF;
    int nArg2 = 0x12345678;

    // now perform each operation in turn
    // first the unary NOT operator
    cout << " nArg1 = 0x" << nArg1  << endl;
    cout << "~nArg1 = 0x" << ~nArg1 << "\n" << endl;
    cout << " nArg2 = 0x" << nArg2  << endl;
    cout << "~nArg2 = 0x" << ~nArg2 << "\n" << endl;

    // now the binary operators
    cout << "  0x" << nArg1 << "\n"
         << "& 0x" << nArg2 << "\n"
         << "  ----------" << "\n"
         << "  0x" << (nArg1 & nArg2) << "\n"
         << endl;

    cout << "  0x" << nArg1 << "\n"
         << "| 0x" << nArg2 << "\n"
         << "  ----------" << "\n"
         << "  0x" << (nArg1 | nArg2) << "\n"
         << endl;

    cout << "  0x" << nArg1 << "\n"
         << "^ 0x" << nArg2 << "\n"
         << "  ----------" << "\n"
         << "  0x" << (nArg1 ^ nArg2) << "\n"
         << endl;

    // wait until user is ready before terminating program
    // to allow the user to see the program results
    system("PAUSE");
    return 0;
}
```

The first two expressions in our program, cout.unsetf(ios::dec) and cout.setf(ios::hex), changes the default output format from decimal to hexadecimal. (You'll have to trust me until Chapter 23 that it works.)

The remainder of the program is straightforward. The program assigns nArg1 the test value 0x78ABCDEF and nArg2 the value 0x12345678. The program then outputs all combinations of bitwise calculations. The extra newlines, such as in the following line, cause a blank line to appear to help group the output to make it easier to read:

```
cout << "~nArg1 = 0x" << ~nArg1 << "\n" << endl;
```

The output appears as follows:

```
 nArg1 = 0x78abcdef
~nArg1 = 0x87543210

 nArg2 = 0x12345678
~nArg2 = 0xedcba987

  0x78abcdef
& 0x12345678
  ----------
  0x10204468

  0x78abcdef
| 0x12345678
  ----------
  0x7abfdfff

  0x78abcdef
^ 0x12345678
  ----------
  0x6a9f9b97

Press any key to continue . . .
```

You can convert each of the digits into binary to check the bitwise arithmetic. For example, from the first digit of each of the examples you can see that 7 & 1 equals 1, 7 | 1 equals 7 and 7 ^ 1 equals 6.

Do something logical with logical calculations

Running through simple and bitwise logical calculations in your head at parties is fun (well, okay, for *some* of us), but a program has to make actual, practical *use* of these values to make them worth the trouble. Coming right up: Chapter 5 demonstrates how logical calculations are used to control program flow.

Chapter 5

Controlling Program Flow

• •

• •

The simple programs that appear in Chapters 1 through 4 process a fixed number of inputs, output the result of that calculation, and quit. However, these programs lack any form of flow control. They cannot make tests of any sort. Computer programs are all about making decisions. If the user presses a key, the computer responds to the command.

For example, if the user presses Ctrl+C, the computer copies the currently selected area to the Clipboard. If the user moves the mouse, the pointer moves on the screen. If the user clicks the right mouse button with the Windows key depressed, the computer crashes. The list goes on and on. Programs that don't make decisions are necessarily pretty boring.

Flow-control commands allow the program to decide what action to take based on the results of the C++ logical operations performed (see Chapter 4). There are basically three types of flow-control statements: the branch, the loop, and the switch.

Controlling Program Flow with the Branch Commands

The simplest form of flow control is the *branch statement*. This instruction allows the program to decide which of two paths to take through C++ instructions, based on the results of a logical expression (see Chapter 4 for a description of logical expressions).

In C++, the branch statement is implemented using the `if` statement:

```
if (m > n)
{
    // Path 1
    // ...instructions to be executed if
    // m is greater than n
}
else
{
    // Path 2
    // ...instructions to be executed if not
}
```

First, the logical expression `m > n` is evaluated. If the result of the expression is `true`, control passes down the path marked `Path 1` in the previous snippet. If the expression is `false`, control passes to `Path 2`. The `else` clause is optional. If it is not present, C++ acts as if it is present but empty.

Actually, the braces are optional if there's only one statement to execute as part of the `if`. If you lose the braces, however, it's embarrassingly easy to make a mistake that the C++ compiler can't catch. The braces serve as a guide marker; it's much safer to include 'em.

The following program demonstrates the `if` statement (note all the lovely braces):

```
// BranchDemo - input two numbers. Go down one path of the
//              program if the first argument is greater
//              than the first or the other path if not
#include <cstdio>
#include <cstdlib>
#include <iostream>
using namespace std;

int main(int nNumberofArgs, char* pszArgs[])
{
    // input the first argument...
    int nArg1;
    cout << "Enter arg1: ";
    cin  >> nArg1;

    // ...and the second
    int nArg2;
    cout << "Enter arg2: ";
    cin  >> nArg2;

    // now decide what to do:
    if (nArg1 > nArg2)
```

```
    {
        cout<< "Argument 1 is greater than argument 2"
            << endl;
    }
    else
    {
        cout<< "Argument 1 is not greater than argument 2"
            << endl;
    }

    // wait until user is ready before terminating program
    // to allow the user to see the program results
    system("PAUSE");
    return 0;
}
```

Here the program reads two integers from the keyboard and compares them.
If nArg1 is greater than nArg2, control flows to the output statement `cout`
`<< "Argument 1 is greater than argument 2"`. If nArg1 is not
greater than nArg2, control flows to the `else` clause where the statement
`cout << "Argument 1 is not greater than argument 2\n"` is
executed. Here's what that operation looks like:

```
Enter arg1: 5
Enter arg2: 6
Argument 1 is not greater than argument 2
Press any key to continue . . .
```

Notice how the instructions within the `if` blocks are indented slightly. This
is strictly for human consumption because C++ ignores whitespace (spaces,
tabs, and newlines). It may seem trivial but a clear coding style increases the
readability of your C++ program. The Code::Blocks editor can enforce this or
any one of several other coding guidelines for you.

Executing Loops in a Program

Branch statements allow you to control the flow of a program's execution
from one path of a program or another. This is a big improvement but still
not enough to write full-strength programs.

Consider the problem of updating the computer display. The typical PC must
update well over a thousand pixels as it paints an image from left to right. It
repeats this process for each of the thousand or so rows on the display. A
program would require several million instructions just to display a single
image if the program did not loop through the same set of instructions for
each pixel.

Looping while a condition is true

The simplest form of looping statement is the `while` loop. Here's what the `while` loop looks like:

```
while(condition)
{
    // ...repeatedly executed as long as condition is true
}
```

The *condition* is tested. This condition could be `if var > 10` or `if var1 == var2` or anything else you might think of. If the condition is `true`, the statements within the braces are executed. Upon encountering the closed brace, C++ returns control to the beginning, and the process starts over. The effect is that the C++ code *within the braces is executed repeatedly* as long as the condition is `true`. (Kind of reminds me of how I get to walk around the yard with my dog until she . . . well, until we're done.)

If the condition were `true` the first time, what would make it be `false` in the future? Consider the following example program:

```
// WhileDemo - input a loop count. Loop while
//             outputting astring arg number of times.
#include <cstdio>
#include <cstdlib>
#include <iostream>
using namespace std;

int main(int nNumberofArgs, char* pszArgs[])
{
    // input the loop count
    int nLoopCount;
    cout << "Enter loop count: ";
    cin  >> nLoopCount;

    // now loop that many times
    while (nLoopCount > 0)
    {
        nLoopCount = nLoopCount - 1;
        cout << "Only " << nLoopCount
             << " loops to go" << endl;
    }

    // wait until user is ready before terminating program
    // to allow the user to see the program results
    system("PAUSE");
    return 0;
}
```

WhileDemo begins by retrieving a loop count from the user, which it stores in the variable nLoopCount. The program then executes a while loop. The while first tests nLoopCount. If nLoopCount is greater than 0, the program enters the body of the loop (the *body* is the code between the braces), where it decrements nLoopCount by 1 and outputs the result to the display. The program then returns to the top of the loop to test whether nLoopCount is still positive.

When executed, the program WhileDemo outputs the results shown in this next snippet. Here I entered a loop count of 5. The result is that the program loops five times, each time outputting a countdown:

```
Enter loop count: 5
Only 4 loops to go
Only 3 loops to go
Only 2 loops to go
Only 1 loops to go
Only 0 loops to go
Press any key to continue . . .
```

If the user enters a negative loop count, the program skips the loop entirely. That's because the specified condition is never true, so control never enters the loop. In addition, if the user enters a very large number, the program loops for a long time before completing.

A separate, less frequently used version of the while loop known as the do . . . while appears identical except the condition isn't tested until the bottom of the loop:

```
do
{
    // ...the inside of the loop
} while (condition);
```

Because the condition isn't tested until the end, the body of the do . . . while is always executed at least once.

The condition is checked only at the beginning of the while loop or at the end of the do . . . while loop. Even if the condition ceases to be true at some time during the execution of the loop, control does not exit the loop until the condition is retested.

Using the autoincrement/ autodecrement feature

Programmers very often use the autoincrement ++ or the autodecrement -- operators with loops that count something. Notice from the following snippet extracted from the `WhileDemo` example that the program decrements the loop count by using assignment and subtraction statements, like this:

```
// now loop that many times
while (nLoopCount > 0)
{
    nLoopCount = nLoopCount - 1;
    cout << "Only " << loopCount
        << " loops to go" << endl;
}
```

A more compact version uses the *autodecrement* feature, which does what you may well imagine:

```
while (nLoopCount > 0)
{
    nLoopCount--;
    cout << "Only " << nLoopCount
        << " loops to go" << endl;
}
```

The logic in this version is the same as in the original. The only difference is the way that `nLoopCount` is decremented.

Because the autodecrement both decrements its argument *and* returns its value, the decrement operation can be combined with the `while` loop. In particular, the following version is the smallest loop yet:

```
while (nLoopCount-- > 0)
{
    cout << "Only " << nLoopCount
        << " loops to go" << endl;
}
```

Believe it or not, `nLoopcount-- > 0` is the version that most C++ programmers would use. It's not that C++ programmers like being cute (although they do). In fact, the more compact version (which embeds the autoincrement or autodecrement feature in the logical comparison) is easier to read, especially as you gain experience.

Both `nLoopCount--` and `--nLoopCount` expressions decrement `nLoop Count`. The former expression, however, returns the value of `loopCount` *before* being decremented; the latter expression does so *after* being decremented.

How often should the autodecrement version of `WhileDemo` execute when the user enters a loop count of 1? If you use the pre-decrement version, the value of `--nLoopCount` is 0, and the body of the loop is never entered. With the post-decrement version, the value of `loopCount--` is 1, and control enters the loop.

Beware thinking that the version of the program with the autodecrement command executes faster (since it contains fewer statements). It probably executes exactly the same. Modern compilers are good at getting the number of machine-language instructions down to a minimum, no matter which of the decrement instructions shown here you actually use.

Using the for loop

The most common form of loop is the `for` loop. The `for` loop is preferred over the more basic `while` loop because it's generally easier to read (there's really no other advantage).

The `for` loop has the following format:

```
for (initialization; conditional; increment)
{
    // ...body of the loop
}
```

The `for` loop is equivalent to the following `while` loop:

```
{
    initialization;
    while(conditional)
    {
        {
            // ...body of the loop
        }
        increment;
    }
}
```

Execution of the `for` loop begins with the *initialization clause,* which got its name because it's normally where counting variables are initialized. The initialization clause is executed only once, when the `for` loop is first encountered.

Execution continues with the *conditional clause*. This clause works just like the while loop: As long as the conditional clause is true, the for loop continues to execute.

After the code in the body of the loop finishes executing, control passes to the increment clause before returning to check the conditional clause — thereby repeating the process. The increment clause normally houses the autoincrement or autodecrement statements used to update the counting variables.

The for loop is best understood by example. The following ForDemo program is nothing more than the WhileDemo converted to use the for loop construct:

```cpp
// ForDemo1 - input a loop count. Loop while
//            outputting astring arg number of times.
#include <cstdio>
#include <cstdlib>
#include <iostream>
using namespace std;

int main(int nNumberofArgs, char* pszArgs[])
{
    // input the loop count
    int nLoopCount;
    cout << "Enter loop count: ";
    cin  >> nLoopCount;

    // count up to the loop count limit
    for (; nLoopCount > 0;)
    {
        nLoopCount = nLoopCount - 1;
        cout << "Only " << nLoopCount
             << " loops to go" << endl;
    }

    // wait until user is ready before terminating program
    // to allow the user to see the program results
    system("PAUSE");
    return 0;
}
```

The program reads a value from the keyboard into the variable loopCount. The for starts out comparing loopCount to 0. Control passes into the for loop if loopCount is greater than 0. Once inside the for loop, the program decrements loopCount and displays the result. That done, the program returns to the for loop control. Control skips to the next line after the for loop as soon as loopCount has been decremented to 0.

All three sections of a `for` loop may be empty. An empty initialization or increment section does nothing. An empty comparison section is treated like a comparison that returns `true`.

This `for` loop has two small problems. First, it's destructive — not in the sense of what my puppy does to a slipper, but in the sense that it changes the value of `loopCount`, "destroying" the original value. Second, this `for` loop counts backward from large values down to smaller values. These two problems are addressed by adding a dedicated counting variable to the `for` loop. Here's what it looks like:

```
// ForDemo2 - input a loop count. Loop while
//            outputting astring arg number of times.
#include <cstdio>
#include <cstdlib>
#include <iostream>
using namespace std;

int main(int nNumberofArgs, char* pszArgs[])
{
    // input the loop count
    int nLoopCount;
    cout << "Enter loop count: ";
    cin  >> nLoopCount;

    // count up to the loop count limit
    for (int i = 1; i <= nLoopCount; i++)
    {
        cout << "We've finished " << i
             << " loops" << endl;
    }

    // wait until user is ready before terminating program
    // to allow the user to see the program results
    system("PAUSE");
    return 0;
}
```

This modified version of `ForDemo` loops the same as it did before. Instead of modifying the value of `nLoopCount`, however, this `ForDemo2` version uses a new counter variable.

This `for` loop declares a counter variable `i` and initializes it to 0. It then compares this counter variable to `nLoopCount`. If `i` is less than `nLoopCount`, control passes to the output statement within the body of the `for` loop. Once the body has completed executing, control passes to the increment clause where `i` is incremented and compared to `nLoopCount` again and so it goes.

The following shows example output from the program:

```
Enter loop count: 5
We've finished 1 loops
We've finished 2 loops
We've finished 3 loops
We've finished 4 loops
We've finished 5 loops
Press any key to continue . . .
```

When declared within the initialization portion of the for loop, the index variable is known only within the for loop itself. Nerdy C++ programmers say that the scope of the variable is the for loop. In the ForDemo2 example just given, the variable i is not accessible from the return statement because that statement is not within the loop.

Avoiding the dreaded infinite loop

An *infinite loop* is an execution path that continues forever. An infinite loop occurs any time the condition that would otherwise terminate the loop can't occur — usually the result of a coding error.

Consider the following minor variation of the earlier loop:

```
while (nLoopCount > 0)
{
    cout << "Only " << nLoopCount
         << " loops to go" << endl;
}
```

The programmer forgot to decrement the variable nLoopCount. The result is a loop counter that never changes. The test condition is either always false or always true. The program executes in a never-ending (infinite) loop.

I realize that nothing's infinite. Eventually the power will fail, the computer will break, Microsoft will go bankrupt, and dogs will sleep with cats. . . . Either the loop will stop executing, or you won't care anymore. But an infinite loop will continue to execute until something outside the control of the program makes it stop.

You can create an infinite loop in many more ways than shown here, most of which are a lot more difficult to spot than this was.

Applying special loop controls

C++ defines two special flow-control commands known as `break` and `con-tinue`. Sometimes the condition for terminating a loop occurs at neither the beginning nor the end of the loop, but in the middle. Consider a program that accumulates numbers of values entered by the user. The loop terminates when the user enters a negative number.

The challenge with this problem is that the program can't exit the loop until the user has entered a value but must exit before the value is added to the sum.

For these cases, C++ defines the `break` command. When encountered, the `break` causes control to exit the current loop immediately. Control passes from the `break` statement to the statement immediately following the closed brace at the end of the loop.

The format of the `break` commands is as follows:

```
while(condition) // break works equally well in for loop
{
    if (some other condition)
    {
        break;    // exit the loop
    }
}                 // control passes here when the
                  // program encounters the break
```

Armed with this new `break` command, my solution to the accumulator problem appears as the program `BreakDemo`:

```
// BreakDemo - input a series of numbers.
//             Continue to accumulate the sum
//             of these numbers until the user
//             enters a negative number.
#include <cstdio>
#include <cstdlib>
#include <iostream>
using namespace std;

int main(int nNumberofArgs, char* pszArgs[])
{
    // input the loop count
    int accumulator = 0;
    cout << "This program sums values entered"
         << "by the user\n";
    cout << "Terminate the loop by entering "
         << "a negative number" << endl;
```

```
// loop "forever"
for(;;)
{
    // fetch another number
    int nValue = 0;
    cout << "Enter next number: ";
    cin  >> nValue;

    // if it's negative...
    if (nValue < 0)
    {
        // ...then exit
        break;
    }

    // ...otherwise add the number to the accumulator
    accumulator += nValue;
}

// now that we've exited the loop
// output the accumulated result
cout << "\nThe total is "
     << accumulator
     << endl;

// wait until user is ready before terminating program
// to allow the user to see the program results
system("PAUSE");
return 0;
}
```

After explaining the rules to the user (entering a negative number to terminate and so on), the program enters what looks like an infinite `for` loop.
Once within the loop, `BreakDemo` retrieves a number from the keyboard.
Only after the program has read the number can it test to see whether that
number matches the exit criteria. If the input number is negative, control
passes to the `break`, causing the program to exit the loop. If the input
number is *not* negative, control skips over the `break` command to the
expression that sums the new value into the accumulator. After the program
exits the loop, it outputs the accumulated value and then exits.

When performing an operation on a variable repeatedly in a loop, make sure
that the variable is initialized properly before entering the loop. In this case,
the program zeros `accumulator` before entering the loop where `nValue` is
added to it.

The result of an example run appears as follows:

```
This program sums values entered by the user
Terminate the loop by entering a negative number
Enter next number: 1
Enter next number: 2
Enter next number: 3
Enter next number: -1

The total is 6
Press any key to continue . . .
```

The similar `continue` command is used less frequently. When the program encounters the `continue` command, it immediately moves back to the top of the loop. The rest of the statements in the loop are ignored for the current iteration.

The following example snippet ignores negative numbers that the user might input. Only a 0 terminates this version (the complete program appears on the CD-ROM as `ContinueDemo`):

```cpp
while(true) // this while() has the same effect as for(;;)
{
    // input a value
    cout << "Input a value:";
    cin  >> nValue;

    // if the value is negative...
    if (nValue < 0)
    {
        // ...output an error message...
        cout << "Negative numbers are not allowed\n";

        // ...and go back to the top of the loop
        continue;
    }

    // ...continue to process input like normal
}
```

Nesting Control Commands

Return to our PC-screen-repaint problem. Surely it must need a loop structure of some type to write each pixel from left to right on a single line. (Do Middle Eastern terminals scan from right to left? I have no idea.) What about repeatedly repainting each scan line from top to bottom? (Do PC screens in Australia scan from bottom to top?) For this particular task, you need to include a left-to-right scan loop within the top-to-bottom scan loop.

A loop command within another loop is known as a *nested loop*. As an example, I have modified the `BreakDemo` program to accumulate any number of sequences. In this `NestedDemo` program, the inner loop sums numbers entered from the keyboard until the user enters a negative number. The outer loop continues accumulating sequences until the sum is 0. Here's what it looks like:

```cpp
// NestedDemo - input a series of numbers.
//              Continue to accumulate the sum
//              of these numbers until the user
//              enters a 0. Repeat the process
//              until the sum is 0.
#include <cstdio>
#include <cstdlib>
#include <iostream>
using namespace std;

int main(int nNumberofArgs, char* pszArgs[])
{
    // the outer loop
    cout << "This program sums multiple series\n"
         << "of numbers. Terminate each sequence\n"
         << "by entering a negative number.\n"
         << "Terminate the series by entering two\n"
         << "negative numbers in a row\n";

    // continue to accumulate sequences
    int accumulator;
    for(;;)
    {
        // start entering the next sequence
        // of numbers
        accumulator = 0;
        cout << "Start the next sequence\n";

        // loop forever
        for(;;)
        {
            // fetch another number
            int nValue = 0;
            cout << "Enter next number: ";
            cin  >> nValue;

            // if it's negative...
            if (nValue < 0)
            {
```

```
            // ...then exit
            break;
        }

        // ...otherwise add the number to the
        // accumulator
        accumulator += nValue;
    }

    // exit the loop if the total accumulated is 0
    if (accumulator == 0)
    {
        break;
    }

    // output the accumulated result and start over
    cout << "The total for this sequence is "
        << accumulator
        << endl << endl;
}

// we're about to quit
cout << "Thank you" << endl;

// wait until user is ready before terminating program
// to allow the user to see the program results
system("PAUSE");
return 0;
}
```

Notice the inner for loop looks like the earlier accumulator example.
Immediately after that loop, however, is an added test. If accumulator is
equal to 0, the program executes a break statement that exits the outer loop.
Otherwise, the program outputs the accumulated value and starts over.

Switching to a Different Subject?

One last control statement is useful in a limited number of cases. The switch
statement resembles a compound if statement by including a number of different possibilities rather than a single test:

```
switch(expression)
{
    case c1:
        // go here if the expression == c1
        break;
```

```
      case c2:
          // go here if expression == c2
          break;
      default:
          // go here if there is no match
}
```

The value of expression must be an integer (int, long, or char). The case
values must be constants. When the switch statement is encountered, the
expression is evaluated and compared to the various case constants. Control
branches to the case that matches. If none of the cases matches, control
passes to the default clause.

Consider the following example code snippet:

```
int choice;
cout << "Enter a 1, 2 or 3:";
cin  >> choice;

switch(choice)
{
    case 1:
        // do "1" processing
        break;

    case 2:
        // do "2" processing
        break;

    case 3:
        // do "3" processing
        break;

    default:
        cout << "You didn't enter a 1, 2 or 3\n";
}
```

Once again, the switch statement has an equivalent, in this case multiple
if statements. However, when there are more than two or three cases, the
switch structure is easier to understand.

The break statements are necessary to exit the switch command. Without
the break statements, control falls through from one case to the next. (Look
out below!)

Part II

Becoming a Functional C++ Programmer

The 5th Wave   By Rich Tennant

"Shoot, that's nothing. Watch me spin him!"

In this part . . .

*I*t's one thing to perform operations such as addition and multiplication — even when we're logical (AND and OR or other operations). It's another thing to write real programs. This section introduces the features necessary to make the leap into programmerdom.

You'll find the program BUDGET1 on the enclosed CD-ROM. This largish program demonstrates the concepts of functional programming. You may want to visit this program and its documentation after you've mastered functional programming concepts.

Chapter 6

Creating Functions

• •

• •

*T*he programs developed in prior chapters have been small enough that they can be easily read as a single unit. Larger, real-world programs are often many thousands if not millions of lines long. Developers need to break up these monster programs into smaller chunks that are easier to conceive, describe, develop, and maintain.

C++ allows programmers to divide their code into exactly such chunks known as *functions*. A function is a small block of code that can be executed as a single entity. This allows the programmer to divide her program into a number of such entities, each solving some well-defined subset of the problem of the overall program. Functions are themselves broken up into smaller, more detailed functions in a pyramid of ever smaller, more detailed solutions that make up the complete program.

This divide-and-conquer approach reduces the complexity of creating a working program of significant size to something achievable by a mere mortal.

Writing and Using a Function

Functions are best understood by example. This section starts with the example program `FunctionDemo`, which simplifies the `NestedDemo` program I discussed in Chapter 5 by defining a function to contain part of the logic. Then this section explains how the function is defined and how it is invoked, using `FunctionDemo` as a pattern for understanding both the problem and the solution.

The NestedDemo program in Chapter 5 contains at least three parts that can be easily separated both in your mind and in fact:

✔ An explanation to the operator as to how data is to be entered

✔ An inner loop that sums up a single sequence of numbers

✔ An outer loop that repeatedly invokes the inner loop until the accumu-lated value is 0

Separating the program along these lines allows the programmer to concen-trate on each piece of the program separately. The following FunctionDemo program shows how NestedDemo can be broken up by creating the functions displayExplanation() and sumSequence():

```cpp
// FunctionDemo - demonstrate the use of functions
//                by breaking the inner loop of the
//                NestedDemo program off into its own
//                function
#include <cstdio>
#include <cstdlib>
#include <iostream>
using namespace std;

// displayExplanation - prompt the user as to the rules
//                      of the game
void displayExplanation(void)
{
    cout << "This program sums multiple series\n"
         << "of numbers. Terminate each sequence\n"
         << "by entering a negative number.\n"
         << "Terminate the series by entering an\n"
         << "empty sequence.\n"
         << endl;
    return;
}

// sumSequence - add a sequence of numbers entered from
//               the keyboard until the user enters a
//               negative number.
//               return - the summation of numbers entered
int sumSequence(void)
{
    // loop forever
    int accumulator = 0;
    for(;;)
    {
        // fetch another number
        int nValue = 0;
        cout << "Enter next number: ";
        cin  >> nValue;
```

```
                // if it's negative...
                if (nValue < 0)
                {
                    // ...then exit from the loop
                    break;
                }

                // ...otherwise add the number to the
                // accumulator
                accumulator += nValue;
            }

        // return the accumulated value
        return accumulator;
    }

int main(int nNumberofArgs, char* pszArgs[])
{
    // display prompt to the user
    displayExplanation();

    // accumulate sequences of numbers...
    for(;;)
    {
        // sum a sequence of numbers entered from
        // the keyboard
        cout << "Enter next sequence" << endl;
        int accumulatedValue = sumSequence();

        // terminate the loop if sumSequence() returns
        // a zero
        if (accumulatedValue == 0)
        {
            break;
        }

        // now output the accumulated result
        cout << "The total is "
             << accumulatedValue
             << "\n"
             << endl;
    }


    cout << "Thank you" << endl;
    // wait until user is ready before terminating program
    // to allow the user to see the program results
    system("PAUSE");
    return 0;
}
```

Defining our first function

The statement `void displayExplanation(void)` is known as a *function declaration* — it introduces the function definition that immediately follows. A function declaration always starts with the name of the function preceded by the type of value the function returns and followed by a pair of open and closed parentheses containing any arguments to the function.

The return type `void` means that `displayExplanation()` does not return a value. The `void` within the argument list means that it doesn't take any arguments either. (We'll get to what that means very soon.) The body of the function is contained in the braces immediately following the function declaration.

Function names are normally written as a multiword description with all the words rammed together. I start function names with lowercase but capitalize all intermediate words. Function names almost always appear followed by an open and close parenthesis pair.

A function doesn't do anything until it is invoked. Our program starts executing with the first line in `main()` just like always. The first non-comment line in `main()` is the call to `displayExplanation()`:

```
displayExplanation();
```

This passes program control to the first line in the `displayExplanation()` function. The computer continues to execute there until it reaches the return statement at the end of `displayExplanation()`.

Defining the sumSequence() function

The declaration `int sumSequence(void)` begins the definition of the `sumSequence()` function. This declaration says that the function does not expect any arguments but returns a value of type `int` to the caller. The body of this function contains the same code previously found in the inner loop of the `NestedDemo` example.

The `sumSequence()` function also contains a return statement to exit the program. This return is not optional since it contains the value to be returned, `accumulator`. The type of value returned must match the type of the function in the declaration, in this case `int`.

Calling the function sumSequence()

Return back to the `main()` function in `FunctionDemo` again. This section of code looks similar to the outer loop in `NestedDemo`.

The main difference is the expression `accumulatedValue = sum Sequence();` that appears where the inner loop would have been. The `sumSequence()` statement invokes the function of that name. The value returned by the function is stored in the variable `accumulatedValue`. Then this value is displayed. The main program continues to loop until `sum Sequence()` returns a sum of 0, which indicates that the user has finished calculating sums.

Divide and conquer

The `FunctionDemo` program has split the outer loop in `main()` from the inner loop into a function `sumSequence()` and created a `display Explanation()` to get things kicked off. This division wasn't arbitrary: Both functions in `FunctionDemo` perform a logically separate operation.

A good function is easy to describe. You shouldn't have to use more than a single sentence, with a minimum of such words as *and, or, unless,* or *but.* For example, here's a simple, straightforward definition: "The function `sum Sequence` accumulates a sequence of integer values entered by the user." This definition is concise and clear. It's a world away from the `NestedDemo` program description: "The program explains to the user how the program works AND then sums a sequence of positive values AND generates an error if the user enters a negative number AND displays the sum AND starts over again until the user enters a zero-length sum."

The output of a sample run of this program appears identical to that generated by the `NestedDemo` program.

Understanding the Details of Functions

Functions are so fundamental to creating C++ programs that getting a handle on the details of defining, creating, and testing them is critical. Armed with the example `FunctionDemo` program, consider the following definition of *function:* A function is a logically separated block of C++ code.

The function construct has the following form:

```
<return type> name(<arguments to the function>)
{
    // ...
    return <expression>;
}
```

The *arguments* to a function are values that can be passed to the function to be used as input information. The *return* value is a value that the function returns. For example, in the call to the function square(10), the value 10 is an argument to the function square(). The returned value is 100 (if it's not, this is one poorly named function).

Both the arguments and the return value are optional. If either is absent, the keyword void is used instead. That is, if a function has a void argument list, the function does not take any arguments when called (this was the case with the FunctionDemo program). If the return type is void, the function does not return a value to the caller.

The default argument type to a function is void, meaning that it takes no arguments. A function int fn(void) may be declared as int fn().

Understanding simple functions

The simple function sumSequence() returns an integer value that it calculates. Functions may return any of the intrinsic variable types described in Chapter 2. For example, a function might return a double or a char. If a function returns no value, the return type of the function is labeled void.

A function may be labeled by its return type — for example, a function that returns an int is often known as an integer function. A function that returns no value is known as a void function.

For example, the following void function performs an operation but returns no value:

```
void echoSquare()
{
    int value;
    cout << "Enter a value:";
    cin >> value;
    cout << "\n The square is:" << (value * value) <<
            "\n";
    return;
}
```

Control begins at the open brace and continues through to the return statement. The return statement in a `void` function is not followed by a value. The
return statement in a `void` function is optional. If it isn't present, execution
returns to the calling function when control encounters the close brace.

Understanding functions with arguments

Functions without arguments are of limited use because the communication
from such functions is one-way — through the return value. Two-way communication is through function arguments.

Functions with arguments

A *function argument* is a variable whose value is passed to the calling function during the call operation. The following SquareDemo example program
defines and uses a function square() that returns the square of a double-
precision float passed to it:

```
// SquareDemo - demonstrate the use of a function
//              which processes arguments

#include <cstdio>
#include <cstdlib>
#include <iostream>
using namespace std;

// square - returns the square of its argument
//          doubleVar - the value to be squared
//          returns - square of doubleVar
double square(double doubleVar)
{
    return doubleVar * doubleVar;
}

// displayExplanation - prompt the user as to the rules
//                       of the game
void displayExplanation(void)
{
    cout << "This program sums the square of multiple\n"
         << "series of numbers. Terminate each sequence\n"
         << "by entering a negative number.\n"
         << "Terminate the series by entering an\n"
         << "empty sequence.\n"
         << endl;
    return;
}
```

```cpp
// sumSquareSequence - accumulate the square of the number
//                 entered at the keyboard into a sequence
//                 until the user enters a negative number
double sumSquareSequence(void)
{
    // loop forever
    double accumulator = 0.0;
    for(;;)
    {
        // fetch another number
        double dValue = 0;
        cout << "Enter next number: ";
        cin  >> dValue;

        // if it's negative...

        if (dValue < 0)
        {
            // ...then exit from the loop
            break;
        }

        // ...otherwise calculate the square
        double value = square(dValue);

        // now add the square to the
        // accumulator
        accumulator += value;
    }

    // return the accumulated value
    return accumulator;
}

int main(int nNumberofArgs, char* pszArgs[])
{
    displayExplanation();

    // Continue to accumulate numbers...
    for(;;)
    {
        // sum a sequence of numbers entered from
        // the keyboard
        cout << "Enter next sequence" << endl;
        double accumulatedValue = sumSquareSequence();

        // terminate if the sequence is zero or negative
        if (accumulatedValue <= 0.0)
```

```
        {
            break;
        }

        // now output the accumulated result
        cout << "\nThe total of the values squared is "
                << accumulatedValue
                << "\n"
                << endl;
    }

    cout << "Thank you" << endl;

    // wait until user is ready before terminating program
    // to allow the user to see the program results
    system("PAUSE");
    return 0;
}
```

This is essentially the same FunctionDemo program, except that the sum
SquareSequence() function accumulates the square of the values entered
and returns them as a double rather than an int. The function square()
returns the value of its one argument multiplied by itself. The change to
the sumSequence() function is simple: Rather than accumulate the value
entered, the function now accumulates the result returned from square().

Functions with multiple arguments

Functions may have multiple arguments that are separated by commas.
Thus, the following function returns the product of its two arguments:

```
int product(int arg1, int arg2)
{
    return arg1 * arg2;
}
```

main () exposed

The "keyword" main() from our standard program template is nothing more
than a function — albeit a function with strange arguments but a function
nonetheless.

When C++ builds a program from source code, it adds some boilerplate code
that executes before your program ever starts. (You can't see this code without digging into the bowels of the C++ library functions.) This code sets up
the environment in which your program operates. For example, this boilerplate code opens the default input and output channels cin and cout.

After the environment has been established, the C++ boilerplate code calls the function main(), thereby beginning execution of your code. When your program finishes, it exits from main(). This enables the C++ boilerplate to clean up a few things before turning control over to the operating system that kills the program.

The arguments to main() are complicated — we'll review those later. The int returned from main() is an error indicator. The program returns a 0 if the program terminates normally. Any other value can be used to indicate the nature of the error that caused the program to quit.

Overloading Function Names

C++ must have a way of telling functions apart. Thus, two functions cannot share the same name and argument list, known as the *extended name* or the *signature*. The following extended function names are all different and can reside in the same program:

```
void someFunction(void)
{
    // ....perform some function
}
void someFunction(int n)
{
    // ...perform some different function
}
void someFunction(double d)
{
    // ...perform some very different function
}
void someFunction(int n1, int n2)
{
    // ....do something different yet
}
```

C++ knows that the functions someFunction(void), someFunction(int), someFunction(double), and someFunction(int, int) are not the same.

This multiple use of names is known as function *overloading*.

Programmers often refer to functions by their shorthand name, which is the name of the function without its arguments, such as someFunction(), in the same way that I have the shorthand name Stephen (actually, my nickname is Randy, but work with me on this one).

Here's a typical application that uses overloaded functions with unique extended names:

```
int intVariable1, intVariable2;
double doubleVariable;

// functions are distinguished by the type of
// the argument passed
someFunction();              // calls someFunction(void)
someFunction(intVariable1);  // calls someFunction(int)
someFunction(doubleVariable);// calls someFunction(double)
someFunction(intVariable1, intVariable2); // calls
                             // someFunction(int, int)

// this works for constants as well
someFunction(1);             // calls someFunction(int)
someFunction(1.0);           // calls someFunction(double)
someFunction(1, 2);          // calls someFunction(int, int)
```

In each case, the type of the arguments matches the extended names of the three functions.

The return type is not part of the extended name of the function. The following two functions have the same name, so they can't be part of the same program:

```
int someFunction(int n);    // full name of the function
                            // is someFunction(int)
double someFunction(int n); // same name
long l = someFunction(10);  // call which function?
```

Here C++ does not know whether to convert the value returned from the `double` version of `someFunction()` to a long or promote the value returned from `int` version.

Defining Function Prototypes

A function must be declared before it can be used. That's so C++ can compare the call against the definition to make sure that any necessary conversions are performed. However, a function does not have to be defined when it is first declared. A function may be defined anywhere in the module. (A *module* is another name for a C++ source file.)

Consider the following code snippet:

```
int main(int nNumberofArgs, char* pszArgs[])
{
    someFunc(1, 2);
}
int someFunc(double dArg1, int nArg2)
{
    // ...do something
}
```

`main()` doesn't know the proper argument types of the function `some Func()` at the time of the call. C++ might surmise from the call that the full function definition is `someFunc(int, int)` and that its return type is `void`; however, the definition of the function that appears immediately after `main()` shows that the programmer wants the first argument converted to a floating point and that the function does actually return a value.

I know, I know — C++ could be less lazy and look ahead to determine the extended name of `someFunc()` on its own, but it doesn't. What is needed is some way to inform `main()` of the full name of `someFunc()` before it is used. This is handled by what we call a *function prototype*.

A prototype declaration appears the same as a function with no body. In use, a prototype declaration looks like this:

```
int someFunc(double, int);
int main(int nNumberofArgs, char* pszArgs[])
{
    someFunc(1, 2);
}
int someFunc(double dArg1, int nArg2)
{
    // ...do something
}
```

The prototype declaration tells the world (at least that part of the world after the declaration) that the extended name for `someFunc()` is `someFunction(double, int)`. The call in `main()` now knows to cast the 1 to a `double` before making the call. In addition, `main()` knows that `some Func()` returns an `int` value to the caller.

It is common practice to include function prototypes for every function in a module either at the beginning of the module or, more often, in a separate file that can be included within other modules at compile time. That's the function of the `include` statements that appear at the beginning of the Official C++ For Dummies program template:

```
#include <cstdio>
#include <cstdlib>
#include <iostream>
```

These three files `cstdio`, `cstdlib` and `iostream` include prototype definitions for the common system functions that we've been using, such as `system("PAUSE")`. The contents of these files are inserted at the point of the `#include` statement by the compiler as part of its normal duties.

Chapter 10 is dedicated to include files and other so-called preprocessor commands.

Variable Storage Types

Variables are also assigned a storage type depending on where and how they are defined in the function as shown in the following example:

```
int globalVariable;
void fn()
{
    int localVariable;
    static int staticVariable = 1;
}
```

Variables declared within a function like `localVariable` are said to be local. The variable `localVariable` doesn't exist until execution passes through its declaration within the function `fn()`. `localVariable` ceases to exist when the function returns. Upon return, whatever value that is stored in `local Variable` is lost. In addition, only `fn()` has access to `localVariable` — other functions cannot reach into the function to access it.

By comparison, the variable `globalVariable` is created when the program begins execution and exists as long as the program is running. All functions have access to `globalVariable` all the time.

The keyword `static` can be used to create a sort of mishling — something between a global and local variable. The static variable `staticVariable` is created when execution reaches the declaration the first time that function `fn()` is called, just like a local variable. The static variable is not destroyed when program execution returns from the function, however. Instead, it retains its value from one call to the next. If `fn()` assigns a value to `static Variable` once, it'll still be there the next time `fn()` is called. The initialization portion of the declaration is ignored every subsequent time execution passes through.

Chapter 7

Storing Sequences in Arrays

· ·

In This Chapter

▶ Considering the need for something like an array

▶ Introducing the array data type

▶ Using an array

▶ Using the most common type of array — the character string

· ·

An *array* is a sequence of variables that shares the same name and that is referenced using an index. Arrays are useful little critters that allow you to store a large number of values of the same type that are related in some way — for example, the batting averages of all the players on the same team might be a good candidate for storage within an array. Arrays can be multidimensional, too, allowing you, for example, to store an array of batting averages within an array of months, which allows you to work with the batting averages of the team as they occur by month.

In this chapter, you find out how to initialize and use arrays for fun and profit. You also find out about an especially useful form of array called a *char string*.

Arraying the Arguments for Arrays

Consider the following problem. You need a program that can read a sequence of numbers from the keyboard and display their sum. You guessed it — the program stops reading in numbers as soon as you enter a negative number. Unlike similar programs in Chapters 5 and 6, however, this program will output all the numbers entered before displaying the average.

You could try to store numbers in a set of independent variables, as in

```
cin >> value1;
if (value1 >= 0)
{
    cin >> value2;
    if (value2 >= 0)
    {
        ...
```

You can see that this approach can't handle sequences involving more than just a few numbers. Besides, it's ugly. What we need is some type of structure that has a name like a variable but that can store more than one value. May I present to you, Ms. A. Ray.

An array solves the problem of sequences nicely. For example, the following snippet declares an array valueArray that has storage for up to 128 int values. It then populates the array with numbers entered from the keyboard:

```
int nValue;

// declare an array capable of holding up to 128 ints
int nValueArray[128];

// define an index used to access subsequent members of
// of the array; don't exceed the 128 int limit
for (int i = 0; i < 128; i++)
{
    cin >> nValue;

    // exit the loop when the user enters a negative
    // number
    if (nValue < 0)
    {
        break;
    }
    nValueArray[i] = nValue;
}
```

The second line of this snippet declares an array nValueArray. Array declarations begin with the type of the array members: in this case, int. This is followed by the name of the array. The last elements of an array declaration are open and closed brackets containing the maximum number of elements that the array can hold. In this code snippet, nValueArray can store up to 128 integers.

This snippet reads a number from the keyboard and stores it into each subsequent member of the array nValueArray. You access an individual element of an array by providing the name of the array followed by brackets containing the index. The first integer in the array is nValueArray[0], the second is nValueArray[1], and so on.

In use, nValueArray[i] represents the ith element in the array. The index variable i must be a counting variable — that is, i must be a char, an int, or a long. If nValueArray is an array of ints, nValueArray[i] is an int.

Using an array

The following program inputs a sequence of integer values from the keyboard until the user enters a negative number. The program then displays the numbers input and reports their sum.

```
// ArrayDemo - demonstrate the use of arrays
//             by reading a sequence of integers
//             and then displaying them and their sum
#include <cstdio>
#include <cstdlib>
#include <iostream>
using namespace std;

// prototype declarations
int readArray(int integerArray[], int maxNumElements);
int sumArray(int integerArray[], int numElements);
void displayArray(int integerArray[], int numElements);

int main(int nNumberofArgs, char* pszArgs[])
{

    // input the loop count
    cout << "This program sums values entered "
         << "by the user\n";
    cout << "Terminate the loop by entering "
         << "a negative number\n";
    cout << endl;

    // read numbers to be summed from the user into a
    // local array
    int inputValues[128];
    int numberOfValues = readArray(inputValues, 128);


    // now output the values and the sum of the values
    displayArray(inputValues, numberOfValues);
    cout << "The sum is "
         << sumArray(inputValues, numberOfValues)
         << endl;

    // wait until user is ready before terminating program
    // to allow the user to see the program results
    system("PAUSE");
    return 0;
}
```

```
// readArray - read integers from the operator into
//              'integerArray' until operator enters neg.
//              Return the number of elements stored.
int readArray(int integerArray[], int maxNumElements)
{
    int numberOfValues;
    for(numberOfValues = 0;
        numberOfValues < maxNumElements;
        numberOfValues++)
    {
        // fetch another number
        int integerValue;
        cout << "Enter next number: ";
        cin  >> integerValue;

        // if it's negative...
        if (integerValue < 0)
        {
            // ...then exit
            break;
        }

        // ... otherwise store the number
        // into the  storage array
        integerArray[numberOfValues] = integerValue;
    }

    // return the number of elements read
    return numberOfValues;
}

// displayArray - display the members of an
//                array of length sizeOfloatArray
void displayArray(int integerArray[], int numElements)
{
    cout << "The value of the array is:" << endl;
    for (int i = 0; i < numElements; i++)
    {
        cout << i << ": " << integerArray[i] << endl;
    }
    cout << endl;
}

// sumArray - return the sum of the members of an
//            integer array
int sumArray(int integerArray[], int numElements)
{
    int accumulator = 0;
    for (int i = 0; i < numElements; i++)
    {
        accumulator += integerArray[i];
    }
    return accumulator;
}
```

The program `ArrayDemo` begins with prototype declarations of the functions `readArray()`, `sumArray()`, and `displayArray()`, which it will need later. The main program starts with a prompt to the user to input data to be summed. The program then declares an array `inputValues[]` to be used to store the values input by the user. The main program passes this array to `readArray()`, along with the length of the array — `readArray()` cannot read more than 128 values even if the user does not enter a negative number since that's all the room allocated in the `inputValues[]` array.

The array `inputValues` is declared as 128 integers long. If you're thinking that this must be more than enough, don't count on it. No matter how large you make the array, always put a check to make sure that you do not exceed the limits of the array. Writing more data than an array can hold causes your program to perform erratically and often to crash.

The main function then calls `displayArray()` to print the contents of the array. Finally, the function calls `sumArray()` to add the elements in the array.

The `readArray()` function takes two arguments: the `integerArray[]` into which to store the values it reads and `maxNumElements`, the maximum number of integer values for which there is room at the inn. The function begins with a `for` loop that reads integer values. Every non-negative value that the function reads is saved into `integerArray[]`. The first element goes into `integerArray[0]`, the second into `integerArray[1]`, and so forth.

Once the user enters a negative number, the program breaks out of the loop and returns the total `numberOfValues` input.

The `displayArray()` function also uses a `for` loop to traverse the elements of the array, starting at 0 and continuing to the last element, which is `numElements - 1`. The final function, `sumArray()`, also iterates through the array but sums the elements stored there into `accumulator`, which it then returns to the caller.

Notice, yet again, that the index i in the `displayArray()` and `sumArray()` functions is initialized to 0 and not to 1. In addition, notice how the `for` loop terminates as soon as i reaches `numElements`. The output from a sample run appears as follows:

```
This program sums values entered by the user
Terminate the loop by entering a negative number

Enter next number: 10
Enter next number: 20
Enter next number: 30
Enter next number: 40
Enter next number: -1
The value of the array is:
0: 10
1: 20
```

```
2: 30
3: 40

The sum is 100
Press any key to continue . . .
```

Just to keep nonprogrammers guessing, the term *iterate* means to traverse through a set of objects such as an array. Programmers say that the preceding functions iterate through the array. In a similar fashion, I "get irate" when my dog iterates from one piece of furniture to another.

Initializing an array

A local variable does not start life with a valid value, not even the value 0. Said another way, a local variable contains garbage until you actually store something in it. Locally declared arrays are the same — each element contains garbage until you actually assign something to it. You should initialize local variables when you declare them. This rule is even truer for arrays. It is far too easy to access uninitialized array elements thinking that they are valid values.

Fortunately, a small array may be initialized at the time it is declared. The following code snippet demonstrates how this is done:

```
float floatArray[5] = {0.0, 1.0, 2.0, 3.0, 4.0};
```

This initializes `floatArray[0]` to 0, `floatArray[1]` to 1.0, `floatArray[2]` to 2.0, and so on.

C++ pads the initialization list with 0s if the number of elements in the list is less than the size of the array. In fact, an empty list can be used to initialize an array to 0:

```
int nArray[128] = {}; // initialize array to all 0's
```

The number of initialization constants can determine the size of the array. For example, you could have determined that `floatArray` has five elements just by counting the values within the braces. C++ can count as well (here's at least one thing C++ can do for itself).

The following declaration is identical to the preceding one:

```
float floatArray[] = {0.0, 1.0, 2.0, 3.0, 4.0};
```

Accessing too far into an array

Mathematicians start counting arrays with 1. Most program languages start with an offset of 1 as well. C++ arrays begin counting at 0. The first member of a C++ array is `valueArray[0]`. That makes the last element of a 128-integer array `integerArray[127]` and not `integerArray[128]`.

Unfortunately for the programmer, C++ does not check to see whether the index you are using is within the range of the array. C++ is perfectly happy giving you access to `integerArray[200]`. Our `integerArray` yard is only 128 integers long — 200 is 72 integers into someone else's yard. No telling who lives there and what he's storing at that location. Reading from `integer Array[200]` will return some unknown and unpredictable value. Writing to that location generates unpredictable results. It may do nothing — the house may be abandoned and the yard unused. On the other hand, it might overwrite some data, thereby confusing the neighbor and making the program act in a seemingly random fashion. Or it might crash the program.

The most common wrong way to access an array is to read or write location `integerArray[128]`. Although it's only one element beyond the end of the array, reading or writing this location is just as dangerous as using any other incorrect address.

Using arrays

On the surface, the `ArrayDemo` program doesn't do anything more than our earlier, non-array-based programs did. True, this version can replay its input by displaying the set of input numbers before calculating their sum, but this feature hardly seems earth shattering.

Yet, the ability to redisplay the input values hints at a significant advantage to using arrays. Arrays allow the program to process a series of numbers multiple times. The main program was able to pass the array of input values to `displayArray()` for display and then repass the same numbers to `sumArray()` for addition.

Defining and using arrays of arrays

Arrays are adept at storing sequences of numbers. Some applications require sequences of sequences. A classic example of this matrix configuration is the spreadsheet. Laid out like a chessboard, each element in the spreadsheet has both an x and a y offset.

C++ implements the matrix as follows:

```
int intMatrix[10][5];
```

This matrix is 10 elements in 1 dimension, and 5 in another, for a total of 50 elements. In other words, `intMatrix` is a 10-element array, each element of which is a 5-`int` array. As you might expect, one corner of the matrix is in `intMatrix[0][0]` while the other corner is `intMatrix[9][4]`.

Whether you consider `intMatrix` to be 10 elements long in the x dimension or in the y dimension is a matter of taste. A matrix can be initialized in the same way that an array is:

```
int intMatrix[2][3] = {{1, 2, 3}, {4, 5, 6}};
```

This line initializes the 3-element array `intMatrix[0]` to 1, 2, and 3; and the 3-element array `intMatrix[1]` to 4, 5, and 6, respectively.

Using Arrays of Characters

The elements of an array can be of any type. Arrays of floats, doubles, and longs are all possible; however, arrays of characters have particular significance.

Creating an array of characters

Human words and sentences can be expressed as an array of characters. An array of characters containing my first name would appear as

```
char sMyName[] = {'S', 't', 'e', 'p', 'h', 'e', 'n'};
```

The following small program displays my name:

```
// CharDisplay - output a character array to
//               standard output, the MS-DOS window
#include <cstdio>
#include <cstdlib>
#include <iostream>
using namespace std;

// prototype declarations
void displayCharArray(char charArray[],
                      int sizeOfArray);
```

```
int main(int nNumberofArgs, char* pszArgs[])
{
    char charMyName[]={'S', 't', 'e', 'p', 'h', 'e', 'n'};
    displayCharArray(charMyName, 7);
    cout << endl;

    // wait until user is ready before terminating program
    // to allow the user to see the program results
    system("PAUSE");
    return 0;
}

// displayCharArray - display an array of characters
//                    by outputting one character at
//                    a time
void displayCharArray(char charArray[],
                      int sizeOfArray)
{
    for(int i = 0; i< sizeOfArray; i++)
    {
        cout << charArray[i];
    }
}
```

The program declares a fixed array of characters `charMyName` containing —
you guessed it — my name (what better name?). This array is passed to the
function `displayCharArray()` along with its length. The `displayChar
Array()` function is identical to the `displayArray()` function in the earlier
example program except that this version displays `char`s rather than `int`s.

This program works fine; however, it is inconvenient to pass the length of the
array with the array itself. If we could come up with a rule for determining
the end of the string of characters, we wouldn't need to pass its length — you
would know that the string was complete when you encountered the special
rule that told you so.

Creating a string of characters

In many cases, all values for each element are possible. However, C++
reserves the special "character" 0 as the noncharacter. We can use `'\0'` to
mark the end of a character array. (The numeric value of `'\0'` is 0, but the
type of `'\0'` is char.)

The character `'\y'` is the character whose octal value is y. The character
`'\0'` is the character with a value of 0, otherwise known as the null character.
Using that rule, the previous small program becomes

```
// DisplayString - output a character array to
//                  standard output, the MS-DOS window
#include <cstdio>
#include <cstdlib>
#include <iostream>
using namespace std;

// prototype declarations
void displayString(char stringArray[]);

int main(int nNumberofArgs, char* pszArgs[])
{
    char charMyName[] =
            {'S', 't', 'e', 'p', 'h', 'e', 'n', '\0'};
    displayString(charMyName);
    cout << endl;

    // wait until user is ready before terminating program
    // to allow the user to see the program results
    system("PAUSE");
    return 0;
}

// displayString - display a character string
//                  one character at a time
void displayString(char stringArray[])
{
    for(int i = 0; stringArray[i] != '\0'; i++)
    {
        cout << stringArray[i];
    }
}
```

The declaration of charMyName declares the character array with the extra null character '\0' on the end. The displayString program iterates through the character array until a null character is encountered.

The function displayString() is simpler to use than its displayChar Array() predecessor because it is no longer necessary to pass along the length of the character array. This secret handshake of terminating a character array with a null is so convenient that it is used throughout the C++ language. C++ even gives such an array a special name.

A *string of characters* is a null-terminated character array. It is officially known as a *null-terminated byte string,* or *NTBS.* The simpler term *C-string* is also used to differentiate from the C++ type string.

The choice of `'\0'` as the terminating character was not random. Remember that 0 is the only numeric value that converts to `false`; all other values translate to `true`. This means that the `for` loop could (and usually is) written as

```
for(int i = 0; stringArray[i]; i++)
```

This whole business of null-terminated character strings is so ingrained in the C++ language psyche that C++ uses a string of characters surrounded by double quotes to be an array of characters automatically terminated with a `'\0'` character. The following are identical declarations:

```
char szMyName[] = "Stephen";
char szAlsoMyName[] =
            {'S', 't', 'e', 'p', 'h', 'e', 'n', '\0'};
```

The naming convention used here is exactly that, a convention. C++ does not care. The prefix `sz` stands for *zero-terminated string*.

The string `Stephen` is eight characters long and not seven — the null character after the n is assumed. The string `" "` is one character long, consisting of just the null character.

Manipulating Strings with Character

The following `Concatenate` program inputs two strings from the keyboard and concatenates them into a single string:

```
// Concatenate - concatenate two strings
//                with a " - " in the middle
#include <cstdio>
#include <cstdlib>
#include <iostream>
using namespace std;

// prototype declarations
void concatString(char szTarget[], const char szSource[]);

int main(int nNumberofArgs, char* pszArgs[])
{
    // read first string...
    char szString1[260];
    cout << "Enter string #1:";
    cin.getline(szString1, 128);
```

```
    // ...now the second string...
    char szString2[128];
    cout << "Enter string #2:";
    cin.getline(szString2, 128);

    // ...concatenate a " - " onto the first...
    concatString(szString1, " - ");

    // ...now add the second string...
    concatString(szString1, szString2);

    // ...and display the result
    cout << "\n" << szString1 << endl;

    // wait until user is ready before terminating program
    // to allow the user to see the program results
    system("PAUSE");
    return 0;
}

// concatString - concatenate the szSource string
//                onto the end of the szTarget string
void concatString(char szTarget[], const char szSource[])
{
    // find the end of the first string
    int targetIndex = 0;
    while(szTarget[targetIndex])
    {
        targetIndex++;
    }

    // tack the second onto the end of the first
    int sourceIndex = 0;
    while(szSource[sourceIndex])
    {
        szTarget[targetIndex] =
            szSource[sourceIndex];
        targetIndex++;
        sourceIndex++;
    }

    // tack on the terminating null
    szTarget[targetIndex] = '\0';
}
```

The Concatenate program reads two character strings and appends them together with a " - " in the middle.

The program begins by reading a string from the keyboard. The program does not use the normal `cin >> szString1` for two reasons. First, the `cin >>` operation stops reading when any type of whitespace is encountered. Characters up to the first whitespace are read, the whitespace character is tossed, and the remaining characters are left in the input hopper for the next `cin >>` statement. Thus, if I were to enter "the Dog", szString2 would be filled with "the" and the word "Dog" would be left in the input buffer.

The second reason is that the `getline()` allows the programmer to specify the size of the buffer. The call to `getline(szString2, 128)` will not read more than 128 bytes no matter how many are input.

Instead, the call to `getline()` inputs an entire line up to but not including the newline at the end. We'll review this function with other file I/O functions in detail in Chapter 23.

After reading the first string into `szString1[]`, the program appends `" - "` onto the end by calling `concatString()`. It concatenates the second string by calling `concatString()` with `szString2[]`.

The `concatString()` function accepts a target string, `szTarget`, and a source string, `szSource`. The function begins by scanning `szTarget` for the terminating null character, which it stores in `targetIndex`. The function then enters a second loop in which it copies characters from the `szSource` into `szTarget` starting at the terminating null. The final statement in `concatString()` slaps a terminating null on the completed string.

An example output from the program appears as follows:

```
Enter string #1:This is a string
Enter string #2:THIS IS A STRING

This is a string - THIS IS A STRING
Press any key to continue . . .
```

Adding Some Library Functions

The C++ programmer is often required to manipulate zero-terminated strings. C++ provides a number of standard string-manipulation functions to make the job easier. A few of these functions are listed in Table 7-1.

Table 7-1	String-Handling Functions
Name	**Operation**
`int strlen(string)`	Returns the number of characters in a string (not including the terminating null).
`char* strcpy(target, source)`	Copies the source string into a target array.
`char* strcat(target, source)`	Concatenates the source string onto the end of the target string.
`char* strncpy(target, source, n)`	Copies a string up to n characters from the source string into a target array.
`char* strncat(target, source, n)`	Concatenates the source string onto the end of the target string or n characters, whichever comes first.
`char* strstr(string, pattern)`	Returns the address of the first occurrence of pattern in string. Returns a null if pattern is not found.
`int strcmp(source1, source2)`	Compares two strings. Returns -1 if source1 occurs before source2 in the dictionary and 1 if later. Returns 0 if the two strings match exactly.
`int strncmp(source1, source2, n)`	Compares the first n characters in two strings.

You need to add the statement `#include <cstring>` to the beginning of any program that uses a `str...` function because this include file contains the prototype declarations that C++ requires to check up on your work.

The arguments to the `str...()` functions appear backward to any reasonable individual (you might consider this an acid test for "reasonable"). For example, the function `strcat(target, source)` tacks the second string `source` onto the end of the first argument `target`.

The `strncpy()` and `strncat()` functions are similar to their `strcpy()` and `strcat()` counterparts except that they accept the length of the target buffer as one of their arguments. The call `strncpy(szTarget, szSource, 128)` says "copy the characters in `szSource` into `szTarget` until you copy a null character or until you've copied 128 characters, whichever comes first." This avoids inadvertently writing beyond the end of the source string array.

Making Room for Wide Strings

The standard C++ library includes similar functions to handle wide character strings. A few of these functions are listed in Table 7-2.

Remember from Chapter 2 that wide characters are used for applications that must support foreign languages, where a measly 255 different characters may not be enough.

Table 7-2	Wide String-Handling Functions
Name	**Operation**
`int wcslen(string)`	Returns the number of wide characters in a string not including the terminating null.
`wchar_t* wcscpy(target, source)`	Copies the source wide string into a target array.
`wchar_t*wcscat(target, source)`	Concatenates the source wide string onto the end of the target wide string.
`wchar_t*wcsncpy(target, source, n)`	Copies a wide string up to *n* characters from the source string into a target array.
`wchar_t*wcsncat(target, source, n)`	Concatenates the source string onto the end of the target string or *n* characters, whichever comes first.
`wchar_t*wcsstr(string, pattern)`	Finds the address of the first occurrence of pattern in string. Returns a null if pattern is not found.
`int wcscmp(source1, source2)`	Compares two wide strings. Returns -1 if source1 occurs before source2 in the dictionary and 1 if later. Returns 0 if the two strings match exactly.
`int wcsncmp(source1, source2, n)`	Compares the first *n* wide characters in two wide strings.

The following shows a wide character version of the `Concatenate` program:

```
// ConcatenateWide - concatenate two wide strings
//       with a " - " in the middle using library routines
#include <cstdio>
#include <cstdlib>
#include <iostream>
using namespace std;
```

```cpp
int main(int nNumberofArgs, char* pszArgs[])
{
    // read first string...
    wchar_t wszString1[260];
    cout << "Enter string #1:";
    wcin.getline(wszString1, 128);

    // ...now the second string...
    wchar_t wszString2[128];
    cout << "Enter string #2:";
    wcin.getline(wszString2, 128);

    // now tack the second onto the end of the first
    // with a dash in between
    wcsncat(wszString1, L" - ", 260);
    wcsncat(wszString1, wszString2, 260);

    wcout << L"\n" << wszString1 << endl;

    // wait until user is ready before terminating program
    // to allow the user to see the program results
    system("PAUSE");
    return 0;
}
```

The wide character string program looks similar to its single-byte character string cousin except for the following differences:

- Variables are declared `wchar_t` rather than `char`.

- Constant characters and constant strings appear preceded by an L, as in `L"This is a wide string"`.

- The objects `wcin` and `wcout` are used in place of `cin` and `cout` for input and output.

- The `wcs...` functions appear in place of the narrow `str...` functions.

The output from `ConcatenateWide` appears identical to that of the `char` based `Concatenate` program to those of us who do most of their input/output in European languages. The topic of writing programs capable of handling multiple languages with different alphabets and rules of grammar is known as *localization* and beyond a beginning book.

ANSI C++ includes a type `string` designed to make it easier to manipulate strings of text. However, this type makes use of features of the language that you haven't seen yet. I return to the `string` type in Chapter 13.

Chapter 8

Taking a First Look at C++ Pointers

So far, the C++ language has been fairly conventional compared with other programming languages. Sure, some computer languages lack (il-)logical operators like those in Chapter 4, and C++ has its own unique symbols for things, but there's been nothing new in the way of concepts. C++ really separates itself from the crowd in its use of pointer variables. A *pointer* is a variable that "points at" other variables. I realize that's a circular argument, but suspend your disbelief at least until you can get into the chapter.

This chapter introduces the pointer variable type. It begins with some concept definitions, flows through pointer syntax, and then introduces some of the reasons for the pointer mania that grips the C++ programming world.

Variable Size

My weight goes up and down all the time, but here I'm really referring to the size of a variable, not my own variable size. Memory is measured in bytes or bits. The keyword `sizeof` returns the size of its argument in bytes. The following program uses this to determine the size of the different variable types:

```
// VariableSize - output the size of each type of
//                variable
#include <cstdio>
#include <cstdlib>
#include <iostream>
using namespace std;

int main(int nNumberofArgs, char* pszArgs[])
{
    bool        b;
    char        c;
    int         n;
    long        l;
    long long   ll;
    float       f;
    double      d;
    long double ld;

    cout << "sizeof a bool        = " << sizeof b << endl;
    cout << "sizeof a char        = " << sizeof c << endl;
    cout << "sizeof an int        = " << sizeof n << endl;
    cout << "sizeof a long        = " << sizeof l << endl;
    cout << "sizeof a long long   = " << sizeof ll<< endl;
    cout << "sizeof a float       = " << sizeof f << endl;
    cout << "sizeof a double      = " << sizeof d << endl;
    cout << "sizeof a long double = " << sizeof ld<< endl;

    // wait until user is ready before terminating program
    // to allow the user to see the program results
    system("PAUSE");
    return 0;
}
```

The VariableSize program generates the following output:

```
sizeof a bool        = 1
sizeof a char        = 1
sizeof an int        = 4
sizeof a long        = 4
sizeof a long long   = 8
sizeof a float       = 4
sizeof a double      = 8
sizeof a long double = 12
Press any key to continue . . .
```

As they say, "Your results may vary." You may get different results if using a compiler other than the one included on the enclosed CD-ROM. For example, you may find that an int is smaller than a long. C++ doesn't say exactly how big a variable type must be; it just says that a long is the same size as or larger than an `int` and that a `double` is the same size as or larger than a `float`. The sizes output by `VariableSize` are typical for a 32-bit processor such as the Pentium class processors.

What's in an Address?

Like the saying goes, "Everyone has to be somewhere." Every C++ variable is stored somewhere in the computer's memory. Memory is broken into individual bytes with each byte carrying its own address numbered 0, 1, 2, and so on.

A variable `intReader` might be at address 0x100, whereas `floatReader` might be over at location 0x180. (By convention, memory addresses are expressed in hexadecimal.) Of course, `intReader` and `floatReader` might be somewhere else in memory entirely — only the computer knows for sure and only at the time that the program is executed.

This is somewhat analogous to a hotel. When you make your reservation, you may be assigned room 0x100. (I know that suite numbers are normally *not* expressed in hexadecimal, but bear with me.) Your buddy may be assigned 80 doors down in room 0x180. Each variable is assigned an address when it is created (more on that later in this chapter when we talk about scope).

Address Operators

The two pointer-related operators are shown in Table 8-1. The & operator says "tell me your address," and * says "the value at the following address."

Table 8-1	Pointer Operators
Operator	*Meaning*
& (unary)	The address of
* (unary)	(In an expression) the thing pointed at by
* (unary)	(In a declaration) pointer to

The ampersand is also used when declaring reference variables, as you will see a little later in this chapter.

The following `Layout` program demonstrates how the & operator can be used to display the layout of variables in memory:

```cpp
// Layout - this program tries to give the
//          reader an idea of the layout of
//          local memory in her compiler
#include <cstdio>
#include <cstdlib>
#include <iostream>
using namespace std;

int main(int nNumberofArgs, char* pszArgs[])
{
    int         start;
    int         n;
    long        l;
    long long   ll;
    float       f;
    double      d;
    long double ld;
    int         end;

    // set output to hex mode
    cout.setf(ios::hex);
    cout.unsetf(ios::dec);

    // output the address of each variable
    // in order to get an idea of how variables are
    // laid out in memory
    cout << "--- = " << &start << endl;
    cout << "&n  = " << &n      << endl;
    cout << "&l  = " << &l      << endl;
    cout << "&ll = " << &ll     << endl;
    cout << "&f  = " << &f      << endl;
    cout << "&d  = " << &d      << endl;
    cout << "&ld = " << &ld     << endl;
    cout << "--- = " << &end    << endl;

    // wait until user is ready before terminating program
    // to allow the user to see the program results
    system("PAUSE");
    return 0;
}
```

The program declares a set of variables of different types. It then applies the & operator to each one to find out its address. The results of one execution of this program with Code::Blocks appear as follows:

```
---  = 0x22ff1c
&n   = 0x22ff18
&l   = 0x22ff14
&ll  = 0x22ff08
&f   = 0x22ff04
&d   = 0x22fef8
&ld  = 0x22fee0
---  = 0x22fedc
Press any key to continue . . .
```

Your results may vary. The absolute address of program variables depends on a lot of factors. In general, it may even vary from one execution of the program to the next. The C++ standard certainly doesn't specify how variables are to be laid out in memory.

Notice how the variable n is exactly 4 bytes from the first variable declared (start), which corresponds to the size of an int (4 bytes). Similarly, the variable l appears 4 bytes down from that, which is also the size of a long. However, the double variable d is a full 12 bytes from its neighboring variable f (0xff04 — 0xfef8 = 0x000c). That's more than the 8 bytes required for a double. Worse than that, the long double variable ld is some 24 bytes away from its neighbor, d.

There is no requirement that the C++ compiler pack variables in memory with no spaces between them.

The Code::Blocks/gcc compiler could be storing variables for its own use in between our variables. Or, more likely, a peculiarity in the way the variables are being laid out in memory is causing the compiler to waste a small amount of space.

Using Pointer Variables

A *pointer variable* is a variable that contains an address, usually the address of another variable. Returning to the analogy of hotel room numbers, I might tell my son that I will be in room 0x100 on my trip. My son can act as a pointer variable of sorts. Anyone can ask him at any time, "Where's your father staying?" Include $5 with that question and he'll spill his guts without hesitation.

By the way, notice something about pointer variables: No matter where my son is, and no matter how many other people he tells of my whereabouts, I'm still in room 0x100.

The following pseudo-C++ demonstrates how the two address operators shown in Table 8-1 are used:

```
mySon = &DadsRoom; // tell mySon the address of Dad's Room
room = *mySon;     // "Dad's room number is"
```

The following C++ code snippet shows these operators used correctly:

```
void fn()
{
    int  nVar;
    int* pnVar;

    nVar  = &nVar;    // pnVar now points to nVar
    *pnVar = 10;      // stores 10 into the int location
}                     // pointed at by pnVar
```

The function fn() begins with the declaration of nVar. The next statement declares the variable pnVar to be a variable of type pointer to an int.

Pointer variables are declared like normal variables except for the addition of the unary * character. This * character can appear anywhere between the base type name — the following two declarations are equivalent:

```
int* pnVar1;
int *pnVar2;
```

Which you use is a matter of personal preference.

The * character is called the *asterisk character* (that's logical enough), but because *asterisk* is hard to say, many programmers have come to call it the star or, less commonly, the *splat* character. Thus, they would say "star pnVar" or "splat pnVar."

In an expression, the unary operator & means "the address of." Thus, we would read the assignment pnVar = &nVar; as "pnVar gets the address of nVar."

Using different types of pointers

Every expression has a type as well as a value. The type of the expression nVar is int; the type of &nVar is "pointer to an integer," written int*. Comparing this with the declaration of pVar, you see that the types match exactly:

```
int* pnVar = &nVar; // both sides of the assignment
                    // are of type int*
```

Similarly, because pnVar is of type int*, the type of *pnVar is int:

```
*pnVar = 10;        // both sides of the assignment are
                    // of type int
```

The type of the thing pointed to by pnVar is int. This is equivalent to saying that, if houseAddress is the address of a house, the thing pointed at by houseAddress must be a house. Amazing, but true.

Pointers to other types of variables are expressed the same way:

```
double doubleVar;
double* pdoubleVar = &doubleVar;
*pdoubleVar = 10.0;
```

A pointer on a Pentium class machine takes 4 bytes no matter what it points to. That is, an address on a Pentium is 4 bytes long, period.

Check out the program LayoutError on the enclosed CD-ROM to see how things can get messed up when casting from one pointer type to another incorrectly.

The house equivalent goes something like this:

```
House* houseAddress = &"123 Main Street";
Hotel* hotelAddress;
hotelAddress = (Hotel*)houseAddress;
*hotelAddress = TheRitz;
```

houseAddress is initialized to point to my house. The variable hotel Address is a pointer to a hotel. Now, the house address is cast into the address of a hotel and saved off into the variable hotelAddress. Finally, TheRitz is plopped down on top of my house. Because TheRitz is slightly bigger than my house (okay, a lot bigger than my house), it isn't surprising that TheRitz wipes out my neighbors' houses as well.

Passing Pointers to Functions

One of the uses of pointer variables is in passing arguments to functions. To understand why this is important, you need to understand how arguments are passed to a function.

Passing by value

By default, arguments are passed to functions by value. This has the somewhat surprising result that changing the value of a variable in a function does not normally change its value in the calling function. Consider the following example code segment:

```
void fn(int nArg)
{
    nArg = 10;
    // value of nArg at this point is 10
}

void parent(void)
{
    int n1 = 0;
    fn(n1);
    // value of n1 at this point is still 0
}
```

Here the `parent()` function initializes the integer variable n1 to 0. The value of n1 is then passed to `fn()`. Upon entering the function, nArg is equal to 0, the value passed. `fn()` changes the value of nArg to 10 before returning to `parent()`. Perhaps surprisingly, upon returning to `parent()`, the value of n1 is still 0.

The reason for this behavior is that C++ doesn't pass a variable to a function. (I'm not even sure what that would mean.) Instead, C++ passes the value contained in the variable at the time of the call. That is, the expression is evaluated, even if it is just a variable name, and the result is passed.

In the example, the value of n1, which is 0, was passed to `fn()`. What the function does with that value has no effect on n1.

It is easy for a speaker to get lazy and say something like, "Pass the variable x to the function `fn()`." This really means to pass the value of the expression x.

Passing pointer values

Like any other intrinsic type, a pointer may be passed as an argument to a function:

```
void fn(int* pnArg)
{
    *pnArg = 10;
}
```

```
void parent(void)
{
    int n = 0;

    fn(&n);         // this passes the address of i
                    // now the value of n is 10
}
```

In this case, the address of n is passed to the function fn() rather than the value of n. The significance of this difference is apparent when you consider the assignment within fn().

Suppose n is located at address 0x100. Rather than the value 10, the call fn(&n) passes the value 0x100. Within fn(), the assignment *pnArg = 10 stores the value 10 in the int variable located at location 0x100, thereby overwriting the value 0. Upon returning to parent(), the value of n is 10 because n is just another name for 0x100.

Passing by reference

C++ provides a shorthand for passing arguments by address — a shorthand that enables you to avoid having to hassle with pointers. The following declaration creates a variable n1 and a second reference to the same n1 but with a new name, nRef:

```
int n1;             // declare an int variable
int& nRef = n1;     // declare a second reference to n1

nRef = 1;           // now accessing the reference
                    // has the same effect as accessing n1;
                    // n1 is now equal to 1
```

A reference variable like nRef must be initialized when it is declared because every subsequent time that its name is used, C++ will assume that you mean the variable that nRef refers to.

Reference variables find their primary application in function calls:

```
void fn(int& rnArg)// declare reference argument
{
    rnArg = 10;     // change the value of the variable...
}                   //...that rnArg refers to

void parent(void)
{
    int n1 = 0;
    fn(n1);         // pass a reference to n1
                    // here the value of n1 is 10
}
```

This is called "passing by reference." The declaration int& rnArg declares rnArg to be a reference to an integer argument. The fn() function stores the value 10 into the int location referenced by rnArg.

Passing by reference is the same as passing the address of a variable. The reference syntax puts the onus on C++ to apply the "address of" operator to the reference rather than requiring the programmer to do so.

You cannot overload a pass by value function with its pass by reference equivalent. Thus, you could not define the two functions fn(int) and fn(int&) in the same program. C++ would not know which one to call.

Constant const Irritation

A program cannot change the value of a variable declared const once it has been defined. However, this introduces an interesting dichotomy in the case of pointer variables. Consider the following declaration:

```
const int* pInt;
```

Exactly what is the constant here? What can we not change? Is it the variable pInt or the integer pointed at by pInt? It turns out that both are possible, but this declaration declares a variable pointer to a constant memory location. Thus the following:

```
const int* pInt;   // declare a pointer to a const int
int nVar;
pInt = &nVar;      // this is allowed
*pInt = 10;        // but this is not
```

We can change the value of pInt, for example, assigning it the address of nVar. But the final assignment in the example snippet generates a compiler error since we cannot change the const int pointed at by pInt.

What if I had intended to create a pointer variable with a constant value? The following snippet shows this in action:

```
int nVar;
int * const cpInt = &nVar; // declare a constant pointer
                           // to a variable integer
*cpInt = 10;               // now this is legal...
cpInt++;                   // ...but this is not
```

The variable `cpInt` is a constant pointer to a variable `int`. The programmer cannot change the value of the pointer but she can change the value of the integer pointed at.

The `const`-ness can be added via an assignment or initialization but cannot be (readily) cast away. Thus, the following:

```
int nVar = 10;
int pVar = &nVar;
const int* pcVar = pVar;    // this is legal
int* pVar2 = pcVar;         // this is not
```

The assignment `pcVar = pVar;` is okay — this is adding the `const` restriction. The final assignment in the snippet is not allowed since it attempts to remove the `const`-ness of `pcVar`.

A variable can be implicitly recast as part of a function call, as in the following example:

```
void fn(const int& nVar);

void mainFn()
{
    int n;

    fn(10);   // calls fn(const int&)
    fn(n);    // calls the same function by treating n
}             // as if it were const
```

The declaration `fn(const int&)` says that the function `fn()` does not modify the value of its argument. That's important when passing a reference to the constant 10. It isn't important when passing a reference to the variable n but it doesn't hurt anything either.

Finally, `const` can be used as a discriminator between functions of the same name:

```
void fn(const int& nVar);
void fn(int& nVar);

void mainFn()
{
    int n;

    fn(10);   // calls the first function
    fn(n);    // calls the second function
}
```

Making Use of a Block of Memory Called the Heap

The *heap* is an amorphous block of memory that your program can access as necessary. This section describes why it exists and how to use it.

Just as it is possible to pass a pointer to a function, it is possible for a function to return a pointer. A function that returns the address of a double is declared as follows:

```
double* fn(void);
```

However, you must be very careful when returning a pointer. To understand the dangers, you must know something about variable scope. (No, I don't mean a variable zoom rifle scope.)

Limited scope

Besides being a mouthwash, *scope* is the range over which a variable is defined. Consider the following code snippet:

```
// the following variable is accessible to
// all functions and defined as long as the
// program is running(global scope)
int intGlobal;

// the following variable intChild is accessible
// only to the function and is defined only
// as long as C++ is executing child() or a
// function which child() calls (function scope)
void child(void)
{
    int intChild;
}

// the following variable intParent has function
// scope
void parent(void)
{
    int intParent = 0;
    child();

    int intLater = 0;
    intParent = intLater;
}
```

```
int main(int nArgs, char* pArgs[])
{
    parent();
}
```

This program fragment starts with the declaration of a variable `intGlobal`. This variable exists from the time the program begins executing until it terminates. We say that `intGlobal` "has program scope." We also say that the variable "goes into scope" even before the function `main()` is called.

The function `main()` immediately invokes `parent()`. The first thing that the processor sees in `parent()` is the declaration of `intParent`. At that point, `intParent` goes into scope — that is, `intParent` is defined and available for the remainder of the function `parent()`.

The second statement in `parent()` is the call to `child()`. Once again, the function `child()` declares a local variable, this time `intChild`. The scope of the variable `intChild` is limited to the function `child()`. Technically, `intParent` is not defined within the scope of `child()` because `child()` doesn't have access to `intParent`; however, the variable `intParent` continues to exist while `child()` is executing.

When `child()` exits, the variable `intChild` goes out of scope. Not only is `intChild` no longer accessible, it no longer exists. (The memory occupied by `intChild` is returned to the general pool to be used for other things.)

As `parent()` continues executing, the variable `intLater` goes into scope at the declaration. At the point that `parent()` returns to `main()`, both `int Parent` and `intLater` go out of scope.

Because `intGlobal` is declared globally in this example, it is available to all three functions and remains available for the life of the program.

Examining the scope problem

The following code segment compiles without error but doesn't work (don't you just hate that):

```
double* child(void)
{
    double dLocalVariable;
    return &dLocalVariable;
}
```

```
void parent(void)
{
    double* pdLocal;
    pdLocal  = child();
    *pdLocal = 1.0;
}
```

The problem with this function is that dLocalVariable is defined only within the scope of the function child(). Thus, by the time the memory address of dLocalVariable is returned from child(), it refers to a variable that no longer exists. The memory that dLocalVariable formerly occupied is probably being used for something else.

This error is very common because it can creep up in a number of ways. Unfortunately, this error does not cause the program to instantly stop. In fact, the program may work fine most of the time — that is, the program continues to work as long as the memory formerly occupied by dLocalVariable is not reused immediately. Such intermittent problems are the most difficult ones to solve.

Providing a solution using the heap

The scope problem originated because C++ took back the locally defined memory before the programmer was ready. What is needed is a block of memory controlled by the programmer. She can allocate the memory and put it back when she wants to — not because C++ thinks it's a good idea. Such a block of memory is called the *heap*.

Heap memory is allocated using the new keyword followed by the type of object to allocate. The new command breaks a chunk of memory off the heap big enough to hold the specified type of object and returns its address. For example, the following allocates a double variable off the heap:

```
double* child(void)
{
    double* pdLocalVariable = new double;
    return pdLocalVariable;
}
```

This function now works properly. Although the variable pdLocalVariable goes out of scope when the function child() returns, the memory to which pdLocalVariable refers does not. A memory location returned by new does not go out of scope until it is explicitly returned to the heap using the keyword delete, which is specifically designed for that purpose:

```
void parent(void)
{
    // child() returns the address of a block
    // of heap memory
    double* pdMyDouble = child();

    // store a value there
    *pdMyDouble = 1.1;

    // ...

    // now return the memory to the heap
    delete pdMyDouble;
    pdMyDouble = 0;

    // ...
}
```

Here the pointer returned by `child()` is used to store a double value. After the function is finished with the memory location, it is returned to the heap. The function `parent()` sets the pointer to 0 after the heap memory has been returned — this is not a requirement, but it is a very good idea. If the programmer mistakenly attempts to store something in `* pdMyDouble` after the `delete`, the program will crash immediately with (I hope) a meaningful error message.

Chapter 9

Taking a Second Look at C++ Pointers

C++ allows the programmer to operate on pointer variables much as she would on simple types of variables. (The concept of pointer variables is introduced in Chapter 8.) How and why this is done along with its implications are the subjects of this chapter.

Defining Operations on Pointer Variables

Some of the same arithmetic operators I cover in Chapter 3 can be applied to pointer types. This section examines the implications of applying these operators to both to pointers and to the array types (I discuss arrays in Chapter 7). Table 9-1 lists the three fundamental operations that are defined on pointers. In Table 9-1, pointer, pointer1, and pointer2 are all of some pointer type, say char*; and offset is an integer, for example, long. C++ also supports the other operators related to addition and subtraction, such as ++ and +=., although they are not listed in Table 9-1.

Table 9-1		The Three Basic Operations Defined on Pointer Types
Operation	*Result*	*Meaning*
`pointer +` `offset`	pointer	Calculate the address of the object `offset` entries from `pointer`
`pointer -` `offset`	pointer	The opposite of addition
`pointer2 -` `pointer1`	offset	Calculate the number of entries between `pointer2` and `pointer1`

The neighborhood memory model is useful to explain how pointer arithmetic works. Consider a city block in which all houses are numbered sequentially. The house at 123 Main Street has 122 Main Street on one side and 124 Main Street on the other.

Now it's pretty clear that the house four houses down from 123 Main Street must be 127 Main Street; thus, you can say `123 Main + 4 = 127 Main`. Similarly, if I were to ask how many houses are there from 123 Main to 127 Main, the answer would be four — `127 Main - 123 Main = 4`. (Just as an aside, a house is zero houses from itself: `123 Main - 123 Main = 0`.)

But it makes no sense to ask how far away from 123 Main Street is 4 or what the sum of 123 Main and 127 Main is. In similar fashion, you can't add two addresses. Nor can you multiply an address, divide an address, square an address, or take the square root — you get the idea. You can perform any operation that can be converted to addition or subtraction. For example, if you increment a pointer to 123 Main Street, it now points to the house next door (at 124 Main, of course!).

Reexamining arrays in light of pointer variables

Now return to the wonderful array for just a moment. Consider the case of an array of 32 1-byte characters called `charArray`. If the first byte of this array is stored at address 0x100, the array will extend over the range 0x100 through 0x11f. `charArray[0]` is located at address 0x100, `charArray[1]` is at 0x101, `charArray[2]` at 0x102, and so on.

After executing the expression

```
ptr = &charArray[0];
```

the pointer `ptr` contains the address 0x100. The addition of an integer offset to a pointer is defined such that the relationships shown in Table 9-2 are true. Table 9-2 also demonstrates why adding an offset n to `ptr` calculates the address of the *n*th element in `charArray`.

Table 9-2	Adding Offsets	
Offset	*Result*	*Is the Address of*
+ 0	0x100	`charArray[0]`
+ 1	0x101	`charArray[1]`
+ 2	0x102	`charArray[2]`
...	...	...
+ n	0x100+ n	`charArray[n]`

The addition of an offset to a pointer is identical to applying an index to an array.

Thus, if

```
char* ptr = &charArray[0];
```

then

```
*(ptr + n) ← corresponds with → charArray[n]
```

Because * has higher precedence than addition, * `ptr` + n adds n to the character that `ptr` points to. The parentheses are needed to force the addition to occur before the indirection. The expression *(ptr + n) retrieves the character pointed at by the pointer `ptr` plus the offset n.

In fact, the correspondence between the two forms of expression is so strong that C++ considers `array[n]` nothing more than a simplified version of *(ptr + n), where `ptr` points to the first element in `array`.

```
array[n] -- C++ interprets as → *(&array[0] + n)
```

To complete the association, C++ takes a second shortcut. If given

```
char charArray[20];
```

`charArray` is defined as `&charArray[0];`. That is, the name of an array without a subscript present is the address of the array itself. Thus, you can further simplify the association to

```
array[n] -- C++ interprets as → *(array + n)
```

TIP

The type of `charArray` is actually `char const*`; that is, "constant pointer to a character" since its address cannot be changed.

Applying operators to the address of an array

The correspondence between indexing an array and pointer arithmetic is useful. For example, a `displayArray()` function used to display the contents of an array of integers can be written as follows:

```
// displayArray - display the members of an
//                array of length nSize
void displayArray(int intArray[], int nSize)
{
    cout << "The value of the array is:\n";

    for(int n; n < nSize; n++)
    {
        cout << n << ": " << intArray[n] << "\n";
    }
    cout << endl;
}
```

This version uses the array operations with which you are familiar. A pointer version of the same appears as follows:

```
// displayArray - display the members of an
//                array of length nSize
void displayArray(int intArray[], int nSize)
{
    cout << "The value of the array is:\n";

    int* pArray = intArray;
    for(int n = 0; n < nSize; n++, pArray++)
    {
        cout << n << ": " << *pArray << "\n";
    }
    cout << endl;
}
```

The new `displayArray()` begins by creating a pointer to an integer `pArray` that points at the first element of `intArray`.

REMEMBER

The `p` in the variable name indicates that the variable is a pointer, but this is just a convention, not a part of the C++ language.

The function then loops through each element of the array. On each loop, `displayArray()` outputs the current integer (that is, the integer pointed at by `pArray`) before incrementing the pointer to the next entry in `intArray`. `displayArray()` can be tested using the following version of `main()`:

```
int main(int nNumberofArgs, char* pszArgs[])
{
    int array[] = {4, 3, 2, 1};
    displayArray(array, 4);

    // wait until user is ready before terminating program
    // to allow the user to see the program results
    system("PAUSE");
    return 0;
}
```

The output from this program is

```
The value of the array is:
0: 4
1: 3
2: 2
3: 1

Press any key to continue . . .
```

You may think this pointer conversion is silly; however, the pointer version of `displayArray()` is actually more common than the array version among C++ programmers in the know. For some reason, C++ programmers don't seem to like arrays but they love pointer manipulation.

The use of pointers to access arrays is nowhere more common than in the accessing of character arrays.

Expanding pointer operations to a string

A null-terminated string is simply a constant character array whose last character is a null. C++ uses the null character at the end to serve as a terminator. This null-terminated array serves as a quasivariable type of its own. (See Chapter 7 for an explanation of null-terminated string arrays.) Often C++ programmers use character pointers to manipulate such strings. The following code examples compare this technique to the earlier technique of indexing in the array.

Character pointers enjoy the same relationship with a character array that any other pointer and array share. However, the fact that strings end in a terminating null makes them especially amenable to pointer-based manipulation, as shown in the following DisplayString program:

```cpp
// DisplayString - display an array of characters using
//                 both a pointer and an array index
#include <cstdio>
#include <cstdlib>
#include <iostream>
using namespace std;

int main(int nNumberofArgs, char* pszArgs[])
{
    // declare a string
    const char* szString = "Randy";
    cout << "The array is '" << szString << "'" << endl;

    // display szString as an array
    cout << "Display the string as an array: ";
    for(int i = 0; i < 5; i++)
    {
        cout << szString[i];
    }
    cout << endl;

    // now using typical pointer arithmetic
    cout << "Display string using a pointer: ";
    const char* pszString = szString;
    while(*pszString)
    {
        cout << *pszString;
        pszString++;
    }
    cout << endl;

    // wait until user is ready before terminating program
    // to allow the user to see the program results
    system("PAUSE");
    return 0;
}
```

The program first makes its way through the array szString by indexing into the array of characters. The for loop chosen stops when the index reaches 5, the length of the string.

The second loop displays the same string using a pointer. The program sets the variable pszString equal to the address of the first character in the array. It then enters a loop that will continue until the char pointed at by pszString is equal to false — in other words, until the character is a null.

The integer value 0 is interpreted as false — all other values are true.

The program outputs the character pointed at by `pszString` and then incre-ments the pointer so that it points to the next character in the string before being returned to the top of the loop.

The dereference and increment can be (and usually are) combined into a single expression as follows:

```
cout << *pszString++;
```

The output of the program appears as follows:

```
The array is 'Randy'
Display the string as an array: Randy
Display string using a pointer: Randy
Press any key to continue . . .
```

Justifying pointer-based string manipulation

The sometimes-cryptic nature of pointer-based manipulation of character strings might lead the reader to wonder, "Why?" That is, what advantage does the `char*` pointer version have over the easier-to-read index version?

The answer is partially (pre-)historic and partially human nature. When C, the progenitor to C++, was invented, compilers were pretty simplistic. These compilers could not perform the complicated optimizations that modern compilers can. As complicated as it might appear to the human reader, a statement such as `*pszString++` could be converted into an amazingly small number of machine-level instructions even by a stupid compiler.

Older computer processors were not very fast by today's standards. In the early days of C, saving a few computer instructions was a big deal. This gave C a big advantage over other languages of the day, notably Fortran, which did not offer pointer arithmetic.

In addition to the efficiency factor, programmers like to generate clever pro-gram statements. After C++ programmers learn how to write compact and cryptic but efficient statements, there is no getting them back to accessing arrays with indices.

Do not generate complex C++ expressions to create a more efficient program. There is no obvious relationship between the number of C++ statements and the number of machine instructions generated.

Applying operators to pointer types other than char

It is not too hard to convince yourself that szTarget + n points to szTarget [n] when szTarget is an array of chars. After all, a char occupies a single byte. If szTarget is stored at 0x100, szTarget [5] is located at 0x105.

It is not so obvious that pointer addition works in exactly the same way for an int array because an int takes 4 bytes for each char's 1 byte (at least it does on a 32-bit Intel processor). If the first element in intArray were located at 0x100, then intArray [5] would be located at 0x114 (0x100 + (5 * 4) = 0x114) and not 0x104.

Fortunately for us, array + n points at array [n] no matter how large a single element of array might be. C++ takes care of the element size for us — it's clever that way.

Once again, the dusty old house analogy works here as well. (I mean dusty analogy, not dusty house.) The third house down from 123 Main is 126 Main, no matter how large the building might be, even if it's a hotel.

Contrasting a pointer with an array

There are some differences between an array and a pointer. For one, the array allocates space for the data, whereas the pointer does not, as shown here:

```
void arrayVsPointer()
{
    // allocate storage for 128 characters
    char charArray[128];

    // allocate space for a pointer but not for
    // the thing pointed at
    char* pArray;
}
```

Here charArray allocates room for 128 characters. pArray allocates only 4 bytes — the amount of storage required by a pointer.

Consider the following example:

```
char charArray[128];
charArray[10] = '0'; // this works fine

char* pArray;
pArray[10] = '0';    // this writes into random location
```

Strings have me constantly confused

You may have noticed that I slipped a `const` declaration into the earlier DisplayString example program. This was necessary to account for differences between an array and a pointer. A string such as "this is a string" is considered a constant address of a string of constant characters. In other words, neither the address of the string nor the characters themselves can be changed. Why is that?

One problem is that you don't know where C++ stores its local strings nor do you know how many times it reuses the same string. Often C++ stores constant strings in the same memory locations as source code, and it very often reuses the same string in several places in the program. For this reason, C++ often marks constant strings as unwritable.

The initialization of a pointer variable is similar to initializing any other simple variable:

```
int i = 1;
const char* pString = "this is a string";
```

Both declarations initialize the variable on the left with the constant value on the right. However, since `pString` points directly at the immutable string "this is a string" it's important that it be declare `const char*`; that is, a pointer to constant characters.

The equivalent array is more complicated than it first appears:

```
char sChars[] = "this is a string"; // declare and init array
```

This declares and allocates memory for an array `sChars[]` and then copies the initialization string into it. Thus, the letter *t* that is the first character in `sChars` is not the same letter *t* that makes up the immutable initialization string.

In fact, the preceding is shorthand for the more long-winded but descriptive

```
char sChars[17];                           // declare the array
   and...
strcpy(sChars, "this is a string"); // ...then initialize it
```

Remember that `strcpy()` copies the string of characters represented by the second argument into the array pointed at by the first argument. And also remember to allocate space for the terminating null.

The expression `pArray[10]` is syntactically equivalent to `charArray[10]`, but `pArray` has not been initialized so `pArray[10]` references some random (garbage) location in memory.

The mistake of referencing memory with an uninitialized pointer variable is generally caught by the CPU when the program executes, resulting in the dreaded *segment violation* error that from time to time issues from your favorite applications under your favorite, or not-so-favorite, operating system. This problem is not generally the fault of the processor or the operating system but of the application.

A second difference between a pointer and the address of an array is that charArray is a constant, whereas pArray is not. Thus, the following for loop used to initialize the array charArray does not work:

```
void arrayVsPointer()
{
char charArray[10];
for (int i = 0; i < 10; i++)
{
    *charArray = '\0';     // this makes sense...
    charArray++;           // ...this does not
}
}
```

The expression charArray++ makes no more sense than 10++. The following version is correct:

```
void arrayVsPointer()
{
char charArray[10];
char* pArray = charArray;
for (int i = 0; i < 10; i++)
{
    *pArray = '\0';     // this works great
    pArray++;
}
}
```

When Is a Pointer Not?

C++ is completely quiet about what is and isn't a legal address, with one exception. C++ predefines the constant nullptr with the following properties:

- ✔ It is a constant value.
- ✔ It can be assigned to any pointer type,
- ✔ It evaluates to false.
- ✔ It is never a legal address.

The constant nullptr is used to indicate when a pointer has not been initialized. It is also often used to indicate the last element in an array of pointers in much the same way that a null character is used to terminate a character string.

Actually the keyword nullptr was introduced in the 2009 standard. Before that, the constant 0 was used to indicate a null pointer.

It is a safe practice to initialize pointers to the `nullptr` (or 0 if your compiler doesn't support `nullptr` yet). You should also clear out the contents of a pointer to heap memory after you invoke `delete` to avoid deleting the same memory block twice:

```
delete pHeap;       // return memory to the heap
pHeap = nullptr;    // now clear out the pointer
```

Passing the same address to delete twice will always cause your program to crash. Passing a `nullptr` (or 0) to `delete` has no effect.

Declaring and Using Arrays of Pointers

If pointers can point to arrays, it seems only fitting that the reverse should be true. Arrays of pointers are a type of array of particular interest.

Just as arrays may contain other data types, an array may contain pointers. The following declares an array of pointers to `int`s:

```
int* pInts[10];
```

Given the preceding declaration, `pInts[0]` is a pointer to an `int` value. Thus, the following is true:

```
void fn()
{
    int n1;
    int* pInts[3];
    pInts[0] = &n1;
    *pInts[0] = 1;
}
```

or

```
void fn()
{
    int n1, n2, n3;
    int* pInts[3] = {&n1, &n2, &n3};
    for (int i = 0; i < 3; i++)
    {
        *pInts[i] = 0;
    }
}
```

or even

```
void fn()
{
    int* pInts[3] = {(new int),
                     (new int),
                     (new int)};
    for (int i = 0; i < 3; i++)
    {
        *pInts[i] = 0;
    }
}
```

The latter declares three int objects off the heap. This type of declaration isn't used very often except in the case of an array of pointers to character strings. The following two examples show why arrays of character strings are useful.

Utilizing arrays of character strings

Suppose I need a function that returns the name of the month corresponding to an integer argument passed to it. For example, if the program is passed a 1, it returns a pointer to the string "January"; if 2, it reports "February", and so on. The month 0 and any numbers greater than 12 are assumed to be invalid. I could write the function as follows:

```
// int2month() - return the name of the month
const char* int2month(int nMonth)
{
    const char* pszReturnValue;

    switch(nMonth)
    {
        case 1: pszReturnValue = "January";
            break;
        case 2: pszReturnValue = "February";
            break;
        case 3: pszReturnValue = "March";
            break;
        // ...and so forth...
        default: pszReturnValue = "invalid";
    }
    return pszReturnValue;
}
```

The switch() control command is like a sequence of if statements.

A more elegant solution uses the integer value for the month as an index into an array of pointers to the names of the months. In use, this appears as follows:

```
// define an array containing the names of the months
const char *const pszMonths[] = {"invalid",
                                 "January",
                                 "February",
                                 "March",
                                 "April",
                                 "May",
                                 "June",
                                 "July",
                                 "August",
                                 "September",
                                 "October",
                                 "November",
                                 "December"};

// int2month() - return the name of the month
const char* int2month(int nMonth)
{
    // first check for a value out of range
    if (nMonth < 1 || nMonth > 12)
    {
        return "invalid";
    }

    // nMonth is valid - return the name of the month
    return pszMonths[nMonth];
}
```

Here int2Month() first checks to make sure that nMonth is a number between 1 and 12, inclusive (the default clause of the switch statement handled that in the previous example). If nMonth is valid, the function uses it as an offset into an array containing the names of the months.

This technique of referring to character strings by index is especially useful when writing your program to work in different languages. For example, a program may declare a ptrMonths of pointers to Julian months in different languages. The program would initialize ptrMonth to the proper names, be they in English, French, or German (for example) at execution time. In that way, ptrMonth[1] points to the correct name of the first Julian month, irrespective of the language.

A program that demonstrates int2Month() is included on the CD-ROM as DisplayMonths.

Accessing the arguments to main ( )

Now the truth can be told — what are all those funny argument declarations to main() in our program template? The second argument to main() is an array of pointers to null-terminated character strings. These strings contain the arguments to the program. The arguments to a program are the strings that appear with the program name when you launch it. These arguments are also known as *parameters*. The first argument to main() is the number of parameters passed to the program. For example, suppose that I entered the following command at the command prompt:

```
MyProgram file.txt /w
```

The operating system executes the program contained in the file MyProgram.exe, passing it the arguments file.txt, and /w.

Consider the following simple program:

```cpp
// PrintArgs - write the arguments to the program
//             to the standard output
#include <cstdio>
#include <cstdlib>
#include <iostream>
using namespace std;

int main(int nNumberofArgs, char* pszArgs[])
{
    // print a warning banner
    cout << "The arguments to "
         << pszArgs[0] << " are:\n";

    // now write out the remaining arguments
    for (int i = 1; i < nNumberofArgs; i++)
    {
        cout << i << ":" << pszArgs[i] << "\n";
    }

    // that's it
    cout << "That's it" << endl;

    // wait until user is ready before terminating program
    // to allow the user to see the program results
    system("PAUSE");
    return 0;
}
```

As always, the function `main()` accepts two arguments. The first argument is an `int` that I have been calling (quite descriptively, as it turns out) `nNum-berofArgs`. This variable is the number of arguments passed to the program. The second argument is an array of pointers of type `char*` that I have been calling `pszArgs`.

Accessing program arguments DOS style

If I were to execute the `PrintArgs` program from the command prompt window as

```
PrintArgs arg1 arg2 arg3 /w
```

`nArgs` would be 5 (one for each argument). The first argument is the name of the program itself. This could be anywhere from the simple "PrintArgs" to the slightly more complicated "PrintArgs.exe" to the full path — the C++ standard doesn't specify. The environment can even supply a null string `""` if it doesn't have access to the name of the program.

The remaining elements in `pszArgs` point to the program arguments. For example, the element `pszArgs[1]` points to "arg1" and `pszArgs[2]` to "arg2". Because Windows does not place any significance on "/w", this string is also passed as an argument to be processed by the program.

Actually C++ includes one final value. The last value in the array, the one after the pointer to the last argument to the program, contains `nullptr`.

To demonstrate how argument passing works, you need to build the program from within Code::Blocks and then execute the program directly from a command prompt. First ensure that Code::Blocks has built an executable by opening the PrintArgs projects and choosing Build⇨Rebuild.

Next open a command prompt window. If you are running Unix or Linux, you're already there. If you are running Windows, choose Programs⇨ Accessories⇨Command Prompt to open an 80-character-wide window with a command prompt.

Now you need to use the CD command to navigate to the directory where Code::Blocks placed the PrintArgs program. If you used the default settings when installing Code::Blocks that directory will be `C:\CPP_Programs\Chap09\PrintArgs\bin\Debug`.

You can now execute the program by typing its name followed by your arguments. The following shows what happened when I did it in Windows Vista:

```
Microsoft Windows [Version 6.0.6001]
Copyright (c) 2006 Microsoft Corporation.   All rights reserved.

C:\Users\Randy>cd \cpp_programs\chap09\printargs\bin\debug

C:\CPP_Programs\Chap09\PrintArgs\bin\Debug>PrintArgs arg1 arg2 arg3 /n
The arguments to PrintArgs are:
1:arg1
2:arg2
3:arg3
4:/n
That's it
Press any key to continue . . .
```

Wild cards such as *.* may or may not be expanded before being passed
to the program — the standard is silent on this point. The Code::Blocks/gcc
compiler included with this book does perform such expansion on Windows
Vista, as the following example shows:

```
C:\CPP_Programs\Chap09\PrintArgs>bin\debug\PrintArgs *.*
The arguments to bin\debug\PrintArgs are:
1:bin
2:main.cpp
3:obj
4:PrintArgs.cbp
That's it
Press any key to continue . . .
```

Here you see the names of the files in the current directory in place of the
. that I entered.

Wild-card expansion is performed under all forms of Unix and Linux as well.
Wild-card expansion was specifically not performed under older versions of
gcc and it isn't performed under Visual C++ Express.

Accessing program arguments Code::Blocks style

You can add arguments to your program when you execute it from
Code::Blocks as well. Choose Project➪Set programs' arguments from within
Code::Blocks. Enter the command line you would like in the program argu-
ments window.

Accessing program arguments Windows-style

Windows passes arguments as a means of communicating with your program
as well. Try the following experiment. Build your program as you would normally. Find the executable file using Windows Explorer. As noted earlier, the

default location for the PrintArgs program is `C:\CPP_Programs\Chap09\PrintArgs\bin\Debug`. Now grab a file and drop it onto the filename. (It doesn't matter what file you choose because the program won't hurt it anyway.) Bam! The PrintArgs program starts right up, and the name of the file that you dropped on the program appears.

Now try again, but drop several files at once. Select multiple filenames while pressing the Ctrl key or by using the Shift key to select a group. Now drag the lot of them onto PrintArgs.exe and let go. The name of each file appears as output.

I dropped a few of the files that appear in my `\Program Files\WinZip` folder onto PrintArgs as an example:

```
The arguments to C:\CPP_Programs\Chap09\PrintArgs\bin\Debug\PrintArgs.exe are:
1:C:\Program Files\WinZip\VENDOR.TXT
2:C:\Program Files\WinZip\WHATSNEW.TXT
3:C:\Program Files\WinZip\WINZIP.CHM
4:C:\Program Files\WinZip\WINZIP.TXT
5:C:\Program Files\WinZip\WINZIP32.EXE
6:C:\Program Files\WinZip\WZ.COM
7:C:\Program Files\WinZip\WZ.PIF
8:C:\Program Files\WinZip\WZ32.DLL
9:C:\Program Files\WinZip\WZCAB.DLL
10:C:\Program Files\WinZip\WZCAB3.DLL
11:C:\Program Files\WinZip\FILE_ID.DIZ
12:C:\Program Files\WinZip\LICENSE.TXT
13:C:\Program Files\WinZip\ORDER.TXT
14:C:\Program Files\WinZip\README.TXT
That's it
Press any key to continue . . .
```

Notice that the name of each file appears as a single argument, even though the filename may include spaces. Also note that Windows passes the full path name of the file.

Chapter 10

The C++ Preprocessor

*Y*ou only thought that all you had to learn was C++. It turns out that C++ includes a preprocessor that works on your source files before the "real C++ compiler" ever gets to see it. Unfortunately, the syntax of the preprocessor is completely different than that of C++ itself.

Before you despair, however, let me hasten to add that the preprocessor is very basic and the C++ '09 standard has added a number of features that make the preprocessor almost unnecessary. Nevertheless, if the conversation turns to C++ at your next Coffee Club meeting, you'll be expected to understand the preprocessor.

What Is a Preprocessor?

Up until now, you may have thought of the C++ compiler as munching on your source code and spitting out an executable program in one step, but that isn't quite true.

First, the preprocessor makes a pass through your program looking for preprocessor instructions. The output of this preprocessor step is an intermediate file that has all the preprocessor commands expanded. This intermediate file gets passed to the C++ compiler for processing. The output from the C++ compiler is an object file that contains the machine instruction equivalent to your C++ source code. During the final step, a separate program known as the linker combines a set of standard libraries with your object file (or files as we'll see in Chapter 21) to create an executable program. (More on the standard library in the next section of this chapter.)

Object files normally carry the extension .o. Executable programs always carry the extension .exe in Windows and have no extension under Unix and Linux. Code::Blocks stores the object and executable files in their own folders. For example, if you've already built the IntAverage program from Chapter 2, you will have on your hard disk a folder C:\CPP_Programs\IntAverage\obj\Debug containing main.o and a folder C:\CPP_Programs\IntAverage\bin\Debug that contains the executable program.

All preprocessor commands start with a # symbol in column 1 and end with the newline.

Like almost all rules in C++, this rule has an exception. You can spread a preprocessor command across multiple lines by ending the line with an escape character: \. We won't have any preprocessor commands that are that complicated, however.

In this book, we'll be working with three preprocessor commands:

- ✔ #include includes the contents of the specified file in place of the #include statement.
- ✔ #define defines a constant or macro.
- ✔ #if includes a section of code in the intermediary file if the following condition is true.

Each of these preprocessor commands is covered in the following sections.

Including Files

The C++ standard library consists of functions that are basic enough that almost everyone needs them. It would be silly to force every programmer to have to write them for herself. For example, the I/O functions, which we have been using to read input from the keyboard and write out to the console, are contained in the standard library.

However, C++ requires a prototype declaration for any function you call, whether it's in a library or not (see Chapter 6 if that doesn't make sense to you). Rather than force the programmer to type all these declarations by hand, the library authors created include files that contain little more than prototype declarations. All you have to do is #include the source file that contains the prototypes for the library routines you intend to use.

Take the following simple example. Suppose I had created a library that contains the trigonometric functions sin(), cosin(), tan(), and a whole lot more. I would likely create an include file mytrig with the following contents to go along with my standard library:

```
// include prototype declarations for my library
double sin(double x);
double cosin(double x);
double tan(double x);
// ...more prototype declarations...
```

Any program that wanted to make use of one of these math functions would #include that file, enclosing the name of the include file either in brackets or quotes as in

```
#include <mytrig>
```

or

```
#include "mytrig"
```

The difference between the two forms of #include is a matter of where the preprocessor goes to look for the mytrig file. When the file is enclosed in quotes, the preprocessor assumes that the include file is locally grown, so it starts looking for the file in the same directory that it found the source file. If it doesn't find the file there, it starts looking in its own include file directories. The preprocessor assumes that include files in angle brackets are from the C++ library, so it skips looking in the source file directory and goes straight to the standard include file folders. Use quotes for any include file that you create and angle brackets for C++ library include files.

Thus, you might write a source file like the following:

```
// MyProgram - is very intelligent
#include "mytrig"

int main(int nArgc, char* pArguments[])
{
    cout << "The sin of .5 is " << sin(0.5) << endl;
    return 0;
}
```

The C++ compiler sees the following intermediary file after the preprocessor gets finished expanding the #include:

```
// MyProgram - is very intelligent
// include prototype declarations for my library
double sin(double x);
double cosin(double x);
double tan(double x);
// ...more prototype declarations...

int main(int nArgc, char* pArguments[])
{
```

```
    cout << "The sin of .5 is " << sin(0.5) << endl;
    return 0;
}
```

Playing in your own name sandbox

(This is truly technical, so feel free to skip this sidebar and come back to it later.) The authors of the C++ standard worry a lot about name collisions. For example, besides my mathematical function `log(x)` that returns the logarithm of x, suppose in another context I had written a function `log(x)` that writes status information to a system log. Clearly, two different functions with the same arguments can't coexist in one program. This is known as a *name collision*.

To avoid this, C++ allows the programmer to bundle declarations into a namespace using the keyword of the same name:

```
namespace Mathematics
{
    double log(double x)
    {
        // ...the definition of the function...
    }
}
namespace SystemLog
{
    int log(double x)
    {
        // ...log the value to file...
    }
}
```

The namespace becomes part of the extended name of the function. Thus, the following code snippet actually logs the logarithm of a value:

```
void myFunc(double x)
{
    // invoke the logarithm function...
    double dl = Mathematics::log(x);

    // ...now log it to disk
    SystemLog::log(dl);
}
```

Fortunately, you don't have to specify the namespace every single time. The keyword `using` allows the programmer to specify a default namespace for a given function:

```
using double Mathematics::log(double);
void myFunc(double x)
{
```

```
        // the default is the mathematics version...
        double dl = log(x);

        // ...however, the other version is still accessible by
        // explicitly specifying the namespace
        SystemLog::log(dl);
}
```

You can automatically default every declaration within a namespace:

```
using namespace Mathematics;
void myFunc(double x)
{
        // look in the Mathematics namespace first...
        double dl = log(x);

        // ...however, the other version is still accessible by
        // explicitly specifying the namespace
        SystemLog::log(dl);
}
```

See the program NamespaceExample on the enclosed CD-ROM for an example of the use of namespaces.

The standard library functions reside in the `std` namespace; the statement `using namespace std;` included at the beginning of each of the programs in this book gives the programs access to the standard library functions without the need to specify the namespace explicitly.

Historically, the convention was to end include files with `.h`. C still uses that standard. However, C++ dropped the extension when it revamped the include file structure. Now, C++ standard include files have no extension.

#Defining Things

The preprocessor also allows the programmer to #define expressions that get expanded during the preprocessor step. For example, you can #define a constant to be used throughout the program.

In usage, you pronounce the # sign as "pound," so you say "pound-define a constant" to distinguish from defining a constant in some other way.

```
#define TWO_PI 6.2831852
```

This makes the following statement much easier to understand:

```
double diameter = TWO_PI * radius;
```

than the equivalent expression, which is actually what the C++ compiler sees after the preprocessor has replaced TWO_PI with its definition:

```
double diameter = 6.2831852 * radius;
```

Another advantage is the ability to #define a constant in one place and use it everywhere. For example, I might include the following #define in an include file:

```
#define MAX_NAME_LENGTH 512
```

Throughout the program, I can truncate the names that I read from the keyboard to a common and consistent MAX_NAME_LENGTH. Not only is this easier to read but it also provides a single place in the program to change should I want to increase or decrease the maximum name length that I choose to process.

The preprocessor also allows the program to #define function-like macros with arguments that are expanded when the definition is used:

```
#define SQUARE(X) X * X
```

In use, such macro definitions look a lot like functions:

```
// calculate the area of a circle
double dArea = HALF_PI * SQUARE(dRadius);
```

Remember that the C++ compiler actually sees the file generated from the expansion of all macros. This can lead to some unexpected results. Consider the following code snippets (these are all taken from the program MacroConfusion, which is included on the CD-ROM):

```
int nSQ = SQUARE(2);
cout << "SQUARE(2) = " << nSQ << endl;
```

Reassuringly, this generates the expected output:

```
SQUARE(2) = 4
```

However, the following line:

```
int nSQ = SQUARE(1 + 2);
cout << "SQUARE(1 + 2) = " << nSQ << endl;
```

generates the surprising result:

```
SQUARE(1 + 2) = 5
```

The preprocesor simply replaced X in the macro definition with 1 + 2. What the C++ compiler actually sees is

```
int nSQ = 1 + 2 * 1 + 2;
```

Since multiplication has higher precedence than addition, this is turned into 1 + 2 + 2 which, of course, is 5. This confusion could be solved by liberal use of parentheses in the macro definition:

```
#define SQUARE(X) ((X) * (X))
```

This version generates the expected:

```
SQUARE(1 + 2) → ((1 + 2) * (1 + 2)) → 9
```

However, some unexpected results cannot be fixed no matter how hard you try. Consider the following snippet:

```
int i = 2;
cout << "i = " << i << endl;
int nSQ = SQUARE(i++);
cout << "SQUARE(i++) = " << nSQ << endl;
cout << "now i = " << i << endl;
```

This generates the following:

```
i = 3;
SQUARE(i++) = 9
now i = 5
```

The value generated by SQUARE is correct but the variable i has been incremented twice. The reason is obvious when you consider the expanded macro:

```
int i = 3;
nSQ = i++ * i++;
```

Since autoincrement has precedence, the two i++ operations are performed first. Both return the current value of i, which is 3. These two values are then multiplied together to return the expected value of 9. However, i is then incremented twice to generate a resulting value of 5.

Okay, how about not #defining things?

The sometimes unexpected results from the preprocessor have created heartburn for the fathers (and mothers) of C++ almost from the beginning. C++ has included features over the years to make most uses of #define unnecessary.

For example, C++ defines the inline function to replace the macro. This looks just like any other function declaration with the addition of the keyword inline tacked to the front:

```
inline int SQUARE(int x) { return x * x; }
```

This inline function definition looks very much like the previous macro definition for SQUARE() (I have written this definition on one line to highlight the similarities). However, an inline function is processed by the C++ compiler rather than by the preprocessor. This definition of SQUARE() does not suffer from any of the strange effects noted previously.

The inline keyword is supposed to suggest to the compiler that it "expand the function inline" rather than generate a call to some code somewhere to perform the operation. This was to satisfy the speed freaks, who wanted to avoid the overhead of performing a function call compared to a macro definition that generates no such call. The best that can be said is that inline functions may be expanded in place, but then again, they may not. There's no way to be sure without performing detailed timing analysis or examining the machine code output by the compiler.

Some C++ compilers allowed programmers to use a variable declared const to take the place of a #define constant so long as the value of the constant was spelled out at compile time. This was formalized in the 2009 C++ standard, which makes the following legal:

```
const int MAX_NAME_LENGTH = 512;
int szName[MAX_NAME_LENGTH];
```

The '09 standard goes so far as to introduce a new declaration type known as a const expression:

```
constexpr int square(int n1, int n2)
    { return n1 * n1 + 2 * n1 * n2 + n2 * n2;}
```

A const expression is valid if every subexpression can be calculated at compile time. This means that a const expression may contain nothing but references to constants and other const expressions.

The compiler included on the enclosed CD-ROM does not implement const expressions.

Enumerating other options

C++ provides a mechanism for defining constants of a separate, user-defined type. Suppose, for example, that I were writing a program that manipulated States of the Union. I could refer to the states by their name, such as "Texas" or "North Dakota." In practice, this is not convenient since repetitive string comparisons are computationally intensive and subject to error.

I could define a unique value for each state as follows:

```
#define DC_OR_TERRITORY 0
#define ALABAMA  1
#define ALASKA   2
#define ARKANSAS 3
// ...and so on...
```

Not only does this avoid the clumsiness of comparing strings; it allows me to use the name of the state as an index into an array of properties such as population:

```
// increment the population of ALASKA (they need it)
population[ALASKA]++;
```

A statement such as this is much easier to understand than the semantically identical `population[2]++`. This is such a common thing to do that C++ allows the programmer to define what's known as an enumeration:

```
enum STATE {DC_OR_TERRITORY,  // gets 0
            ALABAMA,          // gets 1
            ALASKA,           // gets 2
            ARKANSAS,
            // ...and so on...
```

Each element of this enumeration is assigned a value starting at 0, so DC_OR_TERRITORY is defined as 0, ALABAMA is defined as 1, and so on. You can override this incremental sequencing by using as assign statement as follows:

```
enum STATE {DC,
            TERRITORY = 0,
            ALABAMA,
            ALASKA,
            // ...and so on...
```

This version of STATE defines an element DC, which is given the value 0. It then defines a new element TERRITORY, which is also assigned the value 0. ALABAMA picks up with 1 just as before.

The '09 standard extended enumerations by allowing the programmer to create a user-defined enumerated type as follows (note the addition of the keyword `class` in the snippet):

```
enum class STATE {DC,
                  TERRITORIES = 0,
                  ALABAMA,
                  ALASKA,
                  // ...and so on...
```

This declaration creates a new type STATE and assigns it 52 members (ALABAMA through WYOMING plus DC and TERRITORIES). The programmer can now use STATE as she would any other variable type. A variable can be declared to be of type STATE:

```
STATE s = STATE::ALASKA;
```

Function calls can be differentiated by this new type:

```
int getPop(STATE s);            // return population
int setPop(STATE s, int pop);   // set the population
```

The type STATE is not just another word for `int`: arithmetic is not defined for members of type STATE. The following attempt to use STATE as an index into an array is not legal:

```
int getPop(STATE s)
{
    return population[s];   // not legal
}
```

However, the members of STATE can be converted to their integer equivalent (0 for DC and TERRITORIES, 1 for ALABAMA, 2 for ALASKA, and so on) through the application of a cast:

```
int getPop(STATE s)
{
    return population[(int)s];   // is legal
}
```

Including Things #if 1 Say So

The third major class of preprocessor statement is the `#if`, which is a preprocessor version of the C++ `if` statement:

```
#if constexpression
// included if constexpression evaluates to other than 0
#else
// included if constexpression evaluates to 0
#endif
```

This is known as *conditional compilation* because the set of statements between the #if and the #else or #endif are included in the compilation only if a condition is true. The constexpression phrase is limited to simple arithmetic and comparison operators. That's okay because anything more than an equality comparison and the occasional addition is rare.

For example, the following is a common use for #if. I can include the following definition within an include file with a name such as LogMessage:

```
#if DEBUG == 1
inline void logMessage(const char *pMessage)
        { cout << pMessage << endl; }
#else
#define logMessage(X) (0)
#endif
```

I can now sprinkle error messages throughout my program wherever I need them:

```
#define DEBUG 1
#include "LogMessage"
void testFunction(char *pArg)
{
    logMessage(pArg);
    // ...function continues...
```

With DEBUG set to 1, the logMessage() is converted into a call to an inline function that outputs the argument to the display. Once the program is working properly, I can remove the definition of DEBUG. Now the references to logMessage() invoke a macro that does nothing.

A second version of the conditional compilation is the #ifdef (which is pronounced "if def"):

```
#ifdef DEBUG
// included if DEBUG has been #defined
#else
// included if DEBUG has not been #defined
#endif
```

There is also an #ifndef (pronounced "if not def"), which is the logical reverse of #ifdef.

Intrinsically Defined Objects

C++ defines a set of intrinsic constants, which are shown in Table 10-1. These are constants that C++ thinks are just too cool to be without — and that you would have trouble defining for yourself anyway.

Table 10-1	Predefined Preprocessor Constants	
Constant	*Type*	*Meaning*
__FILE__	const char const *	The name of the source file
__LINE__	const int	The current line number
__func__	const char const *	The name of the current function (C++ '09 only)
__DATE__	const char const *	The current date
__TIME__	const char const *	The current time
__TIMESTAMP__	const char const *	The current date and time
__STDC__	int	Set to 1 if the C++ compiler is compliant with the standard
__cplusplus	int	Set to 1 if the compiler is a C++ compiler (as opposed to a C compiler). This allows include files to be shared across environments.

These internal macros are particularly useful when generating error messages. You would think that C++ generates plenty of error messages on its own and doesn't need any more help, but sometimes you want to create your own compiler errors. For you, C++ offers not one, not two, but three options: #error, assert(), and static_assert(). Each of these three mechanisms works slightly differently.

The #error command is a preprocessor directive (as you can tell by the fact that it starts with the # sign). It causes the preprocessor to stop and output a message. Suppose that your program just won't work with anything but standard C++. You could add the following to the beginning of your program:

```
#if !__cplusplus || !__STDC__
#error This is a standard C++ program.
#endif
```

Now if someone tries to compile your program with other than a C++ compiler that strictly adheres to the standards, she will get a single neat error message rather than a raft of potentially meaningless error messages from a confused C compiler.

A more meaningful test would be for a particular compiler. Each compiler defines its own preprocessor constants. If your program required the GNU C++ implementation of the C++ '09 standards, you might add the following, taken straight out of one of the GNU include files:

```
#ifndef __GXX_EXPERIMENTAL_CXX0X__
#error This file requires compiler and library support for the upcoming \
ISO C++ standard, C++0x. This support is currently experimental, and must be \
enabled with the -std=c++0x or -std=gnu++0x compiler options.
#endif
```

The backslash at the end of the line causes the preprocessor to ignore the newline character, effectively turning all three lines of error message into one long preprocessor command.

So, if __GXX_EXPERIMENTAL_CXX0X__ is not defined when the preprocessor gets to this point, the preprocessor stops and spits out the three lines telling you to go back and compile with some silly switch set.

Unlike #error, assert() performs its test when the resulting program is executed. For example, suppose that I had written a factorial program that calculates N * (N - 1) * (N - 2) and so on down to 1 for whatever N I pass it. Factorial is only defined for positive integers; passing a negative number to a factorial is always a mistake. To be careful, I should add a test for a nonpositive value at the beginning of the function:

```
int factorial(int N)
{
    assert(N > 0);
    // ...program continues...
```

The program now checks the argument to factorial() each time it is called. At the first sign of negativity, assert() halts the program with a message to the operator that the assertion failed, along with the file and line number.

Liberal use of assert() throughout your program is a good way to detect problems early during development, but constantly testing for errors that have already been found and removed during testing slows the program needlessly. To avoid this, C++ allows the programmer to "remove" the tests when creating the version of the program to be shipped to users: #define the constant NDEBUG (for "not debug mode"). This causes the preprocessor to convert all the calls to assert() in your module to "do nothing's" (universally known as NO-OPs).

The preprocessor cannot perform certain compile-time tests. For example, suppose that your program works properly only if the default integer size is 32 bits. The preprocessor is of no help since it knows nothing about integers or floating points. To address this situation, C++ '09 introduced the keyword static_assert(), which is interpreted by the compiler (rather than the preprocessor). It accepts two arguments: a const expression and a string, as in the following example:

```
static_assert(sizeof(int) == 4, "int is not 32-bits.");
```

If the const expression evaluates to 0 or false during compilation, the compiler outputs the string and stops. The static_assert() does not generate any runtime code. Remember, however, that the expression is evaluated at compile time so it cannot contain function calls or references to things that are known only when the program executes.

Typedef

The typedef keyword allows the programmer to create a shorthand name for a declaration. The careful application of typedef can make the resulting program easier to read. (Note that typedef is not actually a preprocessor command, but it's largely associated with include files and the preprocessor.)

```
typedef int* IntPtr;
typedef const IntPtr IntConstPtr;

int i;
int *const ptr1 = &i;
IntConstPtr ptr2= ptr1; // ptr1 and ptr2 are the same type
```

The first two declarations in this snippet give a new name to existing types. Thus, the second declaration declares IntConstPtr to be another name for int const*. When this new type is used in the declaration of ptr2, it has the same effect as the more complicated declaration of ptr1.

Although typedef does not introduce any new capability, it can make some complicated declarations a lot easier to read.

Part III
Introduction to Classes

The 5th Wave   By Rich Tennant

In this part . . .

The feature that differentiates C++ from other languages is C++'s support for object-oriented programming. *Object-oriented* is about the most hyped term in the computer world (okay, maybe *.com* has it beat). Computer languages, editors, and databases all claim to be object-oriented, sometimes with justification, but most of the time without.

Check out the BUDGET2 program on the enclosed CD-ROM to see an example program that can help you orient objects of object-oriented concepts.

What is it about being object-oriented that makes it so desired around the world? Read on to find out.

Chapter 11

Examining Object-Oriented Programming

*W*hat, exactly, is object-oriented programming? Object-oriented pro-gramming, or OOP as those in the know prefer to call it, relies on two principles you learned before you ever got out of Pampers: abstraction and classification. To explain, let me tell you a little story.

Abstracting Microwave Ovens

Sometimes when my son and I are watching football (which only happens when my wife can't find the switcher), I whip up a terribly unhealthy batch of nachos. I dump some chips on a plate, throw on some beans, cheese, and lots of jalapeños, and nuke the whole mess in the microwave oven for five min-utes. To use my microwave, I open the door, throw the stuff in, and punch a few buttons. After a few minutes, the nachos are done.

Now think for a minute about all the things I don't do to use my microwave:

✔ I don't rewire or change anything inside the microwave to get it to work. The microwave has an interface — the front panel with all the buttons and the little time display — that lets me do everything I need to do.

✔ I don't have to reprogram the software used to drive the little proces-sor inside my microwave, even if I cooked a different dish the last time I used the microwave.

✔ I don't look inside my microwave's case.

✔ Even if I were a microwave designer and knew all about the inner workings of a microwave, including its software, I would still use it to heat my nachos without thinking about all that stuff.

These are not profound observations. You can deal with only so much stress in your life. To reduce the number of things that you deal with, you work at a certain level of detail. In object-oriented (OO) computerese, the level of detail at which you are working is called the *level of abstraction*. To introduce another OO term while I have the chance, I *abstract away* the details of the microwave's innards.

When I'm working on nachos, I view my microwave oven as a box. (As I'm trying to knock out a snack, I can't worry about the innards of the microwave oven and still follow the Cowboys on the tube.) As long as I operate the microwave only through its interface (the keypad), there should be nothing I can do to

✔ Cause the microwave to enter an inconsistent state and crash.

✔ Turn my nachos into a blackened, flaming mass.

✔ Make the microwave (along with the surrounding house) burst into flames!

Preparing functional nachos

Suppose that I were to ask my son to write an algorithm for how Dad makes nachos. After he understood what I wanted, he would probably write "open a can of beans, grate some cheese, cut the jalapeños," and so on. When it came to the part about microwaving the concoction, he would write something like "cook in the microwave for five minutes."

That description is straightforward and complete. But it's not the way a functional programmer would code a program to make nachos. Functional programmers live in a world devoid of objects such as microwave ovens and other appliances. They tend to worry about flow charts with their myriad functional paths. In a functional solution to the nachos problem, the flow of control would pass through my finger to the front panel and then to the internals of the microwave. Pretty soon, flow would be wiggling around through complex logic paths about how long to turn on the microwave tube and whether to sound the "come and get it" tone.

In a world like this, it's difficult to think in terms of levels of abstraction. There are no objects, no abstractions behind which to hide inherent complexity.

Preparing object-oriented nachos

In an object-oriented approach to making nachos, I would first identify the types of objects in the problem: chips, beans, cheese, and an oven. Then I would begin the task of modeling these objects in software, without regard to the details of how they will be used in the final program.

While I am doing this, I'm said to be working (and thinking) at the level of the basic objects. I need to think about making a useful oven, but I don't have to think about the logical process of making nachos yet. After all, the microwave designers didn't think about the specific problem of my making a snack. Rather, they set about the problem of designing and building a useful microwave.

After the objects I need have been successfully coded and tested, I can ratchet up to the next level of abstraction. I can start thinking at the nacho-making level, rather than the microwave-making level. At this point, I can pretty much translate my son's instructions directly into C++ code.

Classifying Microwave Ovens

Critical to the concept of abstraction is that of classification. If I were to ask my son, "What's a microwave?" he would probably say, "It's an oven that . . ." If I then asked, "What's an oven?" he might reply, "It's a kitchen appliance that . . ." (If I then asked, "What's a kitchen appliance?" he would probably say, "Why are you asking so many stupid questions?")

The answers my son gave to my questions stem from his understanding of our particular microwave as an example of the type of things called micro-wave ovens. In addition, my son sees microwave ovens as just a special type of oven, which itself is just a special type of kitchen appliance.

In object-oriented computerese, the microwave in my kitchen is an *instance* of the class microwave. The class microwave is a subclass of the class oven, and the class oven is a subclass of the class kitchen appliances.

Humans classify. Everything about our world is ordered into taxonomies. We do this to reduce the number of things we have to remember. Take, for example, the first time you saw an SUV. The advertisement probably called the SUV "revolutionary, the likes of which have never been seen." But you and I know that that just isn't so. I like the looks of some SUVs (others need to go back to the factory so the designers can take another crack at it), but, hey, an SUV is a car. As such, it shares all of (or at least most of) the proper-ties of other cars. It has a steering wheel, seats, a motor, brakes, and so on. I bet I could even drive one without first reading the owner's manual.

I don't have to clutter my limited storage with all the things that an SUV has in common with other cars. All I have to remember is "an SUV is a car that . . ." and tack on those few things that are unique to an SUV (like the price tag). I can go further. Cars are a subclass of wheeled vehicles along with other members, such as trucks and pickups. Maybe wheeled vehicles are a subclass of vehicles, which includes boats and planes. And on and on and on.

Why Classify?

Why do we classify? It sounds like a lot of trouble. Besides, people have been using the functional approach for so long, why change now?

It may seem easier to design and build a microwave oven specifically for this one problem, rather than build a separate, more generic oven object. Suppose, for example, that I want to build a microwave to cook nachos and nachos only. I wouldn't need to put a front panel on it, other than a Start button. I always cook nachos the same amount of time, so I could dispense with all that Defrost and Temp Cook nonsense. My nachos-only microwave needs to hold only one flat little plate. Three cubic feet of space would be wasted on nachos.

For that matter, I can dispense with the concept of "microwave oven" alto-gether. All I really need is the guts of the oven. Then, in the recipe, I put the instructions to make it work: "Put nachos in the box. Connect the red wire to the black wire. Bring the radar tube up to about 3,000 volts. Notice a slight hum. Try not to stand too close if you intend to have children." Stuff like that.

But the functional approach has some problems:

- **Too complex:** I don't want the details of oven building mixed into the details of nacho building. If I can't define the objects and pull them out of the morass of details to deal with separately, I must deal with all the complexities of the problem at the same time.

- **Not flexible:** Someday I may need to replace the microwave oven with some other type of oven. I should be able to do so as long as its interface is the same. Without being clearly delineated and developed separately, it becomes impossible to cleanly remove an object type and replace it with another.

- **Not reusable:** Ovens are used to make lots of different dishes. I don't want to create a new oven every time I encounter a new recipe. Having solved a problem once, it would be nice to be able to reuse the solution in future programs.

The remaining chapters in this part demonstrate how object-oriented lan-guage features address these problems.

Chapter 12

Adding Class to C++

. . . .

. . . .

*P*rograms often deal with groups of data: a person's name, rank, and serial number, stuff like that. Any one of these values is not sufficient to describe a person — only in the aggregate do the values make any sense. A simple structure such as an array is great for holding stand-alone values, but it doesn't work well for data groups. This makes good ol' arrays inadequate for storing complex data (such as personal credit records that the Web companies maintain so they can lose them to hackers).

For reasons that will become clear shortly, I'll call such a grouping of data an *object*. A microwave oven is an object (see Chapter 11 if that doesn't make sense). You are an object (no offence). Your savings account information in a database is an object.

Introducing the Class

How nice it would be if we could create objects in C++ that have the relevant properties of the real-world objects we're trying to model. What we need is a structure that can hold all the different types of data necessary to describe a single object. C++ calls the structure that combines multiples pieces of data into a single object a *class*.

The Format of a Class

A class consists of the keyword `class` followed by a name and an open and closed brace. A class used to describe a savings account including account number and balance might appear as follows:

```
class SavingsAccount
{
  public:
    unsigned accountNumber;
    double balance;
};
```

The statement after the open brace is the keyword `public`. (Hold off asking about the meaning of the `public` keyword. I'll make its meaning public a little later.)

The alternative keyword `struct` can be used in place of `class`. The two keywords are identical except that the `public` declaration is assumed in the `struct` and can be omitted. You should stick with `class` for most programs for reasons that will become clear later in this chapter.

Following the `public` keyword are the entries it takes to describe the object. The `SavingsAccount` class contains two elements: an unsigned integer `accountNumber` and the account `balance`. We can also say that `accountNumber` and `balance` are members or properties of the class `SavingsAccount`.

To create an actual savings account object, I type something like the following:

```
SavingsAccount mySavingsAccount;
```

We say that `mySavingsAccount` is an *instance* of the class `SavngsAccount`.

The naming convention used here is common: Class names are normally capitalized. In a class name with multiple words such as `SavingsAccount`, each word is capitalized, and the words are jammed together without an underscore. Object names follow the same rule of jamming multiple words together, but they normally start with a small letter, as in `mySavingsAccount`. As always, these norms (I hesitate to say rules) are to help out the human reader — C++ doesn't care one way or the other.

Accessing the Members of a Class

The following syntax is used to access the property of a particular object:

```
// Create a savings account object
SavingsAccount mySave;
mySave.accountNumber = 1234;
mySave.balance = 0;

// Input a second savings account from the keyboard
cout << "Input your account number and balance" << endl;
SavingsAccount urSave;
cin >> urSave.accountNumber;
cin >> urSave.balance;
```

This code snippet declares two objects of class `SavingsAccount`, `mySave` and `urSave`. The snippet initializes `mySave` by assigning a value to the account number and a 0 to the balance (as per usual for my savings account). It then creates a second object of the same class, `urSave`. The snippet reads the account number and balance from the keyboard.

An important point to note in this snippet is that `mySave` and `urSave` are separate, independent objects. Manipulating the members of one has no effect on the members of the other (lucky for `urSave`).

In addition, the name of the member without an associated object makes no sense. I cannot say either of the following:

```
balance = 0;                    // illegal; no object
SavingsAccount.balance = 0;  // class but still no object
```

Every savings account has its own unique account number and maintains a separate balance. (There may be properties that are shared by all savings accounts — we'll get to those soon enough — but account and balance don't happen to be among them.)

Activating Our Objects

You use classes to simulate real-world objects. The `Savings` class tries to represent a savings account. This allows you to think in terms of objects rather than simply lines of code. The closer C++ objects are to modeling the real world, the easier it is to deal with them in programs. This sounds simple enough. However, the `Savings` class doesn't do a very good job of simulating a savings account.

Simulating real-world objects

Real-world objects have data-type properties such as account numbers and balances, the same as the `Savings` class. This makes `Savings` a good starting point for describing a real object. But real-world objects do things. Ovens cook. Savings accounts accumulate interest; CDs charge a substantial penalty for early withdrawal — stuff like that.

Functional programs "do things" through functions. A C++ program might call `strcmp()` to compare two character strings or `max()` to return the maximum of two values. In fact, Chapter 23 explains that even stream I/O (`cin >>` and `cout <<`) is a special form of function `call`.

The `Savings` class needs active properties of its own if it's to do a good job of representing a real concept:

```
class Savings
{
  public:
    double deposit(double amount)
    {
        balance += amount;
        return balance;
    }

    unsigned accountNumber;
    double balance;
};
```

In addition to the account number and balance, this version of `Savings` includes the function `deposit()`. This gives `Savings` the ability to control its own future. A class `MicrowaveOven` has the function `cook()`, the class `Savings` has the function `accumulateInterest()`, and the class `CD` has a function to `penalizeForEarlyWithdrawal()`.

Functions defined in a class are called *member functions*.

Why bother with member functions?

Why should you bother with member functions? What's wrong with the good ol' days of functional programming?

```
class Savings
{
  public:
    unsigned accountNumber;
```

```
    double balance;
};
double deposit(Savings& s, double amount)
{
    s.balance += amount;
    return s.balance;
}
```

Here, `deposit()` implements the "deposit into savings account" function. This functional solution relies on an outside function, `deposit()`, to implement an activity that savings accounts perform but that `Savings` lacks. This gets the job done, but it does so by breaking the object-oriented (OO) rules.

The microwave oven has internal components that it "knows" how to use to cook, defrost, and burn to a crisp. Class data members are similar to the parts of a microwave — the member functions of a class perform cook-like functions.

When I make nachos, I don't have to start hooking up the internal components of the oven in a certain way to make it work. Nor do I rely on some external device to reach into a mess of wiring for me. I want my classes to work the same way my microwave does (and, no, I don't mean "not very well"). I want my classes to know how to manipulate their internals without outside intervention.

Adding a Member Function

To demonstrate member functions, start by defining a class `Student`. One possible representation of such a class follows (taken from the program CallMemberFunction):

```
class Student
{
  public:
    // add a completed course to the record
    float addCourse(int hours, float grade)
    {
        // calculate the sum of all courses times
        // the average grade
        float weightedGPA;
        weightedGPA = semesterHours * gpa;

        // now add in the new course
        semesterHours += hours;
        weightedGPA += grade * hours;
        gpa = weightedGPA / semesterHours;
```

```
        // return the new gpa
        return gpa;
    }

    int  semesterHours;
    float gpa;
};
```

The function `addCourse(int, float)` is called a member function of the class `Student`. In principle, it's a property of the class like the data members `semesterHours` and `gpa`.

Sometimes functions that are not members of a class are class "plain ol' functions," but I'll refer to them simply as *nonmembers*.

The member functions do not have to precede the data members as in this example. The members of a class can be listed in any order — I just prefer to put the functions first.

For historical reasons, member functions are also called *methods*. This term originated in one of the original object-oriented languages. The name made sense there, but it makes no sense in C++. Nevertheless, the term has gained popularity in OO circles because it's easier to say than "member function." (The fact that it sounds more impressive probably doesn't hurt, either.) So, if your friends start spouting off at a dinner party about "methods of the class," just replace *methods* with *member functions* and reparse anything they say.

Calling a Member Function

The following `CallMemberFunction` program shows how to invoke the member function `addCourse()`:

```
//
// CallMemberFunction - define and invoke a function
//                      that's a member of the class Student
//
#include <cstdio>
#include <cstdlib>
#include <iostream>
using namespace std;

class Student
{
  public:
    // add a completed course to the record
    float addCourse(int hours, float grade)
    {
```

```
            // calculate the sum of all courses times
            // the average grade
            float weightedGPA;
            weightedGPA = semesterHours * gpa;

            // now add in the new course
            semesterHours += hours;
            weightedGPA += grade * hours;
            gpa = weightedGPA / semesterHours;

            // return the new gpa
            return gpa;
        }

    int   semesterHours;
    float gpa;
};

int main(int nNumberofArgs, char* pszArgs[])
{
    // create a Student object and initialize it
    Student s;
    s.semesterHours = 3;
    s.gpa = 3.0;

    // the values before the call
    cout << "Before: s = (" << s.semesterHours
         << ", "     << s. gpa
         << ")" << endl;

    // the following subjects the data members of the s
    // object to the member function addCourse()
    cout << "Adding 3 hours with a grade of 4.0" << endl;
    s.addCourse(3, 4.0); // call the member function

    // the values are now changed
    cout << "After: s = (" << s.semesterHours
         << ", "     << s. gpa
         << ")"      << endl;

    // wait until user is ready before terminating program
    // to allow the user to see the program results
    system("PAUSE");
    return 0;
}
```

The syntax for calling a member function looks like a cross between the syntax for accessing a data member and that used for calling a function. The right side of the dot looks like a conventional function call, but an object is on the left of the dot.

In the call s.addCourse(), we say that "addCourse() operates on the object s" or, said another way, "*s* is the student to which the course is to be added." You can't fetch the number of semester hours without knowing from which student to fetch those hours — you can't add a student to a course without knowing which student to add. Calling a member function without an object makes no more sense than referencing a data member without an object.

Accessing other members from a member function

I can see it clearly: You repeat to yourself, "Accessing a member without an object makes no sense. Accessing a member without an object. Accessing . . ." Just about the time you've accepted this, you look at the member function Student::addCourse() and *Wham!* It hits you: addCourse() accesses other class members without reference to an object. Just like the TV show: "How Do They Do That?"

Okay, which is it, can you or can't you? Believe me, you can't. When you reference a member of Student from addCourse(), that reference is against the Student object with which the call to addCourse() was made. Huh? Go back to the CallMemberFunction example. A stripped-down version appears here:

```
int main(int nNumberofArgs, char* pszArgs[])
{
    Student s;
    s.semesterHours = 10;
    s.gpa        = 3.0;
    s.addCourse(3, 4.0); // call the member function

    Student t;
    t.semesterHours = 6;
    t.gpa        = 1.0;    // not doing so good
    t.addCourse(3, 1.5);  // things aren't getting
                           // much better

    system("PAUSE");
    return 0;
}
```

When addCourse() is invoked with the object s, all of the otherwise unqualified member references in addCourse() refer to s as well. Thus, the reference to semesterHours in addCourse() refers to s.semesterHours, and gpa refers to s.gpa. But when addCourse() is invoked with the Student t object, these same references are to t.semesterHours and t.gpa instead.

Naming the current object

How does the member function know what the current object is? It's not magic — the address of the object is passed to the member function as an implicit and hidden first argument. In other words, the following conversion is taking place:

```
s.addCourse(3, 2.5)
```

is like

```
Student::addCourse(&s, 3, 2.5)
```

(Note that you can't actually use the explicit syntax; this is just the way C++ sees it.)

Inside the function, this implicit pointer to the current object has a name, in case you need to refer to it. It is called `this`, as in "Which object? *This* object." Get it? The type of `this` is always a pointer to an object of the appropriate class.

Anytime a member function refers to another member of the same class without providing an object explicitly, C++ assumes `this`. You also can refer to `this` explicitly, if you like. I could have written `Student::addCourse()` as follows:

```
float Student::addCourse(int hours, float
            grade)
{
      float weightedGPA;
      weightedGPA = this->semesterHours *
            this->gpa;

      // now add in the new course
      this->semesterHours += hours;
      weightedGPA += hours * grade;
      this->gpa = weightedGPA / this-
            >semesterHours;
      return this->gpa;
}
```

The effect is the same whether you explicitly include `this`, as in the preceding example, or leave it implicit, as you did before.

The object with which the member function was invoked is the "current" object, and all unqualified references to class members refer to this object. Put another way, unqualified references to class members made from a member function are always against the current object.

Scope Resolution (And I Don't Mean How Well Your Microscope Works)

The `::` between a member and its class name is called the *scope resolution operator* because it indicates the class to which a member belongs. The class name before the colon is like the family last name, while the function name after the colons is like the first name — the order is similar to a Chinese name, family name first.

You use the `::` operator to describe a nonmember function by using a null class name. The nonmember function `addCourse`, for example, can be referred to as `::addCourse(int, float)`, if you prefer. This is like a function without a home.

Normally the `::` operator is optional, but there are a few occasions when this is not so, as illustrated here:

```
// addCourse - combine the hours and grade into
//             a weighted grade
float addCourse(int hours, float grade)
{
    return hours * grade;
}


class Student
{
  public:
    // add a completed course to the record
    float addCourse(int hours, float grade)
    {
        // call some external function to calculate the
        // weighted grade
        float weightedGPA= ::addCourse(semesterHours,gpa);

        // now add in the new course
        semesterHours += hours;

        // use the same function to calculate the weighted
        // grade of this new course
        weightedGPA += ::addCourse(hours, grade);
        gpa = weightedGPA / semesterHours;

        // return the new gpa
        return gpa;
    }

    int  semesterHours;
    float gpa;

};
```

Here, I want the member function `Student::addCourse()` to call the nonmember function `::addCourse()`. Without the `::` operator, however, a call to `addCourse()` from `Student` refers to `Student::addCourse()`. This would result in the function calling itself.

Defining a Member Function in the Class

A member function can be defined either in the class or separately. When defined in the class definition, the function looks like the following, which is contained in the include file `Savings.h`:

```
// Savings - define a class that includes the ability
//           to make a deposit
class Savings
{
  public:
    // define a member function deposit()
    float deposit(float amount)
    {
        balance += amount;
        return balance;
    }

    unsigned int accountNumber;
    float  balance;
};
```

Inlining member functions

Member functions defined in the class default to inline (unless they have been specifically outlined by a compiler switch or because they contain a loop). Mostly, this is because a member function defined in the class is usually very small, and small functions are prime candidates for inlining.

Remember that an inline function is expanded where it is invoked. (See Chapter 10 for a comparison of inline functions and macros.) An inline function executes faster because the processor doesn't have to jump over to where the function is defined — inline functions take up more memory because they are copied into every call instead of being defined just once.

There is another good but more technical reason to inline member functions defined within a class. Remember that C++ structures are normally defined in include files, which are then included in the .CPP source files that need them. Such include files should not contain data or functions because these files are compiled multiple times. Including an inline function is okay, however, because it (like a macro) expands in place in the source file. The same applies to C++ classes. By defaulting member functions defined in classes inline, you avoid the preceding problem.

Using an include like this is pretty slick. Now a program can include the class definition (along with the definition for the member function), as follows in the venerable SavingsClass_inline program:

```
//
//   SavingsClassInline - invoke a member function that's
//                        both declared and defined within
//                        the class Student
//
#include <cstdio>
#include <cstdlib>
#include <iostream>

using namespace std;
#include "Savings.h"

int main(int nNumberofArgs, char* pszArgs[])
{
    Savings s;
    s.accountNumber = 123456;
    s.balance = 0.0;

    // now add something to the account
    cout << "Depositing 10 to account "
         << s.accountNumber << endl;
    s.deposit(10);
    cout << "Balance is " << s.balance << endl;

    // wait until user is ready before terminating program
    // to allow the user to see the program results
    system("PAUSE");
    return 0;
}
```

This is cool because everyone other than the programmer of the `Savings` class can concentrate on the act of performing a deposit rather the details of banking. These details are neatly tucked away in their own include files.

The `#include` directive inserts the contents of the file during the compilation process. The C++ compiler actually "sees" your source file with the contents of the `Savings.h` file included. See Chapter 10 for details on include files.

Keeping a Member Function After Class

For larger functions, putting the code directly in the class definition can lead to some large, unwieldy class definitions. To prevent this, C++ lets you define member functions outside the class.

A function that is defined outside the class is said to be an *outline function*. This term is meant to be the opposite of an inline function that has been defined within the class. Your basic functions such as those we have defined since Chapter 5 are also outline functions.

When written outside the class declaration, the `Savings.h` file declares the `deposit()` function without defining it as follows:

```
// Savings - define a class that includes the ability
//           to make a deposit
class Savings
{
  public:
    // declare but don't define member function
    float deposit(float amount);
    unsigned int accountNumber;
    float  balance;
};
```

The definition of the `deposit()` function must be included in one of the source files that make up the program. For simplicity, I defined it within `main.cpp`.

You would not normally combine the member function definition with the rest of your program. It is more convenient to collect the outlined member function definitions into a source file with an appropriate name (such as `Savings.cpp`). This source file is combined with other source files as part of building the executable program. I describe this in Chapter 21.

```
//
//   SavingsClassOutline - invoke a member function that's
//                         declared within a class but
//                         defined in a separate file
//
#include <cstdio>
#include <cstdlib>
#include <iostream>

using namespace std;
#include "Savings.h"

// define the member function Savings::deposit()
// (normally this is contained in a separate file that is
// then combined with a different file that is combined)
float Savings::deposit(float amount)
{
    balance += amount;
    return balance;
}
```

```
// the main program
int main(int nNumberofArgs, char* pszArgs[])
{
    Savings s;
    s.accountNumber = 123456;
    s.balance = 0.0;

    // now add something to the account
    cout << "Depositing 10 to account "
         << s.accountNumber << endl;
    s.deposit(10);
    cout << "Balance is " << s.balance << endl;

    // wait until user is ready before terminating program
    // to allow the user to see the program results
    system("PAUSE");
    return 0;
}
```

This class definition contains nothing more than a prototype declaration for the function `deposit()`. The function definition appears separately. The member function prototype declaration in the structure is analogous to any other prototype declaration and, like all prototype declarations, is required.

Notice how the function nickname `deposit()` was good enough when the function was defined within the class. When defined outside the class, however, the function requires its extended name, `Savings::deposit()`.

Overloading Member Functions

Member functions can be overloaded in the same way that conventional functions are overloaded. (See Chapter 6 if you don't remember what that means.) Remember, however, that the class name is part of the extended name. Thus, the following functions are all legal:

```
class Student
{
  public:
    // grade -- return the current grade point average
    float grade();
    // grade -- set the grade and return previous value
    float grade(float newGPA);
    // ...data members and other stuff...
};
```

```
class Slope
{
  public:
    // grade -- return the percentage grade of the slope
    float grade();
    // ...stuff goes here too...
};

// grade - return the letter equivalent of a number grade
char grade(float value);

int main(int argcs, char* pArgs[])
{
    Student s;
    s.grade(3.5);            // Student::grade(float)
    float v = s.grade();  // Student::grade()

    char c = grade(v);     // ::grade(float)

    Slope o;
    float m = o.grade();  // Slope::grade()
    return 0;
}
```

Each call made from `main()` is noted in the comments with the extended name of the function called.

When calling overloaded functions, not only the arguments of the function but also the type of the object (if any) with which the function is invoked are used to resolve the call. (The term *resolve* is object-oriented talk for "decide at compile time which overloaded function to call." A mere mortal might say "differentiate.")

Chapter 13

Point and Stare at Objects

C++ programmers are forever generating arrays of things — arrays of ints, arrays of floats — so why not arrays of students? Students stand in line all the time — a lot more than they care to. The concept of Student objects all lined up quietly awaiting their name to jump up to perform some mundane task is just too attractive to pass up.

Declaring Arrays of Objects

Arrays of objects work the same way arrays of simple variables work. (Chapter 7 goes into the care and feeding of arrays of simple — intrinsic — variables, and Chapters 8 and 9 describe simple pointers in detail.) Take, for example, the following snippet from the ArrayOfStudents program:

```
// ArrayOfStudents - define an array of Student objects
//                   and access an element in it. This
//                   program doesn't do anything
class Student
{
  public:
    int   semesterHours;
    float gpa;
    float addCourse(int hours, float grade);
};

void someFn()
```

```
{
    // declare an array of 10 students
    Student s[10];

    // assign the 5th student a gpa of 4.0 (lucky guy)
    s[4].gpa = 4.0;
    s[4].semesterHours = 32;

    // add another course to the 5th student;
    // this time he failed - serves him right
    s[4].addCourse(3, 0.0);
}
```

Here s is an array of Student objects. s[4] refers to the fifth Student object in the array. By extension, s[4].gpa refers to the GPA of the 5th student. Further, s[4].addCourse() adds a course to the 5th Student object.

Declaring Pointers to Objects

Pointers to objects work like pointers to simple types, as you can see in the example program ObjPtr:

```
// ObjPtr - define and use a pointer to a Student object
#include <cstdio>
#include <cstdlib>
#include <iostream>
using namespace std;

class Student
{
  public:
    int   semesterHours;
    float gpa;
    float addCourse(int hours, float grade);
};

int main(int argc, char* pArgs[])
{
    // create a Student object
    Student s;
    s.gpa = 3.0;

    // now create a pointer pS to a Student object
    Student* pS;

    // make pS point to our Student object
    pS = &s;
```

```
    // now output the gpa of the object, once thru
    // the variable name and a second time thru  pS
    cout << "s.gpa    = " << s.gpa    << "\n"
         << "pS->gpa = " << pS->gpa << endl;

    // wait until user is ready before terminating program
    // to allow the user to see the program results
    system("PAUSE");
    return 0;
}
```

The program declares a variable s of type Student. It then goes on to declare a pointer variable pS of type "pointer to a Student object," also written as Student*. The program initializes the value of one of the data members in s. It then proceeds to assign the address of s to the variable pS. Finally, it refers to the same Student object, first using the object's name, s, and then using the pointer to the object, pS. I explain the strange notation pS->gpa; in the next section of this chapter.

Dereferencing an object pointer

By analogy of pointers to simple variables, you might think that the following refers to the GPA of student s:

```
int main(int argc, char* pArgs[])
{
    Student s;
    Student* pS = &s; // create a pointer to s

    // access the gpa member of the obj pointed at by pS
    // (this doesn't work)
    *pS.gpa = 3.5;

    return 0;
}
```

As the comments indicate, this doesn't work. The problem is that the dot operator (.) is evaluated before the pointer (*). Parentheses are necessary to force the pointer operator to be evaluated before the dot:

```
int main(int argc, char* pArgs[])
{
    Student s;
    Student* pS = &s; // create a pointer to s
```

```
    // access the gpa member of the obj pointed at by pS
    // (this works as expected)
    (*pS).gpa = 3.5;

    return 0;
}
```

The *pS evaluates to the pointer's Student object pointed at by pS. The
.gpa refers to the gpa member of that object.

Pointing toward arrow pointers

Using the asterisk operator together with parentheses works just fine for
dereferencing pointers to objects; however, even the most hardened techies
would admit that this mixing of asterisks and parentheses is a bit tortured.

C++ offers a more convenient operator for accessing members of an object
to avoid clumsy object pointer expressions. The -> operator is defined as
follows:

```
ps->gpa is equivalent to (*pS).gpa
```

This leads to the following:

```
int main(int argc, char* pArgs[])
{
    Student s;
    Student* pS = &s; // create a pointer to s

    // access the gpa member of the obj pointed at by pS
    pS->gpa = 3.5;

    return 0;
}
```

The arrow operator is used almost exclusively because it is easier to read;
however, the two forms are completely equivalent.

Passing Objects to Functions

Passing pointers to functions is just one of the ways to entertain yourself
with pointer variables.

Calling a function with an object value

As you know, C++ passes arguments to functions by reference when the argument type is flagged with the & property (see Chapter 8). However, by default, C++ passes arguments to functions by value. (You can check Chapter 6, on this one, if you insist.)

Complex, user-defined class objects are passed the same as simple int values, as shown in the following PassObjVal program:

```
// PassObjVal - attempts to change the value of an object
//              in a function fail when the object is
//              passed by value
#include <cstdio>
#include <cstdlib>
#include <iostream>
using namespace std;

class Student
{
  public:
    int   semesterHours;
    float gpa;
};

void someFn(Student copyS)
{
    copyS.semesterHours = 10;
    copyS.gpa           = 3.0;
    cout << "The value of copyS.gpa = "
         << copyS.gpa << endl;
}

int main(int argc, char* pArgs[])
{
    Student s;
    s.gpa = 0.0;

    // display the value of s.gpa before calling someFn()
    cout << "The value of s.gpa = " << s.gpa << endl;

    // pass the address of the existing object
    cout << "Calling someFn(Student)" << endl;
    someFn(s);
    cout << "Returned from someFn(Student)" << endl;

    // the value of s.gpa remains 0
    cout << "The value of s.gpa = " << s.gpa << endl;
```

```
        // wait until user is ready before terminating program
        // to allow the user to see the program results
        system("PAUSE");
        return 0;
}
```

The function `main()` creates an object `s` and then passes `s` to the function `someFn()`.

It is not the object `s` itself that is passed, but a copy of `s`.

The object `copyS` in `someFn()` begins life as an exact copy of the variable `s` in `main()`. Since it is a copy, any change to `copyS` made within `someFn()` has no effect on `s` back in `main()`. Executing this program generates the following understandable but disappointing response:

```
The value of s.gpa = 0
Calling someFn(Student)
The value of copyS.gpa = 3
Returned from someFn(Student)
The value of s.gpa = 0
Press any key to continue . . .
```

Calling a function with an object pointer

Most of the time, the programmer wants any changes made in the function to be reflected in the calling function as well. For this, the C++ programmer must pass either the address of an object or a reference to the object rather than the object itself. The following PassObjPtr program uses the address approach:

```
// PassObjPtr - change the contents of an object in
//              a function by passing a pointer to the
#include <cstdio>
#include <cstdlib>
#include <iostream>
using namespace std;

class Student
{
  public:
    int   semesterHours;
    float gpa;
};
```

```
void someFn(Student* pS)
{
    pS->semesterHours = 10;
    pS->gpa           = 3.0;
    cout << "The value of pS->gpa = "
         << pS->gpa << endl;
}

int main(int nNumberofArgs, char* pszArgs[])
{
    Student s;
    s.gpa = 0.0;

    // display the value of s.gpa before calling someFn()
    cout << "The value of s.gpa = " << s.gpa << endl;

    // pass the address of the existing object
    cout << "Calling someFn(Student*)" << endl;
    someFn(&s);
    cout << "Returned from someFn(Student*)" << endl;

    // the value of s.gpa is now 3.0
    cout << "The value of s.gpa = " << s.gpa << endl;

    // wait until user is ready before terminating program
    // to allow the user to see the program results
    system("PAUSE");
    return 0;
}
```

The type of the argument to someFn() is a pointer to a Student object
(otherwise known as Student*). This is reflected in the way that the program calls someFn(), passing the address of s rather than the value of s.
Giving someFn() the address of s allows him to modify whatever value that
is stored there. Conceptually, this is akin to writing down the address of the
house s on the piece of paper pS and then passing that paper to someFn().
The function someFn() uses the arrow syntax for dereferencing the pS
pointer.

The output from PassObjPtr is much more satisfying (to me anyway):

```
The value of s.gpa = 0
Calling someFn(Student*)
The value of pS->gpa = 3
Returned from someFn(Student*)
The value of s.gpa = 3
Press any key to continue . . .
```

Calling a function by using the reference operator

The reference operator described in Chapter 9 works for user-defined objects. The following PassObjRef demonstrates references to user-defined objects:

```
// PassObjRef - change the contents of an object in
//               a function by using a reference
#include <cstdio>
#include <cstdlib>
#include <iostream>
using namespace std;

class Student
{
  public:
    int   semesterHours;
    float gpa;
};

// same as before, but this time using references
void someFn(Student& refS)
{
    refS.semesterHours = 10;
    refS.gpa       = 3.0;
    cout << "The value of copyS.gpa = "
         << refS.gpa << endl;
}

int main(int nNumberofArgs, char* pszArgs[])
{
    Student s;
    s.gpa = 0.0;

    // display the value of s.gpa before calling someFn()
    cout << "The value of s.gpa = " << s.gpa  << endl;

    // pass the address of the existing object
    cout << "Calling someFn(Student*)" << endl;
    someFn(s);
    cout << "Returned from someFn(Student&)" << endl;

    // the value of s.gpa is now 3.0
    cout << "The value of s.gpa = " << s.gpa << endl;

    // wait until user is ready before terminating program
    // to allow the user to see the program results
    system("PAUSE");
    return 0;
}
```

In this example, C++ passes a reference to `s` rather than a copy. Changes made in `someFn()` are retained in `main()`.

Passing by reference is just another way of passing the address of the object. C++ keeps track of the address of a reference, whereas you manipulate the address in a pointer.

Why Bother with Pointers or References?

Okay, so both pointers and references provide relative advantages, but why bother with either one? Why not just always pass the object? I mentioned one obvious answer earlier in this chapter: You can't modify the object from a function that gets nothing but a copy of the structure object.

Here's a second reason: Some objects are large — I mean *really* large. An object representing a screen image can be many megabytes in length. Passing such an object by value means copying the entire thing into the function's memory.

The object will need to be copied again should that function call another, and so on. After a while, you can end up with dozens of copies of this object. That consumes memory, and copying all the objects can make execution of your program slower than booting up Windows.

The problem of copying objects gets worse. You see in Chapter 17 that making a copy of an object can be even more painful than simply copying some memory around.

Returning to the Heap

The problems that exist for simple types of pointers plague class object pointers as well. In particular, you must make sure that the pointer you're using actually points to a valid object. For example, don't return a reference to an object defined local to the function:

```
MyClass* myFunc()
{
    // the following does not work
    MyClass  mc;
    MyClass* pMC = &mc;
    return pMC;
}
```

Upon return from `myFunc()`, the `mc` object goes out of scope. The pointer returned by `myFunc()` is not valid in the calling function.

The problem of returning memory that's about to go out of scope is discussed in Chapter 9.

Allocating the object off the heap solves the problem:

```
MyClass* myFunc()
{
    MyClass* pMC = new MyClass;
    return pMC;
}
```

Here the memory allocated off the heap is not returned when the variable pMC goes out of scope.

Programmers allocate memory from the heap when they don't want the memory to be lost when any particular variable goes out of scope. The programmer is responsible for both allocating and returning heap memory.

Allocating heaps of objects

It is also possible to allocate an array of objects off the heap using the following syntax:

```
class MyClass
{
  public:
    int nValue;
};
void fn()
{
    MyClass* pMC = new MyClass[5]

    // reference individual members like any array
    for (int i = 0; i < 5; i++)
    {
        pMC[i].nValue = i;
    }

    // uses a different delete keyword to return memory
    // to the heap
    delete[] pMC;
};
```

Notice that once allocated, pMC can be used like any other array, with pMC[i] referring to the i'th object of type MyClass. Notice also that you use the slightly different keyword delete[] to return arrays of class objects to the heap.

Comparing Pointers to References

I hate to keep referencing pointers and pointing to references, but new programmers often wonder why both are needed.

Actually, you could argue that you don't need both. C# and most other languages don't use pointers. However, pointer variables are an ingrained part of good ol' standard C++.

Linking Up with Linked Lists

The second most common structure after the array is called a *list*. Lists come in different sizes and types; however, the most common one is the *linked list*. In the linked list, each object points to the next member in a sort of chain that extends through memory. The program can simply point the last element in the list to an object to add it to the list. This means that the user doesn't have to declare the size of the linked list at the beginning of the program — you can add and remove objects from the list by merely unlinking them. In addition, you can sort the members of a linked list — without actually moving data objects around — by changing the links.

The cost of such flexibility is speed of access. You can't just reach in and grab the tenth element, for example, like you would in the case of an array. Instead, you have to start at the beginning of the list and link ten times from one object to the next.

A linked list has one other feature besides its runtime expandability (that's good) and its difficulty in accessing an object at random (that's bad): A linked list makes significant use of pointers. This makes linked lists a great tool for giving you experience in manipulating pointer variables.

The C++ standard library offers a number of different types of lists. You can see them in action in Chapter 27; however, it's always good to implement your first linked list yourself to get practice in manipulating pointers.

Not every class can be used to create a linked list. You declare a linkable class as follows:

```
class LinkableClass
{
    public:
        LinkableClass* pNext;

        // other members of the class
};
```

The key to a linkable class is the pNext pointer. At first blush, this seems odd indeed — a class contains a pointer to itself? Actually, pNext is not a pointer to itself but to another, different object of the same type.

The pNext pointer is similar to the appendage used to form a chain of children crossing the street. The list of children consists of a number of objects, all of type child. Each child holds onto another child.

Somewhere outside the linked list is a pointer to the first element of the list, the *head pointer*. The head pointer is simply a pointer of type LinkableClass*: To keep torturing the child chain analogy, the teacher points to an object of class child.

Always initialize any pointer to nullptr, the pointer that doesn't point to anything, the nonpointer.

```
LinkableClass* pHead = nullptr;
```

For C++ compilers prior to the '09 standard that don't implement nullptr, use a hardcoded 0 or an equivalent #define instead:

```
LinkableClass* pHead = 0;
```

To see how linked lists work in practice, consider the following function, which adds the argument passed it to the beginning of a list:

```
void addHead(LinkableClass* pLC)
{
    pLC->pNext = pHead;
    pHead = pLC;
}
```

Here, the pNext pointer of the object is set to point to the first member of the list. This is akin to grabbing the hand of the first kid in the chain. For one instruction, both you and the teacher have hold of this first kid in the list. The second line points the head pointer to the object, sort of like having the teacher let go of the kid you're holding onto and grabbing you. That makes you the first kid in the chain.

Performing other operations on a linked list

Adding an object to the head of a list is the simplest operation on a linked list. Moving through the elements in a list gives you a better idea about how a linked list works:

```
// navigate through a linked list
LinkableClass* pL = pHead;
while(pL)
{
    // perform some operation here

    // get the next entry
    pL = pL->pNext;
}
```

The program initializes the pL pointer to the first object of a list of LinkableClass objects through the pointer pHead. (Grab the first kid's hand.) The program then enters the while loop. If the pL pointer is non-null, it points to some LinkableClass object. Control enters the loop, where the program can then perform whatever operations it wants on the object pointed at by pL.

The assignment pL = pL->pNext "moves" the pL pointer over to the next kid in the list of objects. The program checks to see if pL is null, meaning that we've exhausted the list . . . I mean run out of kids, not exhausted all the kids in the list.

Hooking up with a LinkedListData program

The LinkedListData program shown here implements a linked list of objects containing a person's name. The program could easily contain whatever other data you might like, such as social security number, grade point average, height, weight, and bank account balance. I've limited the information to just a name to keep the program as simple as possible.

```
// LinkedListData - store data in a linked list of objects
#include <cstdio>
#include <cstdlib>
#include <iostream>
#include <string.h>

using namespace std;

// NameDataSet - stores a person's name (these objects
//               could easily store any other information
//               desired).
class NameDataSet
{
  public:
    string sName;
```

```
        // the link to the next entry in the list
        NameDataSet* pNext;
};

// the pointer to the first entry in the list
NameDataSet* pHead = 0;

// add - add a new member to the linked list
void add(NameDataSet* pNDS)
{
    // point the current entry to the beginning of
    // the list
    pNDS->pNext = pHead;

    // point the head pointer to the current entry
    pHead = pNDS;
}

// getData - read a name and social security
//           number; return null if no more to
//           read
NameDataSet* getData()
{
    // read the first name
    string name;
    cout << "\nEnter name:";
    cin  >> name;

    // if the name entered is 'exit'...
    if (name == "exit")
    {
        // ...return a null to terminate input
        return 0;
    }

    // get a new entry and fill in values
    NameDataSet* pNDS = new NameDataSet;
    pNDS->sName = name;
    pNDS->pNext = 0; // zero link

    // return the address of the object created
    return pNDS;
}

int main(int nNumberofArgs, char* pszArgs[])
{
    cout << "Read names of students\n"
         << "Enter 'exit' for first name to exit"
         << endl;

    // create (another) NameDataSet object
    NameDataSet* pNDS;
```

```
while (pNDS = getData())
{
    // add it to the list of NameDataSet objects
    add(pNDS);
}

// to display the objects, iterate through the
// list (stop when the next address is NULL)
cout << "\nEntries:" << endl;
for(NameDataSet *pIter = pHead;
                 pIter; pIter = pIter->pNext)
{
    // display name of current entry
    cout << pIter->sName << endl;
}

// wait until user is ready before terminating program
// to allow the user to see the program results
system("PAUSE");
return 0;
}
```

Although somewhat lengthy, the LinkedListData program is simple if you take it in parts. The `NameDataSet` structure has room for a person's name and a link to the next `NameDataSet` object in a linked list. I mentioned earlier that this class would have other members in a real-world application.

I have used the class `string` to contain the person's name. Although I don't describe all the methods of the `string` class until Chapter 27, it is much easier to use than zero-terminated character strings. You will see the `string` class used in preference to character strings in most applications these days. The `string` class has become about as close to an intrinsic type in the C++ language as possible.

The `main()` function starts looping, calling `getData()` on each iteration to fetch another `NameDataSet` entry from the user. The program exits the loop if `getData()` returns a null, the "nonaddress," for an address.

The `getData()` function prompts the user for a name and reads in whatever the user enters. If the string entered is equal to `exit`, the function returns a null to the caller, thereby exiting the `while` loop. If the string entered is not `exit`, the program creates a new `NameDataSet` object, populates the name, and zeroes out the `pNext` pointer.

Never leave link pointers uninitialized. Use the old programmer's wives' tale: "When in doubt, zero it out." (I mean "Old tale," not "Tale of an old wife.")

Finally, `getData()` returns the object's address to `main()`.

`main()` adds each object returned from `getData()` to the beginning of the linked list pointed at by the global variable `pHead`. Control exits the initial `while` loop when `getData()` returns a null. `main()` then enters a second section that iterates through the completed list, displaying each object.

This time I used a `for` loop that is functionally equivalent to the earlier `while` loop. The `for` loop initializes the iteration pointer `pIter` to point to the first element in the list through the assignment `pIter = pHead`. It next checks to see if `pIter` is null, which will be the case when the list is exhausted. It then enters the loop. On each round trip through the `for` loop, the third clause moves `pIter` from one object to the next with the assignment `pIter = pIter->pNext` before repeating the test and the body of the loop. This pattern is commonly followed for all list types.

The output of a sample run of the program appears as follows:

```
Read names of students
Enter 'exit' for first name to exit
Enter name:Randy
Enter name:Loli
Enter name:Bodi
Enter name:exit

Entries:
Bodi
Loli
Randy
Press any key to continue . . .
```

The program outputs the names in the opposite order in which they were entered. This is because each new object is added to the beginning of the list. Alternatively, the program could have added each object to the end of the list — doing so just takes a little more code. I included just such a version on the enclosed CD-ROM. Called LinkedListForward, it links newly added objects to the end of the list so that the list comes out in the same order it was entered. The only difference is in the `add()` function. See if you can create this forward version before you peek at my solution.

A Ray of Hope: A List of Containers Linked to the C++ Library

I believe everyone should walk before they run, should figure out how to perform arithmetic in their head before using a calculator, and should write a linked list program before using a list class written by someone else. That being said, in Chapter 27, I describe the list class provided by the C++ environment.

Chapter 14

Protecting Members: Do Not Disturb

....

....

C hapter 12 introduces the concept of the class. That chapter describes the public keyword as though it were part of the class declaration — just something you do. In this chapter, you find out about an alternative to public.

Protecting Members

The members of a class can be marked protected, which makes them inaccessible outside the class. The alternative is to make the members public. Public members are accessible to all.

Please understand the term *inaccessible* in a weak sense. Any programmer can go into the source code, remove the protected keyword, and do whatever she wants. Further, any hacker worth his salt can code into a protected section of code. The protected keyword is designed to protect a programmer from herself by preventing inadvertent access.

Why you need protected members

To understand the role of protected, think about the goals of object-oriented programming:

✔ To protect the internals of the class from outside functions. Suppose, for example, that you have a plan to build a software microwave (or whatever), provide it with a simple interface to the outside world, and then put a box around it to keep others from messing with the insides. The protected keyword is that box.

✔ To make the class responsible for maintaining its internal state. It's not fair to ask the class to be responsible if others can reach in and manipulate its internals (any more than it's fair to ask a microwave designer to be responsible for the consequences of my mucking with a microwave's internal wiring).

✔ To limit the interface of the class to the outside world. It's easier to figure out and use a class that has a limited interface (the public members). Protected members are hidden from the user and need not be learned. The interface becomes the class; this is called *abstraction* (see Chapter 11 for more on abstraction).

✔ To reduce the level of interconnection between the class and other code. By limiting interconnection, you can more easily replace one class with another or use the class in other programs.

Now, I know what you functional types out there are saying: "You don't need some fancy feature to do all that. Just make a rule that says certain members are publicly accessible and others are not."

Although that is true in theory, it doesn't work. People start out with all kinds of good intentions, but as long as the language doesn't at least discourage direct access of protected members, these good intentions get crushed under the pressure to get the product out the door.

Discovering how protected members work

Adding the keyword `public` to a class makes subsequent members public, which means that they are accessible by nonmember functions. Adding the keyword `protected` makes subsequent members of the class protected, which means they are not accessible by nonmembers of the class. You can switch between `public` and `protected` as often as you like.

Suppose you have a class named `Student`. In this example, the following capabilities are all that a fully functional, upstanding `Student` needs (notice the absence of `spendMoney()` and `drinkBeer()` — this is a highly stylized student):

`addCourse(inthours, float grade)` — adds a course

`grade()` — returns the current grade point average

`hours()` — returns the number of hours earned toward graduation

The remaining members of Student can be declared protected to keep other functions' prying expressions out of Student's business.

```
class Student
{
  public:
    // grade - return the current grade point average
    float grade()
    {
        return gpa;
    }

    // hours - return the number of semester hours
    int hours()
    {
        return semesterHours;
    }
    // addCourse - add a course to the student's record
    float addCourse(int hours, float grade);

    // the following members are off-limits to others
  protected:
    int   semesterHours; // hours earned toward graduation
    float gpa;           // grade point average
};
```

Now the members semester hours and gpa are accessible only to other members of Student. Thus, the following doesn't work:

```
Student s;
int main(int argcs, char* pArgs[])
{
  // raise my grade (don't make it too high; otherwise, no
  // one would believe it)
  s.gpa = 3.5;           // <- generates compiler error
  float gpa = s.grade(); // <- this public function reads
                         // a copy of the value, but you
                         // can't change it from here

  return 0;
}
```

The application's attempt to change the value of gpa is flagged with a compiler error.

It's considered good form not to rely on the default and specify either public or protected at the beginning of the class. Most of the time, people start with the public members because they make up the interface of the class. Protected members are saved until later.

A class member can also be protected by declaring it private. In this book, I use the protected keyword exclusively. The difference between private and protected has to do with inheritance, which is presented in Chapter 19.

Making an Argument for Using Protected Members

Now that you know a little more about how to use protected members in an actual class, I can replay the arguments for using protected members.

Protecting the internal state of the class

Making the gpa member protected precludes the application from setting the grade point average to some arbitrary value. The application can add courses, but it can't change the grade point average.

If the application has a legitimate need to set the grade point average directly, the class can provide a member function for that purpose, as follows:

```cpp
class Student
{
  public:
    // same as before
    float grade()
    {
        return gpa;
    }
    // here we allow the grade to be changed
    float grade(float newGPA)
    {
        float oldGPA = gpa;
        // only if the new value is valid
        if (newGPA > 0 && newGPA <= 4.0)
        {
            gpa = newGPA;
        }
        return oldGPA;
    }
    // ...other stuff is the same including the data
          members:
  protected:
    int   semesterHours; // hours earned toward graduation
    float gpa;
};
```

The addition of the member function grade(float) allows the application to set the gpa. Notice, however, that the class still hasn't given up control completely. The application can't set gpa to any old value; only a gpa in the legal range of values (from 0 through 4.0) is accepted.

Thus, the Student class has provided access to an internal data member without abdicating its responsibility to make sure that the internal state of the class is valid.

Using a class with a limited interface

A class provides a limited interface. To use a class, you need to know only its public members as well as what they do and their arguments. This can drastically reduce the number of things you need to master and remember to use the class.

As conditions change or as bugs are found, you want to be able to change the internal workings of a class. Changes to those details are less likely to require changes in the external application code if you can hide the internal workings of the class.

A second, perhaps more important, reason lies in the limited ability of humans (I can't speak for dogs and cats) to keep a large number of things in their minds at any given instant. Using a strictly defined class interface allows the programmer to forget the details that go on behind it. Likewise, a programmer building the class need not concentrate to quite the same degree on exactly how each of the functions is being used.

Giving Nonmember Functions Access to Protected Members

Occasionally, you want a nonmember function to have access to the protected members of a class. You do so by declaring the function to be a friend of the class by using the keyword friend.

The friend declaration appears in the class that contains the protected member. The friend declaration is like a prototype declaration in that it includes the extended name and the return type. In the following example, the function initialize() can now access anything it wants in Student:

```
class Student
{
    friend void initialize(Student*);
  public:
    // same public members as before...
  protected:
    int   semesterHours; // hours earned toward graduation
    float gpa;
};
```

```
// the following function is a friend of Student
// so it can access the protected members
void initialize(Student *pS)
{
    pS->gpa = 0;          // this is now legal...
    pS->semesterHours = 0;  // ...when it wasn't before
}
```

A single function can be declared a friend of two classes at the same time. Although this can be convenient, it tends to bind the two classes together. This binding of classes is normally considered bad because it makes one class dependent on the other. If the two classes naturally belong together, however, it's not all bad, as shown here:

```
class Student;    // forward declaration
class Teacher
{
    friend void registration(Teacher& t, Student& s);
  public:
    void assignGrades();
  protected:
    int   noStudents;
    Student *pList[100];
};
class Student
{
    friend void registration(Teacher& t, Student& s);
  public:
    // same public members as before...
  protected:
    Teacher *pT;
    int  semesterHours; // hours earned toward graduation
    float gpa;
};

void registration(Teacher& t, Student& s)
{
    // initialize the Student object
    s.semesterHours = 0;
    s.gpa = 0;

    // if there's room...
    if (t.noStudents < 100)
    {
        // ...add it onto the end of the list
        t.pList[t.noStudents] = &s;
        t.noStudents++;
    }
}
```

In this example, the `registration()` function can reach into both the `Student` and `Teacher` classes to tie them together at registration time, without being a member function of either one.

The first line in the example declares the class `Student`, but none of its members. This is called a *forward declaration* and just defines the name of the class so that other classes, such as `Teacher`, can define a pointer to it. Forward declarations are necessary when two classes refer to each other.

A member function of one class may be declared a friend of another class, as shown here:

```
class Teacher
{
    // ...other members as well...
  public:
    void assignGrades();
};
class Student
{
    friend void Teacher::assignGrades();
  public:
    // same public members as before...
  protected:
    int   semesterHours; // hours earned toward graduation
    float gpa;
};
void Teacher::assignGrades()
{
    // can access protected members of Teacher from here
}
```

Unlike in the nonmember example, the member function `assignGrades()` must be declared before the class `Student` can declare it to be a friend.

An entire class can be named a friend of another. This has the effect of making every member function of the class a friend:

```
class Student;   // forward declaration
class Teacher
{
  protected:
    int    noStudents;
    Student *pList[100];
  public:
    void assignGrades();
};
class Student
```

```
{
    friend class Teacher; // make entire class a friend
public:
    // same public members as before...
protected:
    int  semesterHours; // hours earned toward graduation
    float gpa;
};
```

Now, any member function of Teacher has access to the protected members of Student. Declaring one class a friend of the other inseparably binds the two classes together.

Chapter 15

Why Do You Build Me Up, Just to Tear Me Down Baby?

*O*bjects in programs are built and scrapped just like objects in the real world. If the class is to be responsible for its well-being, it must have some control over this process. As luck would have it (I suppose some planning was involved as well), C++ provides just the right mechanism. But first, a discussion of what it means to create an object.

Creating Objects

Some people get a little sloppy in using the terms *class* and *object*. What's the difference? What's the relationship?

I can create a class Dog that describes the relevant properties of man's best friend. At my house, we have two dogs. Thus, my class Dog has two instances, Trude (pronounced "Troo-duh") and Scooter. (Well, I *think* there are two instances — I haven't seen Scooter in a few days.)

A class describes a type of thing. An object is one of those things. An object is an instance of a class. There is only one class Dog, no matter how many dogs I have.

Objects are created and destroyed, but classes simply exist. My pets, Trude and Scooter, come and go, but the class Dog (evolution aside) is perpetual.

Different types of objects are created at different times. *Global objects* are created when the program first begins execution. *Local objects* are created when the program encounters their declaration.

A global object is one that is declared outside a function. A local object is one that is declared within a function and is, therefore, local to the function. In the following example, the variable me is global, and the variable notMe is local to the function pickOne():

```
int me = 0;
void pickOne()
{
    int notMe;
}
```

According to the rules, global objects are initialized to all zeros when the program starts executing. Objects declared local to a function have no particular initial value. Having all data members have a random state may not be a valid condition for all classes.

C++ allows the class to define a special member function that is invoked automatically when an object of that class is created. This member function, called the *constructor,* initializes the object to a valid initial state. In addition, the class can define a destructor to handle the destruction of the object. These two functions are the topics of this chapter.

Using Constructors

The constructor is a member function that is called automatically when an object is created. Its primary job is to initialize the object to a legal initial value for the class. (It's the job of the remaining member functions to ensure that the state of the object stays legal.)

The constructor carries the same name as the class to differentiate it from the other members of the class. The designers of C++ could have made up a different rule, such as: "The constructor must be called init()." It wouldn't have made any difference, as long as the compiler can recognize the constructor. In addition, the constructor has no return type, not even void, because it is called only automatically — if the constructor did return something, there would be no place to put it. A constructor cannot be invoked manually.

Constructing a single object

With a constructor, the class `Student` appears as follows:

```
//
//   Constructor - example that invokes a constructor
//
#include <cstdio>
#include <cstdlib>
#include <iostream>
using namespace std;

class Student
{
  public:
    Student()
    {
        cout << "constructing student" << endl;
        semesterHours = 0;
        gpa = 0.0;
    }
    // ...other public members...
  protected:
    int   semesterHours;
    float gpa;
};

int main(int nNumberofArgs, char* pszArgs[])
{
    cout << "Creating a new Student object" << endl;
    Student s;

    cout << "Creating a new object off the heap" << endl;
    Student* pS = new Student;

    // wait until user is ready before terminating program
    // to allow the user to see the program results
    system("PAUSE");
    return 0;
}
```

At the point of the declaration of `s`, the compiler inserts a call to the constructor `Student::Student()`. Allocating a new `Student` object from the heap has the same effect, as demonstrated by the output from the program:

```
Creating a new Student object
constructing student
Creating a new object off the heap
constructing student
Press any key to continue . . .
```

This simple constructor was written as an inline member function. Constructors can be written also as outline functions, as shown here:

```
class Student
{
  public:
    Student();
    // ...other public members...
  protected:
    int  semesterHours;
    float gpa;
};
Student::Student()
{
    cout << "constructing student" << endl;
    semesterHours = 0;
    gpa = 0.0;
}
```

Constructing multiple objects

Each element of an array must be constructed on its own. For example, the following ConstructArray program creates five Student objects by declaring a single five-element array:

```
//
//   ConstructArray - example that invokes a constructor
//                    on an array of objects
//
#include <cstdio>
#include <cstdlib>
#include <iostream>
using namespace std;

class Student
{
  public:
    Student()
    {
        cout << "constructing student" << endl;
        semesterHours = 0;
        gpa = 0.0;
    }
    // ...other public members...
  protected:
    int  semesterHours;
    float gpa;
};
```

```
int main(int nNumberofArgs, char* pszArgs[])
{
    cout << "Creating an array of 5 Student objects"
         << endl;
    Student s[5];

    // wait until user is ready before terminating program
    // to allow the user to see the program results
    system("PAUSE");
    return 0;
}
```

Executing the program generates the following output:

```
Creating an array of 5 Student objects
constructing student
constructing student
constructing student
constructing student
constructing student
Press any key to continue . . .
```

Constructing a duplex

If a class contains a data member that is an object of another class, the constructor for that class is called automatically as well. Consider the following ConstructMembers example program. I added output statements so that you can see the order in which the objects are invoked.

```
//
//  ConstructMembers - the member objects of a class
//                     are each constructed before the
//                     container class constructor gets
//                     a shot at it
//
#include <cstdio>
#include <cstdlib>
#include <iostream>
using namespace std;

class Course
{
  public:
    Course()
    {
        cout << "constructing course" << endl;
    }
};
```

```
class Student
{
  public:
    Student()
    {
        cout << "constructing student" << endl;
        semesterHours = 0;
        gpa = 0.0;
    }
  protected:
    int  semesterHours;
    float gpa;
};
class Teacher
{
  public:
    Teacher()
    {
        cout << "constructing teacher" << endl;
    }
  protected:
    Course c;
};
class TutorPair
{
  public:
    TutorPair()
    {
        cout << "constructing tutorpair" << endl;
        noMeetings = 0;
    }
  protected:
    Student student;
    Teacher teacher;
    int    noMeetings;
};

int main(int nNumberofArgs, char* pszArgs[])
{
    cout << "Creating TutorPair object" << endl;
    TutorPair tp;

    // wait until user is ready before terminating program
    // to allow the user to see the program results
    system("PAUSE");
    return 0;
}
```

Executing this program generates the following output:

```
Creating TutorPair object
constructing student
constructing course
constructing teacher
constructing tutorpair
Press any key to continue . . .
```

Creating the object `tp` in `main` automatically invokes the constructor for `TutorPair`. Before control passes into the body of the `TutorPair` constructor, however, the constructors for the two-member objects, `student` and `teacher`, are invoked.

The constructor for `Student` is called first because it is declared first. Then the constructor for `Teacher` is called.

The member `Teacher.c` of class `Course` is constructed as part of building the `Teacher` object. The `Course` constructor gets a shot first. Each object within a class must construct itself before the class constructor can be invoked. Otherwise, the main constructor would not know the state of its data members.

After all member data objects have been constructed, control returns to the open brace, and the constructor for `TutorPair` is allowed to construct the remainder of the object.

Dissecting a Destructor

Just as objects are created, so are they destroyed (ashes to ashes, dust to dust). If a class can have a constructor to set things up, it should also have a special member function to take the object apart. This member is called the *destructor.*

Why you need the destructor

A class may allocate resources in the constructor; these resources need to be deallocated before the object ceases to exist. For example, if the constructor opens a file, the file needs to be closed before leaving that class or the program. Or, if the constructor allocates memory from the heap, this memory must be freed before the object goes away. The destructor allows the class to do these cleanup tasks automatically without relying on the application to call the proper member functions.

Working with destructors

The destructor member has the same name as the class but with a tilde (~) added at the front. (C++ is being cute again — the tilde is the symbol for the logical NOT operator. Get it? A destructor is a "not constructor." Très clever.) Like a constructor, the destructor has no return type. For example, the class Student with a destructor added appears as follows:

```
class Student
{
  public:
    Student()
    {
        semesterHours = 0;
        gpa = 0.0;
    }
    ~Student()
    {
        // ...whatever assets are returned here...
    }
  protected:
    int   semesterHours;
    float gpa;
};
```

The destructor is invoked automatically when an object is destroyed, or in C++ parlance, when an object is *destructed*. That sounds sort of circular ("the destructor is invoked when an object is destructed"), so I've avoided the term until now. For non-heap memory, you can also say, "when the object goes out of scope." A local object goes out of scope when the function returns. A global or static object goes out of scope when the program terminates.

But what about heap memory? A pointer may go out of scope, but heap memory doesn't. By definition, it is memory that is not part of a given function. An object that has been allocated off the heap is destructed when it's returned to the heap using the delete command. This is demonstrated in the following DestructMembers program:

```
//
//  DestructMembers - this program both constructs and
//                    destructs a set of data members
//
#include <cstdio>
#include <cstdlib>
#include <iostream>
using namespace std;
```

```
class Course
{
  public:
    Course()  { cout << "constructing course" << endl; }
    ~Course() { cout << "destructing course" << endl;  }
};

class Student
{
  public:
    Student() { cout << "constructing student" << endl;}
    ~Student(){ cout << "destructing student" << endl; }
  protected:
    int   semesterHours;
    float gpa;
};
class Teacher
{
  public:
    Teacher()
    {
        cout << "constructing teacher" << endl;
        pC = new Course;
    }
    ~Teacher()
    {
        cout << "destructing teacher" << endl;
        delete pC;
    }
  protected:
    Course* pC;
};
class TutorPair
{
  public:
    TutorPair(){cout << "constructing tutorpair" << endl;}
    ~TutorPair(){cout << "destructing tutorpair" << endl; }
  protected:
    Student student;
    Teacher teacher;
};

TutorPair* fn()
{
    cout << "Creating TutorPair object in function fn()"
         << endl;
    TutorPair tp;

    cout << "Allocating TutorPair off the heap" << endl;
    TutorPair*  pTP = new TutorPair;
```

```
        cout << "Returning from fn()" << endl;
        return pTP;
}


int main(int nNumberofArgs, char* pszArgs[])
{
        // call function fn() and then return the
        // TutorPair object returned to the heap
        TutorPair* pTPReturned = fn();
        cout << "Return heap object to the heap" << endl;
        delete pTPReturned;

        // wait until user is ready before terminating program
        // to allow the user to see the program results
        system("PAUSE");
        return 0;
}
```

The function main() invokes a function fn() that defines the object tp —
this is to allow you to watch the variable go out of scope when control exits
the function. fn() also allocates heap memory that it returns to main()
where the memory is returned to the heap.

If you execute this program, it generates the following output:

```
Creating TutorPair object in function fn()
constructing student
constructing teacher
constructing course
constructing tutorpair
Allocating TutorPair off the heap
constructing student
constructing teacher
constructing course
constructing tutorpair
Returning from fn()
destructing tutorpair
destructing teacher
destructing course
destructing student
Return heap object to the heap
destructing tutorpair
destructing teacher
destructing course
destructing student
Press any key to continue . . .
```

Each constructor is called in turn as the TutorPair object is built up, starting from the smallest data member and working up to the TutorPair::TutorPair() constructor function.

Two TutorPair objects are created. The first, tp, is defined locally to the function fn(); the second, pTP, is allocated off the heap. tp goes out of scope and is destructed when control passes out of the function. The heap memory whose address is returned from fn() is not destructed until main() deletes it.

When an object is destructed, the sequence of destructors is invoked in the reverse order in which the constructors were called.

It is important to use the delete[] keyword when destructing arrays of class objects allocated on the heap:

```
Student* pS = new Student[5];   // construct 5 Students

// ...later in the program...
delete[] pS;              // delete heap memory and invoke
                          // destructor on each object
```

Only the delete[] keyword knows to invoke the destructor for each object allocated.

Chapter 16

Making Constructive Arguments

A class represents a type of object in the real world. For example, in earlier chapters, I use the class Student to represent the properties of a student. Just like students, classes are autonomous. Unlike a student, a class is responsible for its own care and feeding — a class must keep itself in a valid state at all times.

The default constructor presented in Chapter 15 isn't always enough. For example, a default constructor can initialize the student ID to 0 so that it doesn't contain a random value; however, a Student ID of 0 is probably not valid.

C++ programmers require a constructor that accepts some type of argument to initialize an object to other than its default value. This chapter examines constructors with arguments.

Outfitting Constructors with Arguments

C++ enables programmers to define a constructor with arguments, as shown here:

```
class Student
{
  public:
    Student(const char *pName);

    // ...class continues...
};
```

Using a constructor

Conceptually, the idea of adding an argument is simple. A constructor is a member function, and member functions can have arguments. Therefore, constructors can have arguments.

Remember, though, that you don't call the constructor like a normal function. Therefore, the only time to pass arguments to the constructor is when the object is created. For example, the following program creates an object s of the class Student by calling the Student(const char*) constructor. The object s is destructed when the function main() returns.

```
//
//   ConstructorWArg - a class may pass along arguments
//                     to the members' constructors
//
#include <cstdio>
#include <cstdlib>
#include <iostream>
using namespace std;
class Student
{
  public:
    Student(const char* pName)
    {
        cout << "constructing Student " << pName << endl;
        name = pName;
        semesterHours = 0;
        gpa = 0.0;
    }

    // ...other public members...
  protected:
    string   name;
    int      semesterHours;
    float    gpa;
};

int main(int argcs, char* pArgs[])
{
    // create a student locally and one off the heap
    Student s1("Chester");
    Student* pS2 = new Student("Trude");

    // be sure to delete the heap student
    delete pS2;

    // wait until user is ready before terminating program
    // to allow the user to see the program results
```

```
    system("PAUSE");
    return 0;
}
```

The `Student` constructor here looks like the constructors shown in Chapter 15 except for the addition of the `const char*` argument pName. The constructor initializes the data members to their empty start-up values, except for the data member `name`, which gets its initial value from `pName` because a `Student` object without a name is not a valid student.

The object `s1` is created in `main()`. The argument to be passed to the constructor appears in the declaration of `s1`, right next to the name of the object. Thus, the student `s1` is given the name `Chester` in this declaration.

A second student is allocated off the heap on the very next line. The arguments to the constructor in this case appear next to the name of the class.

The third executable line in the program returns the newly allocated object to the heap before exiting the program. This may not be necessary; for example, Windows or Unix will close any files you may have open and return all heap memory when a program terminates even if you forget to do so yourself. However, it's good practice to delete your heap memory when you're finished.

The `const` in the constructor declaration `Student::Student(const char*)` is necessary to allow statements such as the following:

```
Student s1("Chester");
```

The type of "Chester" is `const char *`. I could not pass a pointer to a constant character string to a constructor declared `Student(char*)`. A function, including a constructor, declared this way might attempt to modify the character string, which would not be good. You cannot strip away the `const` part of a declaration.

You can add `const`-ness, however, as in the following:

```
void fn(char* pName)
{
    // the following is allowed even though constructor
    // declared Student(const char*)
    Student s(pName);
    // ...do whatever...
}
```

The function `fn()` passes a `char*` string to a constructor that promises to treat the string as if it were a constant.

Placing Too Many Demands on the Carpenter: Overloading the Constructor

I can draw one more parallel between constructors and other more normal member functions in this chapter: Constructors can be overloaded.

Overloading a function means to define two functions with the same short name but with different types of arguments. See Chapter 6 for the latest news on function overloading.

C++ chooses the proper constructor based on the arguments in the declaration of the object. For example, the class `Student` can have all three constructors shown in the following snippet at the same time:

```cpp
//
//   OverloadConstructor - provide the class multiple
//                         ways to create objects by
//                         overloading the constructor
//
#include <cstdio>
#include <cstdlib>
#include <iostream>
using namespace std;

class Student
{
  public:
    Student()
    {
        cout << "constructing student No Name" << endl;
        name = "No Name";
        semesterHours = 0;
        gpa = 0.0;
    }
    Student(const char *pName)
    {
        cout << "constructing student " << pName << endl;
        name = pName;
        semesterHours = 0;
        gpa = 0;
    }
    Student(const char *pName, int xfrHours, float xfrGPA)
    {
        cout << "constructing student " << pName << endl;
        name = pName;
        semesterHours = xfrHours;
        gpa = xfrGPA;
    }
```

```
   protected:
      string  name;
      int     semesterHours;
      float   gpa;
};

int main(int argcs, char* pArgs[])
{
    // the following invokes three different constructors
    Student noName;
    Student freshman("Marian Haste");
    Student xferStudent("Pikumup Andropov", 80, 2.5);

    // wait until user is ready before terminating program
    // to allow the user to see the program results
    system("PAUSE");
    return 0;
}
```

Because the object `noName` appears with no arguments, it's constructed using the constructor `Student::Student()`. This constructor is called the default constructor. The `freshMan` is constructed using the constructor that has only a `const char*` argument, and the `xferStudent` uses the constructor with three arguments.

Notice the similarity in all three constructors. The number of semester hours and the GPA default to 0 if only the name is provided. Otherwise, there is no difference between the two constructors. You wouldn't need both constructors if you could just specify a default value for the two arguments.

C++ enables you to specify a default value for a function argument in the declaration to be used in the event that the argument is not present. By adding defaults to the last constructor, all three constructors can be combined into one. For example, the following class combines all three constructors into a single, clever constructor:

```
//
//   ConstructorWDefaults - multiple constructors can often
//                          be combined with the definition
//                          of default arguments
//
#include <cstdio>
#include <cstdlib>
#include <iostream>
using namespace std;

class Student
```

```
{
  public:
    Student(const char *pName  = "No Name",
            int xfrHours = 0,
            float xfrGPA = 0.0)
    {
        cout << "constructing student " << pName << endl;
        name = pName;
        semesterHours = xfrHours;
        gpa = xfrGPA;
    }

  protected:
    string  name;
    int     semesterHours;
    float   gpa;
};

int main(int argcs, char* pArgs[])
{
    // the following invokes three different constructors
    Student noName;
    Student freshman("Marian Haste");
    Student xferStudent("Pikumup Andropov", 80, 2.5);

    // wait until user is ready before terminating program
    // to allow the user to see the program results
    system("PAUSE");
    return 0;
}
```

Now all three objects are constructed using the same constructor; defaults are provided for nonexistent arguments in noName and freshMan.

Defaulting Default Constructors

As far as C++ is concerned, every class must have a constructor; otherwise, you can't create objects of that class. If you don't provide a constructor for your class, C++ should probably just generate an error, but it doesn't. To provide compatibility with existing C code, which knows nothing about constructors, C++ automatically provides a default constructor (sort of a default default constructor) that sets each data member to the default value for its type: 0 for int, 0.0 for float and double, and so on.

If you define a constructor for your class, C++ doesn't provide the automatic default constructor on its own. (Having tipped your hand that this isn't a C program, C++ doesn't feel obliged to do any extra work to ensure compatibility.)

The following code snippets help demonstrate this point. This is legal:

```
class Student
{

    string  name;
};

int main(int argcs, char* pArgs[])
{
    Student noName;
    return 0;
}
```

The automatically provided default constructor invokes the default `string` constructor to create an empty `name` object. The following code snippet does not compile properly:

```
class Student
{
  public:
    Student(const char *pName) {name = pName;}

    string name;
};

int main(int argcs, char* pArgs[])
{
    Student noName;    // doesn't compile
    return 0;
}
```

The seemingly innocuous addition of the `Student(const char*)` constructor precludes C++ from automatically providing a `Student()` constructor with which to build object `noName`.

The C++ '09 standard allows you to "get the default constructor back" via the new keyword `default`, as follows:

```
class Student
{
  public:
    Student(const char *pName) { name = pName; }
    Student() = default;
```

```
      string name;
};

int main(int argcs, char* pArgs[])
{
    Student noName;
    return 0;
}
```

The `default` keyword says, in effect, "I know that I defined a constructor but I still want my automatic default constructor back."

The '09 standard also allows a default method such as the default constructor to be explicitly removed using the new keyword `delete`:

```
class Student
{
  public:
     Student() = delete; // remove the default constructor

     string name;
};
```

This makes more sense when applied to automatic methods other than the default constructor, as you see later in the book.

Constructing Class Members

In the previous examples, all data members are of simple types, such as `int` and `float`. With simple types, it's sufficient to assign a value to the variable within the constructor. Problems arise when initializing certain types of data members, however.

Constructing a complex data member

Members of a class have the same problems as any other variable. It makes no sense for a `Student` object to have some default ID of 0. This is true even if the object is a member of a class. Consider the following example that creates a new class `StudentId` to manage the student identification numbers instead of relying on a plain ol' integer variable:

```
//
//   ConstructingMembers - a class may pass along arguments
//                         to the members' constructors
//
```

```
//
#include <cstdio>
#include <cstdlib>
#include <iostream>
using namespace std;

int nextStudentId = 1000; // first legal Student ID
class StudentId
{
  public:
    // default constructor assigns id's sequentially
    StudentId()
    {
        value = nextStudentId++;
        cout << "take next student id " << value << endl;
    }

    // int constructor allows user to assign id
    StudentId(int id)
    {
        value = id;
        cout << "assign student id " << value << endl;
    }
  protected:
    int value;
};

class Student
{
  public:
    Student(const char* pName)
    {
        name = pName;
    }

  // ...other public members...
  protected:
    string    name;
    StudentId id;
};

int main(int argcs, char* pArgs[])
{
    // create a couple of students
    Student s1("Chester");
    Student s2("Trude");

    // wait until user is ready before terminating program
    // to allow the user to see the program results
    system("PAUSE");
    return 0;
}
```

A student ID is assigned to each student as the `student` object is constructed. In this example, the default constructor for `StudentId` assigns IDs sequentially using the global variable `nextStudentId` to keep track.

The `Student` class invokes the default constructor for the two students `s1` and `s2`. The output from the program shows that this is working properly:

```
take next student id 1000
constructing Student Chester
take next student id 1001
constructing Student Trude
Press any key to continue . . .
```

Notice that the message from the `StudentId` constructor appears before the output from the `Student` constructor. This implies that the constructor `StudentId` was invoked even before the `Student` constructor got underway.

If the programmer does not provide a constructor, the default constructor provided by C++ automatically invokes the default constructors for data members. The same is true come harvesting time. The destructor for the class automatically invokes the destructor for data members that have destructors. The C++–provided destructor does the same.

Okay, this is all great for the default constructor. But what if you want to invoke a constructor other than the default? Where do you put the object? The `StudentId` class provides a second constructor that allows the student ID to be assigned to any arbitrary value. The question is, how do we invoke it?

Let me first show you what doesn't work. Consider the following program segment (only the relevant parts are included here — the entire program, ConstructSeparateID, is on the CD-ROM that accompanies this book):

```
class Student
{
  public:
    Student(const char *pName, int ssId)
    {
        cout << "constructing student " << pName << endl;
        name = pName;
        // don't try this at home kids. It doesn't work
        StudentId id(ssId);     // construct a student id
    }
  protected:
    string    name;
    StudentId id;
};
```

```
int main(int argcs, char* pArgs[])
{
    Student s("Chester", 1234);
    cout << "This message from main" << endl;

    // wait until user is ready before terminating program
    // to allow the user to see the program results
    system("PAUSE");
    return 0;
}
```

Within the constructor for Student, the programmer (that's me) has (cleverly) attempted to construct a StudentId object named id. (I also added a destructor to StudentId that does nothing but output the ID of the object being destroyed.)

If you look at the output from this program, you can see the problem:

```
take next student id 1000
constructing student Chester
assign student id 1234
destructing 1234
This message from main
Press any key to continue . . .
```

We seem to be constructing two StudentId objects: The first one is created with the default constructor as before. After control enters the constructor for Student, a second StudentId is created with the assigned value of 1234. Mysteriously, this 1234 object is then destroyed as soon as the program exits the Student constructor.

The explanation for this rather bizarre behavior is clear. The data member id already exists by the time the body of the constructor is entered. Instead of constructing the existing data member id, the declaration provided in the constructor creates a local object of the same name. This local object is destructed upon returning from the constructor.

Somehow, we need a different mechanism to indicate "construct the existing member; don't create a new one." This mechanism needs to appear after the function argument list but before the open brace. C++ provides a construct for this, as shown in the following subset taken from the ConstructDataMembers program (the only change between this program and its predecessor is to the Student class constructor — the entire program is on the CD-ROM):

```
class Student
{
  public:
    Student(const char *pName, int ssId)
```

```
        : name(pName), id(ssId)
   {
       cout << "constructing student " << pName << endl;
   }
 protected:
   string name;
   StudentId id;
};
```

Notice in particular the first line of the constructor. Here's something you haven't seen before. The : means that what follows are calls to the constructors of data members of the current class. To the C++ compiler, this line reads "Construct the members `name` and `id` using the arguments `pName` and `ssId`, respectively, of the `Student` constructor. Whatever data members are not called out in this fashion are constructed using their default constructor."

The `string` type is actually a conventional class defined in an include file which is included by `iostream`. Programs prior to this example have been using the default `string` constructor to create an empty `name` and then copying the student's name into the object within the body of the constructor. It is more efficient to assign the `string` object a value when it's created, if possible.

This new program generates the expected result:

```
assign student id 1234
constructing student Chester
This message from main
Press any key to continue . . .
```

Constructing a constant data member

A problem also arises when initializing a member that has been declared `const`. Remember that a `const` variable is initialized when it is declared and cannot be changed thereafter. How can the constructor assign a `const` data member a value? The problem is solved with the following member initializer syntax:

```
class Mammal
{
  public:
    Mammal(int nof) : numberOfFeet(nof) {}
  protected:
    const int numberOfFeet;
};
```

Ostensibly, a given `Mammal` has a fixed number of feet (barring amputation). The number of feet can, and should, be declared `const`. This declaration assigns a value to the variable `numberOfFeet` when the object is created. The numberOfFeet cannot be modified once it's been declared and initialized.

Reconstructing the Order of Construction

When there are multiple objects, all with constructors, programmers usually don't care about the order in which things are built. If one or more of the constructors has side effects, however, the order can make a difference.

The rules for the order of construction are as follows:

- ✔ Local and static objects are constructed in the order in which their declarations are invoked.
- ✔ Static objects are constructed only once.
- ✔ All global objects are constructed before `main()`.
- ✔ Global objects are constructed in no particular order.
- ✔ Members are constructed in the order in which they are declared in the class.
- ✔ Objects are destructed in the opposite order in which they were constructed.

A *static variable* is a variable that is local to a function but retains its value from one function invocation to the next. A *global variable* is a variable declared outside a function.

Now we'll consider each of the preceding rules in turn.

Local objects construct in order

Local objects are constructed in the order in which the program encounters their declaration. Normally, this is the same as the order in which the objects appear in the function, unless the function jumps around particular declarations. (By the way, jumping around declarations is a bad thing. It confuses the reader and the compiler.)

Static objects construct only once

Static objects are similar to local variables, except that they are constructed
only once. C++ waits until the first time control passes through the static's
declaration before constructing the object. Consider the following trivial
ConstructStatic program:

```
//
//   ConstructStatic - demonstrate that statics are only
//                     constructed once
//
#include <cstdio>
#include <cstdlib>
#include <iostream>
using namespace std;

class DoNothing
{
  public:
    DoNothing(int initial) : nValue(initial)
    {
        cout << "DoNothing constructed with a value of "
             << initial
             << endl;
    }
    ~DoNothing()
    {
        cout << "DoNothing object destructed" << endl;
    }
    int nValue;
};
void fn(int i)
{
    cout << "Function fn passed a value of " << i << endl;
    static DoNothing dn(i);
}

int main(int argcs, char* pArgs[])
{
    fn(10);
    fn(20);
    system("PAUSE");
    return 0;
}
```

Executing this program generates the following results:

```
Function fn passed a value of 10
DoNothing constructed with a value of 10
Function fn passed a value of 20
Press any key to continue . . .
DoNothing object destructed
```

Notice that the message from the function fn() appears twice, but the message from the constructor for DoNothing appears only the first time fn() is called. This indicates that the object is constructed the first time that fn() is called but not thereafter. Also notice that the destructor is not invoked until the program returns from main() as part of the program shutdown process.

All global objects construct before main ()

All global variables go into scope as soon as the program starts. Thus, all global objects are constructed before control is passed to main().

Initializing global variables can cause real debugging headaches. Some debuggers try to execute up to main() as soon as the program is loaded and before they hand over control to the user. This can be a problem because the constructor code for all global objects has already been executed by the time you can wrest control of your program. If one of these constructors has a fatal bug, you never even get a chance to find the problem. In this case, the program appears to die before it even starts!

The best way I've found to detect this type of problem is to set a breakpoint in every constructor that you even remotely suspect as well as the first statement in main(). You will hit a breakpoint for each global object declared as soon as you start the program. Press Continue after each breakpoint until the program crashes — now you know that you pressed Continue once too often. Restart the program and repeat the process, but stop on the constructor that caused the program to crash. You can now single-step through the constructor until you find the problem. If you make it all the way to the breakpoint in main(), the program did not crash while constructing global objects.

Global objects construct in no particular order

Figuring out the order of construction of local objects is easy. An order is implied by the flow of control. With globals, no such flow is available to give order. All globals go into scope simultaneously — remember? Okay, you argue, why can't the compiler just start at the top of the file and work its way down the list of global objects?

That would work fine for a single file (and I presume that's what most compilers do). Most programs in the real world consist of several files that are compiled separately and then linked. Because the compiler has no control over the order in which these files are linked, it cannot affect the order in which global objects are constructed from file to file.

Most of the time, the order of global construction is pretty ho-hum stuff. Once in a while, though, global variables generate bugs that are extremely difficult to track down. (It happens just often enough to make it worth mentioning in a book.)

Consider the following example:

```
class Student
{
  public:
    Student (int id) : studentId(id) {}
    const int studentId;
};
class Tutor
{
  public:
    Tutor(Student& s) : tutoredId(s.studentId) {}
    int tutoredId;
};

// set up a student
Student randy(1234);

// assign that student a tutor
Tutor   jenny(randy);
```

Here the constructor for `Student` assigns a student ID. The constructor for `Tutor` records the ID of the student to help. The program declares a student `randy` and then assigns that student a tutor `jenny`.

The problem is that the program makes the implicit assumption that `randy` is constructed before `jenny`. Suppose it were the other way around. Then `jenny` would be constructed with a block of memory that had not yet been turned into a `Student` object and, therefore, had garbage for a student ID.

The preceding example is not too difficult to figure out and more than a little contrived. Nevertheless, problems deriving from global objects being constructed in no particular order can appear in subtle ways. To avoid this problem, don't allow the constructor for one global object to refer to the contents of another global object.

Members construct in the order in which they are declared

Members of a class are constructed according to the order in which they're declared within the class. This isn't quite as obvious as it may sound. Consider the following example:

```
class Student
{
  public:
    Student (int id, int age) : nAge(age), nId(id){}
    const int   nId;
    const int   nAge;
        double dAverage = 0.0;
};
```

In this example, nId is constructed before nAge, even though nId appears second in the constructor's initialization list because it appears before nAge in the class definition. The data member dAverage is constructed last for the same reason. The only time you might detect a difference in the construction order is when both data members are an instance of a class that has a constructor that has some mutual side effect.

The Code::Blocks/gcc compiler generates a warning message if your declaration lists the data members in an order other than the order they are constructed.

Destructors destruct in the reverse order of the constructors

Finally, no matter in what order the constructors kick off, you can be assured that the destructors are invoked in the reverse order. (It's nice to know that at least one rule in C++ has no ifs, ands, or buts.)

Constructors as a Form of Conversion

C++ views constructors with a single argument as way of converting from one type to another. Consider a user-defined type Complex designed to represent complex numbers. Without getting too technical (for me, not for you), there is a natural conversion between real numbers and complex numbers just like the conversion from integers to real numbers, as in the following example:

```
double d = 1;    // this is legal
Complex c = d;   // this should be allowed as well
```

In fact, C++ looks for ways to try to make sense out of statements like this. If the class `Complex` has a constructor that takes as its argument a `double`, C++ will use that constructor as a form of conversion, as if the preceding statement had been written as follows:

```
double d = 1;
Complex c(d);
```

Some constructor-introduced conversions do not make sense. For example, you may not want C++ to convert an integer into a `Student` object just because a `Student(int)` constructor exists. Unexpected conversions can lead to strange runtime errors when C++ tries to make sense out of simple coding mistakes.

The programmer can use the keyword `explicit` to avoid creating unexpected and unintended conversion paths. A constructor marked `explicit` cannot be used as an implicit conversion path:

```
class Student
{
  public:
    // the following "No Name" constructor cannot be used
    // as an implicit conversion path from int to Student
    explicit Student(int nStudentID);
};

Student s = 1;          // generates compiler error
Student t(123456);      // this is still allowed
```

The declaration of `s` does not implicitly invoke the `Student(int)` constructor since it is flagged as "explicitly invokable only." The explicit invoking of the constructor to create the object `t` is still okay.

A complete TypeConversion program to demonstrate this principle is included on the CD-ROM.

Chapter 17

Copying the Copy Copy Copy Constructor

The constructor is a special function that C++ invokes automatically when an object is created to allow the object to initialize itself. Chapter 15 introduces the concept of the constructor, whereas Chapter 16 describes other types of constructors. This chapter examines a particular variation of the constructor known as the *copy constructor*.

Copying an Object

A copy constructor is the constructor that C++ uses to make copies of objects. It carries the name $X::X(X\&)$, where X is the name of the class. That is, it's the constructor of class X, which takes as its argument a reference to an object of class X. Now, I know that this sounds really useless, but just give me a chance to explain why C++ needs such a beastie.

Why you need the copy constructor

Think for a moment about what happens when you call a function like the following:

```
void fn(Student fs)
{
    // ...same scenario; different argument...
}
int main(int argcs, char* pArgs[])
{
    Student ms;
    fn(ms);
    return 0;
}
```

In the call to `fn()`, C++ passes a copy of the object `ms` and not the object itself.

Now consider what it means to create a copy of an object. First, it takes a constructor to create an object, even a copy of an existing object. C++ could create a default copy constructor that copies the existing object into the new object one byte at a time. That's what older languages such as C do. But what if the class doesn't want a simple copy of the object? What if something else is required? (Ignore the "why?" for a little while.) The class needs to be able to specify exactly how the copy should be created.

Thus, C++ uses a copy constructor in the preceding example to create a copy of the object `ms` on the stack during the call of function `fn()`. This particular copy constructor would be `Student::Student(Student&)` — say that three times quickly.

Using the copy constructor

The best way to understand how the copy constructor works is to see one in action. Consider the following CopyConstructor program:

```
//
//  CopyConstructor - demonstrate a copy constructor
//
#include <cstdio>
#include <cstdlib>
#include <iostream>
```

```cpp
using namespace std;

class Student
{
  public:
    // conventional constructor
    Student(const char *pName = "no name", int ssId = 0)
      : name(pName), id(ssId)
    {
        cout << "Constructed "  << name << endl;
    }

    // copy constructor
    Student(Student& s)
      : name("Copy of " + s.name), id(s.id)
    {
        cout << "Constructed "  << name << endl;
    }

    ~Student()
    {
        cout << "Destructing " << name << endl;
    }

  protected:
    string name;
    int  id;
};

// fn - receives its argument by value
void fn(Student copy)
{
    cout << "In function fn()" << endl;
}

int main(int nNumberofArgs, char* pszArgs[])
{
    Student chester("Chester", 1234);
    cout << "Calling fn()" << endl;
    fn(chester);
    cout << "Back in main()" << endl;

    // wait until user is ready before terminating program
    // to allow the user to see the program results
    system("PAUSE");
    return 0;
}
```

The output from executing this program appears as follows:

```
Constructed Chester
Calling fn()
Constructed Copy of Chester
In function fn()
Destructing Copy of Chester
Back in main()
Press any key to continue . . .
```

The normal `Student` constructor generates the first message from the dec-laration on the first line of `main()` about creating `chester`. `main()` then outputs the `Calling...` message before calling `fn()`. As part of the func-tion call process, C++ invokes the copy constructor to make a copy of `ches-ter` to pass to `fn()`. The copy constructor outputs a message. The function `fn()` outputs the `In function...` message. The copied `Student` object `copy` is destructed at the return from `fn()`. The original object, `chester`, is destructed at the end of `main()`.

The assignment operator is defined on the `string` class to concatenate two strings or a string and a null-terminated character string. You see how to define operators on user-defined classes in Chapter 22.

The copy constructor copies the name of the object provided it is prepended with "Copy of" into its own name field. It then copies the `id` field from `s` into the `id` field of the current object. The constructor outputs the resulting name field before returning.

The first line of output shows the `chester` object being created. The third line demonstrates the copy `Student` being generated from the copy con-structor in the call to `fn()`. The function `fn()` does nothing more than output a message. The copy is destructed as part of the return, which gener-ates the `destructing...` message.

The Automatic Copy Constructor

Like the default constructor, the copy constructor is important; important enough that C++ thinks no class should be without one. If you don't provide your own copy constructor, C++ generates one for you. (This differs from the default constructor that C++ provides unless your class has constructors defined for it.)

The copy constructor provided by C++ performs a member-by-member copy of each data member. The copy constructor that early versions of C++ provided performed a bit-wise copy. The difference is that a member-by-member copy invokes all copy constructors that might exist for the members of the class, whereas a bit-wise copy does not. You can see the effects of this difference in the following DefaultCopyConstructor sample program. (I left out the definition of the `Student` class to save space — it's identical to that shown in the CopyConstructor program. The entire DefaultCopyConstructor program is on the enclosed CD-ROM.)

```
class Tutor
{
  public:
    Tutor(Student& s)
       : student(s), id(0)
    {
        cout << "Constructing Tutor object" << endl;
    }
  protected:
    Student student;
    int id;
};

void fn(Tutor tutor)
{
    cout << "In function fn()" << endl;
}

int main(int argcs, char* pArgs[])
{
    Student chester("Chester");
    Tutor tutor(chester);
    cout << "Calling fn()" << endl;
    fn(tutor);
    cout << "Back in main()" << endl;

    // wait until user is ready before terminating program
    // to allow the user to see the program results
    system("PAUSE");
    return 0;
}
```

Executing this program generates the following output:

```
Constructed Chester
Constructed Copy of Chester
Constructing Tutor object
Calling fn()
Constructed Copy of Copy of Chester
In function fn()
Destructing Copy of Copy of Chester
Back in main()
Press any key to continue . . .
```

Constructing the `chester` object generates the first output message from the "plain Jane" constructor. The constructor for the `tutor` object invokes the `Student` copy constructor to generate its own `student` data member and then outputs its own message. This accounts for the next two lines of output.

The program then passes a copy of the `Tutor` object to the function `fn()`. Because the `Tutor` class does not define a copy constructor, the program invokes the default copy constructor to make a copy to pass to `fn()`.

The default `Tutor` copy constructor invokes the copy constructor for each data member. The copy constructor for `int` does nothing more than copy the value. You've already seen how the `Student` copy constructor works. This is what generates the `Constructed Copy of Copy of Chester` message. The destructor for the copy is invoked as part of the return from function `fn()`.

Creating Shallow Copies versus Deep Copies

Performing a member-by-member copy seems the obvious thing to do in a copy constructor. Other than adding the capability to tack on silly things such as "`Copy of` " to the front of students' names, when would you ever want to do anything but a member-by-member copy?

Consider what happens if the constructor allocates an asset, such as memory off the heap. If the copy constructor simply makes a copy of that asset without allocating its own asset, you end up with a troublesome situation: two objects thinking they have exclusive access to the same asset. This becomes nastier when the destructor is invoked for both objects and they both try to put the same asset back. To make this more concrete, consider the following example class:

```
//
//   ShallowCopy - performing a byte-by-byte (shallow) copy
//                 is not correct when the class holds
//          assets
//
#include <cstdio>
#include <cstdlib>
#include <iostream>
using namespace std;
```

```
class Person
{
  public:
    Person(const char *pN)
    {
        cout << "Constructing " << pN << endl;
        pName = new string(pN);
    }
    ~Person()
    {
        cout << "Destructing " << pName
             << " (" << *pName << ")" << endl;
        *pName = "already destructed memory";
        // delete pName;
    }
 protected:
    string *pName;
};

void fn()
{
    // create a new object
    Person p1("This_is_a_very_long_name");

    // copy the contents of p1 into p2
    Person p2(p1);
}

int main(int argcs, char* pArgs[])
{
    cout << "Calling fn()" << endl;
    fn();
    cout << "Back in main()" << endl;

    // wait until user is ready before terminating program
    // to allow the user to see the program results
    system("PAUSE");
    return 0;
}
```

This program generates the following output:

```
Calling fn()
Constructing This_is_a_very_long_name
Destructing 0x360f78 (This_is_a_very_long_name)
Destructing 0x360f78 (already destructed memory)
Back in main()
Press any key to continue . . .
```

The constructor for `Person` allocates memory off the heap to store the person's name. The destructor would normally return this memory to the heap using the `delete` keyword; however, in this case, I've replace the call to `delete` with a statement that replaces the name with a message. The main program calls the function `fn()`, which creates one person, `p1`, and then makes a copy of that person, `p2`. Both objects are destructed automatically when the program returns from the function.

Only one constructor output message appears when this program is executed. That's not too surprising because the C++ provided copy constructor used to build `p2` performs no output. The `Person` destructor is invoked twice, however, as both `p1` and `p2` go out of scope. The first destructor outputs the expected `This_is_a_very_long_name`. The second destructor indicates that the memory has already been deleted. Notice also that the address of the memory block is the same for both objects (0x360F78).

If the program really were to delete the name, the program would become unstable after the second delete and might not even complete properly without crashing.

The problem is shown graphically in Figure 17-1. The object `p1` is copied into the new object `p2`, but the assets are not. Thus, `p1` and `p2` end up pointing to the same assets (in this case, heap memory). This is known as a shallow copy because it just "skims the surface," copying the members themselves.

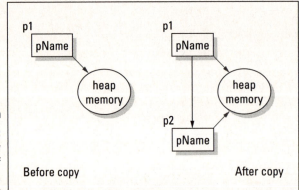

Figure 17-1:
Shallow
copy of
p1 to p2.

The solution to this problem is demonstrated visually in Figure 17-2. This figure represents a copy constructor that allocates its own assets to the new object.

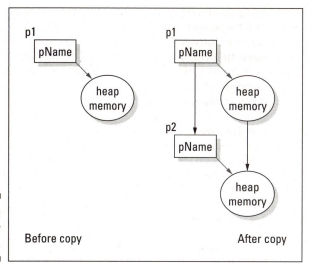

Figure 17-2:
Deep copy
of p1 to p2.

Before copy   After copy

The following shows an appropriate copy constructor for class `Person`,
the type you've seen up until now. (This class is embodied in the program
DeepCopy, which is on this book's CD-ROM.)

```cpp
class Person
{
  public:
    Person(const char *pN)
    {
        cout << "Constructing " << pN << endl;
        pName = new string(pN);
    }
    Person(Person& person)
    {
        cout << "Copying " << *(person.pName) << endl;
        pName = new string(*person.pName);
    }
    ~Person()
    {
        cout << "Destructing " << pName
             << " (" << *pName << ")" << endl;
        *pName = "already destructed memory";
        // delete pName;
    }
  protected:
    string *pName;
};
```

Here you see that the copy constructor allocates its own memory block for the name and then copies the contents of the source object name into this new name block. This is a situation similar to that shown in Figure 17-2. *Deep copy* is so-named because it reaches down and copies all the assets. (Okay, the analogy is pretty strained, but that's what they call it.)

The output from this program is as follows:

```
Calling fn()
Constructing This_is_a_very_long_name
Copying This_is_a_very_long_name
Destructing 0x270fb0 (This_is_a_very_long_name)
Destructing 0x270f60 (This_is_a_very_long_name)
Back in main()
Press any key to continue . . .
```

The destructor for Person now indicates that the string pointers in p1 and p2 don't point to the same block of memory: the addresses of the two objects are different, and the name in the version owned by the copy has not been overwritten indicating that it's been deleted.

It's a Long Way to Temporaries

Passing arguments by value to functions is the most obvious but not the only example of the use of the copy constructor. C++ creates a copy of an object under other conditions as well.

Consider a function that returns an object by value. In this case, C++ must create a copy using the copy constructor. This situation is demonstrated in the following code snippet:

```
Student fn();          // returns object by value
int main(int argcs, char* pArgs[])
{
  Student s;
  s = fn();            // call to fn() creates temporary

  // how long does the temporary returned by fn() last?
  return 0;
}
```

The function `fn()` returns an object by value. Eventually, the returned object is copied to `s`, but where does it reside until then?

C++ creates a temporary object into which it stuffs the returned object. "Okay," you say. "C++ creates the temporary, but how does it know when to destruct it?" Good question. In this example, it doesn't make much difference, because you'll be through with the temporary when the copy constructor copies it into `s`. But what if `s` is defined as a reference? It makes a big difference how long temporaries live because `refS` exists for the entire function:

```
int main(int argcs, char* pArgs[])
{
    Student& refS = fn();
    // ...now what?...
    return 0;
}
```

Temporaries created by the compiler are valid throughout the extended expression in which they were created and no further.

In the following function, I mark the point at which the temporary is no longer valid:

```
Student fn1();
int fn2(Student&);
int main(int argcs, char* pArgs[])
{
    int x;
    // create a Student object by calling fn1().
    // Pass that object to the function fn2().
    // fn2() returns an integer that is used in some
    // silly calculation.
    // All this time the temporary returned from fn1()
    // remains valid.
    x = 3 * fn2(fn1()) + 10;

    // the temporary returned from fn1() is now no longer
            valid
    // ...other stuff...
    return 0;
}
```

This makes the reference example invalid because the object may go away before `refS` does, leaving `refS` referring to a nonobject.

Avoiding temporaries, permanently

It may have occurred to you that all this copying of objects hither and yon can be a bit time-consuming. What if you don't want to make copies of everything? The most straightforward solution is to pass objects to functions and return objects from functions by reference. Doing so avoids the majority of temporaries.

But what if you're still not convinced that C++ isn't out there craftily constructing temporaries that you know nothing about? Or what if your class allocates unique assets that you don't want copied? What do you do then?

You can add an output statement to your copy constructor. The presence of this message when you execute the program warns you that a copy has just been made.

A more crafty approach is to declare the copy constructor protected, as follows:

```
class Student
{
  protected:
    Student(Student&s){}

  public:
    // ...everything else normal...
};
```

The C++ '09 standard also allows the programmer to delete the copy constructor:

```
class Student
{
    Student(Student&s) = delete;

    // ...everything else normal...
};
```

Either declaring the copy constructor protected or deleting it entirely precludes any external functions, including C++, from constructing a copy of your Student objects. If no one can invoke the copy constructor, no copies are being generated. Voilà.

Chapter 18

Static Members: Can Fabric Softener Help?

*B*y default, data members are allocated on a per-object basis. For example, each person has his or her own name. You can also declare a member to be shared by all objects of a class by declaring that member static. The term *static* applies to both data members and member functions, although the meaning is slightly different. This chapter describes both types, beginning with static data members.

Defining a Static Member

The programmer can make a data member common to all objects of the class by adding the keyword `static` to the declaration. Such members are called *static data members*. (I would be a little upset if they were called something else.)

Why you need static members

Most properties are properties of the object. Using the well-worn (one might say, threadbare) student example, properties such as name, ID number, and courses are specific to the individual student. However, all students share some properties — for example, the number of students currently enrolled, the highest grade of all students, or a pointer to the first student in a linked list.

It's easy enough to store this type of information in a common, ordinary, garden-variety global variable. For example, you could use a lowly `int` variable to keep track of the number of `Student` objects. The problem with this solution, however, is that global variables are outside the class. It's like putting the voltage regulator for my microwave outside the enclosure. Sure, I could do it, and it would probably work — the only problem is that I wouldn't be too happy if my dog got into the wires, and I had to peel him off the ceiling (the dog wouldn't be thrilled about it, either).

If a class is going to be held responsible for its own state, objects such as global variables must be brought inside the class, just as the voltage regulator must be inside the microwave lid, away from prying paws. This is the idea behind static members.

You may hear static members referred to as *class members;* this is because all objects in the class share them. By comparison, normal members are referred to as *instance members,* or *object members,* because each object receives its own copy of these members.

Using static members

A static data member is one that has been declared with the `static` storage class, as shown here:

```
class Student
{
  public:
    Student(char *pName = "no name") : name(pName)
    {
        noOfStudents++;
    }
    ~Student(){ noOfStudents--; }

    static int noOfStudents;
    string name;
};

Student s1;
Student s2;
```

The data member `noOfStudents` is part of the class `Student` but is not part of either s1 or s2. That is, for every object of class `Student`, there is a separate name, but there is only one `noOfStudents`, which all `Students` must share.

"Well then," you ask, "if the space for noOfStudents is not allocated in any of the objects of class Student, where is it allocated?" The answer is, "It isn't." You have to specifically allocate space for it, as follows:

```
int Student::noOfStudents = 0;
```

This somewhat peculiar-looking syntax allocates space for the static data member and initializes it to 0. (You don't have to initialize a static member when you declare it; C++ will invoke the default constructor if you don't.) Static data members must be global — a static variable cannot be local to a function.

The name of the class is required for any member when it appears outside its class boundaries.

This business of allocating space manually is somewhat confusing until you consider that class definitions are designed to go into files that are included by multiple source code modules. C++ has to know in which of those .cpp source files to allocate space for the static variable. This is not a problem with nonstatic variables because space is allocated in every object created.

Referencing static data members

The access rules for static members are the same as the access rules for normal members. From within the class, static members are referenced like any other class member. Public static members can be referenced from outside the class, whereas well-protected static members can't. Both types of reference are shown in the following code snippet using the declaration of Student from the previous section:

```
void fn(Student& s1, Student& s2)
{
    // reference public static
    cout << "No of students "
         << s1.noOfStudents // reference from outside
         << endl;           // of the class
}
```

In fn(), noOfStudents is referenced using the object s1. But s1 and s2 share the same member noOfStudents. How did I know to choose s1? Why didn't I use s2 instead? It doesn't make any difference. You can reference a static member using any object of that class.

In fact, you don't need an object at all. You can use the class name directly instead, if you prefer, as in the following:

```
// ...class defined the same as before...
void fn(Student& s1, Student& s2)
{
   // the following produce identical results
   cout << "Number of students "
        << Student::noOfStudents
        << endl;
}
```

If you do use an object name when accessing a static member, C++ uses only the declared class of the object.

This is a minor technicality, but in the interest of full disclosure: The object used to reference a static member is not evaluated even if it's an expression. For example, consider the following case:

```
class Student
{
   public:
      static int noOfStudents;
      Student& nextStudent();
      // ...other stuff the same...
};

void fn(Student& s)
{
      cout << s.nextStudent().noOfStudents << "\n"
}
```

The member function nextStudent() is not actually called. All C++ needs to access noOfStudents is the return type, and it can get that without bothering to evaluate the expression. This is true even if nextStudent() should do other things, such as wash windows or shine your shoes. None of those things will be done. Although the example is obscure, it does happen. That's what you get for trying to cram too much stuff into one expression.

Uses for static data members

Static data members have umpteen uses, but let me touch on a few here. First, you can use static members to keep count of the number of objects floating about. In the Student class, for example, the count is initialized to 0, the constructor increments it, and the destructor decrements it. At any given instant, the static member contains the count of the number of existing

Student objects. Remember, however, that this count reflects the number of Student objects (including any temporaries) and not necessarily the number of students.

A closely related use for a static member is as a flag to indicate whether a particular action has occurred. For example, a class Radio may need to initialize hardware before sending the first tune command but not before subsequent tunes. A flag indicating that this is the first tune is just the ticket. This includes flagging when an error has occurred.

Another common use is to provide space for the pointer to the first member of a list — the so-called head pointer (see Chapter 13 if this doesn't sound familiar). Static members can allocate bits of common data that all objects in all functions share (overuse of this common memory is a really bad idea because doing so makes tracking errors difficult).

Declaring Static Member Functions

Member functions can be declared static as well. Static member functions are useful when you want to associate an action to a class, but you don't need to associate that action with a particular object. For example, the member function Duck::fly() is associated with a particular duck, whereas the rather more drastic member function Duck::goExtinct() is not.

Like static data members, static member functions are associated with a class and not with a particular object of that class. This means that, like a reference to a static data member, a reference to a static member function does not require an object. If an object is present, only its type is used.

Thus, both calls to the static member function number() in the following example are legal. This brings us to our first static program — I mean our first program using static members — CallStaticMember:

```
//
// CallStaticMember - demonstrate two ways to call a
//                    static member function
//
#include <cstdio>
#include <cstdlib>
#include <iostream>
using namespace std;

class Student
{
  public:
```

```
        Student(const char* pN = "no name") : sName(pN)
        {
            noOfStudents++;
        }
        ~Student() { noOfStudents--; }
        const string& name() { return sName; }
        static int number() { return noOfStudents; }

  protected:
    string sName;
    static int noOfStudents;
};
int Student::noOfStudents = 0;

int main(int argcs, char* pArgs[])
{
    // create two students and ask the class "how many?"
    Student s1("Chester");
    Student* pS2 = new Student("Scooter");

    cout << "Created " << s1.name()
        << " and "    << pS2->name() << endl;
    cout << "Number of students is "
        << s1.number() << endl;

    // now get rid of a student and ask again
    cout << "Deleting " << pS2->name() << endl;
    delete pS2;
    cout << "Number of students is "
        << Student::number() << endl;

    // wait until user is ready before terminating program
    // to allow the user to see the program results
    system("PAUSE");
    return 0;
}
```

This program creates two Student objects, one locally and one off the heap. It then displays their names and the count of the number of students. Next the program deletes one of the students and asks the class how many students are out there. The output from the program appears as follows:

```
Created Chester and Scooter
Number of students is 2
Deleting Scooter
Number of students is 1
Press any key to continue . . .
```

This class keeps its data members protected and provides access functions that allow outside (non-Student) code to read but not modify them.

Declaring the return type of `name()` method to be `string&` rather than simply `string` causes the function to return a reference to the object's existing name rather than create a temporary string object. (See Chapter 17 for a brilliant treatise on constructing and avoiding temporaries.) Adding the `const` to the declaration keeps the caller from modifying the class's name member.

Notice how the static member function `number()` can access the static data member `noOfStudents`. In fact, that's the only member of the class that it can access — a static member function is not associated with any object. Were I to declare `name()` to be static, I could refer to `Student::name()`, which would immediately beg the question, "Which name?"

What Is This About Anyway?

How does a nonstatic object method know what object it's referring to? In other words, when I ask the `Student` object for its name, how does `name()` know which `sName` to return?

The address of the current object is passed as an implied first argument to every nonstatic method. When it is necessary to refer to this object, C++ gives it the name `this`. `this` is a keyword in every object method meaning "the current object. This is illustrated in the following code snippet:

```
class SC
{
  public:
    void dyn(int a); // like SC::dyn(SC *this, int a)
    static void stat(int a); // like SC::stat(int a)
};

void fn(SC& s)
{
    s.dyn(10);  // -converts to-> SC::dyn(&s, 10);
    s.stat(10); // -converts to-> SC::stat(10);
}
```

That is, the function `dyn()` is interpreted almost as though it were declared `void SC::dyn(SC *this, int a)`. The call to `dyn()` is converted by the compiler as shown, with the address of s passed as the first argument. (You can't actually write the call this way, but this is what the compiler is doing.)

References to other nonstatic members within `SC::dyn()` automatically use the `this` argument as the pointer to the current object. When `SC::stat()` was called, no object address was passed. Thus, it has no `this` pointer to use when referencing nonstatic functions, which is why I say that a static member function is not associated with any current object.

You can see `this` used explicitly in an object-oriented version of the linked list program from Chapter 9 called LinkedListClass. The entire program is included on the CD-ROM; this critical `NameDataSet` class appears here:

```
// NameDataSet - stores a person's name (these objects
//                could easily store any other information
//                desired).
class NameDataSet
{
  public:
    NameDataSet(string& refName)
      : sName(refName), pNext(nullptr) {}

    // add self to beginning of list
    void add()
    {
        pNext = pHead;
        pHead = this;
    }

    // access methods
    static NameDataSet* first() { return pHead; }
           NameDataSet* next()  { return pNext; }
           const string& name() { return sName; }
  protected:
    string sName;

    // the link to the first and next member of list
    static NameDataSet* pHead;
    NameDataSet* pNext;
};

// allocate space for the head pointer
NameDataSet* NameDataSet::pHead = nullptr;
```

Here you can see that the pHead pointer to the beginning of the list has been converted into a static data member because it applies to the entire class. In addition, pNext has been made a data member and access methods have been provided to give other programs access to the now protected members of the class.

The add() method adds the current object to the list by first setting its pNext pointer to the beginning of the list. The next statement causes the head pointer to point to the current object via the assignment pHead = this.

Part IV
Inheritance

"Now, when someone rings my doorbell, the current goes to a scanner that digitizes the audio impulses and sends the image to my PC where it's converted to a Pict file. The image is then automated, compressed, and sent via high-speed modem to an automated phone service that sends me an e-mail message back to tell me someone was at my door 40 minutes ago."

In this part . . .

In the discussions of object-oriented philosophy in Part III, I explain that two main features of real-world solutions are seemingly not shared by functional programming solutions.

The first is the capability of treating objects separately. I present the example of using a microwave oven to whip up a snack. The microwave oven provides an interface (the front panel) that I use to control the oven, without worrying about its internal workings. This is true even if I know all about how the darn thing works (which I don't).

A second aspect of real-world solutions is the capability of categorizing like objects — recognizing and exploiting their similarities. If my recipe calls for an oven of any type, I should be okay because a microwave is an oven.

In Part III I present the mechanism that C++ uses to implement the first feature, the class. To support the second aspect of object-oriented programming, C++ uses a concept known as *inheritance,* which extends classes. Inheritance is the central topic of this part and the central message of the BUDGET3 program on the enclosed CD-ROM.

Chapter 19

Inheriting a Class

. . . .

In This Chapter

▶ Defining inheritance

▶ Inheriting a base class

▶ Constructing the base class

▶ Exploring meaningful relationships: The IS_A versus the HAS_A relationship

. . . .

his chapter discusses *inheritance,* the ability of one class to inherit capabilities or properties from another class.

Inheritance is a common concept. I am a human (except when I first wake up in the morning). I inherit certain properties from the class Human, such as my ability to converse (more or less) intelligently and my dependence on air, water, and carbohydrate-based nourishment (a little too dependent on the latter, I'm afraid). These properties are not unique to humans. The class Human inherits the dependencies on air, water, and nourishment from the class Mammal, which inherited it from the class Animal.

The capability of passing down properties is a powerful one. It enables you to describe things in an economical way. For example, if my son asks, "What's a duck?" I can say, "It's a bird that goes quack." Despite what you may think, that answer conveys a considerable amount of information. He knows what a bird is, and now he knows all those same things about a duck plus the duck's additional property of "quackness." (Refer to Chapter 11 for a further discussion of this and other profound observations.)

Object-oriented (OO) languages express this inheritance relationship by allowing one class to inherit from another. Thus, OO languages can generate a model that's closer to the real world (remember that real-world stuff!) than the model generated by languages that don't support inheritance.

C++ allows one class to inherit another class as follows:

```
class Student
{
};

class GraduateStudent : public Student
{
};
```

Here, a `GraduateStudent` inherits all the members of `Student`. Thus, a `GraduateStudent` IS_A `Student`. (The capitalization of IS_A stresses the importance of this relationship.) Of course, `GraduateStudent` may also contain other members that are unique to a `GraduateStudent`.

Do 1 Need My Inheritance?

Inheritance was introduced into C++ for several reasons. Of course, the major reason is the capability of expressing the inheritance relationship. (I'll return to that in a moment.) A minor reason is to reduce the amount of typing. Suppose that you have a class `Student`, and you're asked to add a new class called `GraduateStudent`. Inheritance can drastically reduce the number of things you have to put in the class. All you really need in the class `GraduateStudent` are things that describe the differences between students and graduate students.

Another minor side effect has to do with software modification. Suppose you inherit from some existing class. Later, you find that the base class doesn't do exactly what the subclass needs. Or perhaps the class has a bug. Modifying the base class might break any code that uses that base class. Creating and using a new subclass that overloads the incorrect feature solves your problem without causing someone else further problems.

This IS_A-mazing

To make sense of our surroundings, humans build extensive taxonomies. Fido is a special case of dog, which is a special case of canine, which is a special case of mammal, and so it goes. This shapes our understanding of the world.

To use another example, a student is a (special type of) person. Having said this, I already know a lot of things about students (American students, anyway). I know they have social security numbers, they watch too much TV, and they daydream about the opposite sex (the male ones, anyway). I know all these things because these are properties of all people.

In C++, we say that the class `Student` inherits from the class `Person`. Also, we say that `Person` is a *base class* of `Student`, and `Student` is a *subclass* of `Person`. Finally, we say that a `Student` IS_A `Person` (using all caps is a common way of expressing this unique relationship — I didn't make it up).

C++ shares this terminology with other object-oriented languages.

Notice that although `Student` IS_A `Person`, the reverse is not true. A `Person` IS not a `Student`. (A statement like this always refers to the general case. It could be that a particular `Person` is, in fact, a `Student`.) A lot of people who are members of class `Person` are not members of class `Student`. In addition, class `Student` has properties it does not share with class `Person`. For example, `Student` has a grade point average, but `Person` does not.

The inheritance property is transitive. For example, if I define a new class `GraduateStudent` as a subclass of `Student`, `GraduateStudent` must also be `Person`. It has to be that way: If a `GraduateStudent` IS_A `Student` and a `Student` IS_A `Person`, a `GraduateStudent` IS_A `Person`.

How Does a Class Inherit?

Here's the `GraduateStudent` example filled out into a program InheritanceExample:

```
//
// InheritanceExample - demonstrate an inheritance
//            relationship in which the subclass
//            constructor passes argument information
//            to the constructor in the base class
//
#include <cstdio>
#include <cstdlib>
#include <iostream>
```

```cpp
using namespace std;
class Advisor {}; // define an empty class

class Student
{
  public:
    Student(const char *pName = "no name")
        : name(pName), average(0.0), semesterHours(0)
    {
        cout << "Constructing student " << name << endl;
    }

    void addCourse(int hours, float grade)
    {
        cout << "Adding grade to " << name << endl;
        average = semesterHours * average + grade;
        semesterHours += hours;
        average = average / semesterHours;
    }

    int hours( ) { return semesterHours;}
    float gpa( ) { return average;}

  protected:
    string name;
    double average;
    int    semesterHours;
};

class GraduateStudent : public Student
{
  public:
    GraduateStudent(const char *pName, Advisor adv,
                    double qG = 0.0)
        : Student(pName), advisor(adv), qualifierGrade(qG)
    {
        cout << "Constructing graduate student "
             << pName << endl;
    }

    double qualifier( ) { return qualifierGrade; }

  protected:
    Advisor advisor;
    double qualifierGrade;
};

int main(int nNumberofArgs, char* pszArgs[])
{
    // create a dummy advisor to give to GraduateStudent
    Advisor adv;

    // create two Student types
    Student llu("Cy N Sense");
```

```
      GraduateStudent gs("Matt Madox", adv, 1.5);

      // now add a grade to their grade point average
      llu.addCourse(3, 2.5);
      gs.addCourse(3, 3.0);

      // display the graduate student's qualifier grade
      cout << "Matt's qualifier grade = "
           << gs.qualifier() << endl;

      // wait until user is ready before terminating program
      // to allow the user to see the program results
      system("PAUSE");
      return 0;
}
```

This program demonstrates the creation and use of two objects, one of class
Student and a second of GraduateStudent. The output of this program is
as follows:

```
Constructing student Cy N Sense
Constructing student Matt Madox
Constructing graduate student Matt Madox
Adding grade to Cy N Sense
Adding grade to Matt Madox
Matt's qualifier grade = 1.5
Press any key to continue . . .
```

Using a subclass

The class Student has been defined in the conventional fashion. The class
GraduateStudent is a bit different, however. The colon followed by the
phrase public Student at the beginning of the class definition declares
GraduateStudent to be a subclass of Student.

The appearance of the keyword public implies that there is probably protected inheritance as well. All right, it's true, but *protected* inheritance is
beyond the scope of this book.

Programmers love inventing new terms or giving new meaning to existing
terms. Heck, programmers even invent new terms and then give them a
second meaning. Here is a set of equivalent expressions that describes the
same relationship:

✔ GraduateStudent is a subclass of Student.

✔ Student is the base class or is the parent class of GraduateStudent.

✔ GraduateStudent inherits or is derived from Student.

✔ GraduateStudent extends Student.

As a subclass of Student, GraduateStudent inherits all its members. For example, a GraduateStudent has a name even though that member is declared up in the base class. However, a subclass can add its own members, for example qualifierGrade. After all, gs quite literally IS_A Student plus a little bit more.

The main() function declares two objects, llu of type Student and gs of type GraduateStudent. It then proceeds to access the addCourse() member function for both types of students. main() then accesses the qualifier() function that is only a member of the subclass.

Constructing a subclass

Even though a subclass has access to the protected members of the base class and could initialize them, each subclass is responsible for initializing itself.

Before control passes beyond the open brace of the constructor for GraduateStudent, control passes to the proper constructor of Student. If Student were based on another class, such as Person, the constructor for that class would be invoked before the Student constructor got control. Like a skyscraper, the object is constructed starting at the "base"-ment class and working its way up the class structure one story at a time.

Just as with member objects, you often need to be able to pass arguments to the base class constructor. The example program declares the subclass constructor as follows:

```
GraduateStudent(const char *pName, Advisor adv,
                double qG = 0.0)
   : Student(pName), advisor(adv), qualifierGrade(qG)
{
    // whatever else the constructor does
}
```

Here the constructor for GraduateStudent invokes the Student constructor, passing it the argument pName. C++ then initializes the members advisor and qualifierGrade before executing the statements within the constructor's open and close braces.

The default constructor for the base class is executed if the subclass makes no explicit reference to a different constructor. Thus, in the following code snippet, the Pig base class is constructed before any members of LittlePig, even though LittlePig makes no explicit reference to that constructor:

```
class Pig
{
  public:
    Pig() : pHouse(nullptr) {}
  protected:
    House* pHouse;
};
class LittlePig : public Pig
{
  public:
    LittlePig(double volStraw, int numSticks,
              int numBricks)
      : straw(volStraw), sticks(numSticks),
        bricks(numBricks)
    { }

  protected:
    double straw;
    int sticks;
    int bricks;
};
```

Similarly, the copy constructor for a base class is invoked automatically.

Destructing a subclass

Following the rule that destructors are invoked in the reverse order of the constructors, the destructor for GraduateStudent is given control first. After it's given its last full measure of devotion, control passes to the destructor for Advisor and then to the destructor for Student. If Student were based on a class Person, the destructor for Person would get control after Student.

This is logical. The blob of memory is first converted to a Student object. Only then is it the job of the GraduateStudent constructor to transform this simple Student into a GraduateStudent. The destructor simply reverses the process.

Having a HAS_A Relationship

Notice that the class GraduateStudent includes the members of class Student and Advisor, but in a different way. By defining a data member of class Advisor, you know that a Student has all the data members of an `Advisor` within it. However, you can't say that a `GraduateStudent` is an `Advisor` — instead you say that a `GraduateStudent` HAS_A `Advisor`. What's the difference between this and inheritance?

Use a car as an example. You could logically define a car as being a subclass of vehicle, so it inherits the properties of other vehicles. At the same time, a car has a motor. If you buy a car, you can logically assume that you are buying a motor as well. (Unless you go to the used-car lot where I got my last junk heap.)

If friends ask you to show up at a rally on Saturday with your vehicle of choice and you go in your car, they can't complain (even if someone else shows up on a bicycle) because a car IS_A vehicle. But, if you appear on foot carrying a motor, your friends will have reason to laugh at you because a motor is not a vehicle. A motor is missing certain critical properties that vehicles share — such as radios without AUX plugs for your MP-3 player.

From a programming standpoint, the HAS_A relationship is just as straight-forward. Consider the following:

```
class Vehicle {};
class Motor {};
class Car : public Vehicle
{
  public:
    Motor motor;
};

void VehicleFn(Vehicle& v);
void MotorFn(Motor& m);

int main(int nNumberofArgs, char* pszArgs[])
{
    Car car;
    VehicleFn(car);    // this is allowed
    MotorFn(car);      // this is not allowed
    MotorFn(car.motor);// this is
    return 0;
}
```

The call `VehicleFn(c)` is allowed because `car` IS_A vehicle. The call `MotorFn(car)` is not because `car` is not a `Motor`, even though it contains a `Motor`. If the intention were to pass the `Motor` portion of c to the function, this must be expressed explicitly, as in the call `MotorFn(car.motor)`.

Chapter 20

Examining Virtual Member Functions: Are They for Real?

*T*he number and type of a function's arguments are included in its full, or *extended,* name. This enables you to give two functions the same name as long as the extended name is different:

```
void someFn(int);
void someFn(char*);
void someFn(char*, double);
```

In all three cases, the short name for these functions is someFn() (hey! this is some fun). The extended names for all three differ: someFn(int) versus someFn(char*), and so on. C++ is left to figure out which function is meant by the arguments during the call.

Member functions can be overloaded. The number of arguments, the type of arguments, and the class name are all part of the extended name.

Inheritance introduces a whole new wrinkle, however. What if a function in a base class has the same name as a function in the subclass? Consider, for example, the following simple code snippet:

```
class Student
{
  public:
    double calcTuition();
};
```

```
class GraduateStudent : public Student
{
  public:
    double calcTuition();
};

int main(int argcs, char* pArgs[])
{
    Student s;
    GraduateStudent gs;
    s.calcTuition(); //calls Student::calcTuition()
    gs.calcTuition();//calls GraduateStudent::calcTuition()
    return 0;
}
```

As with any overloading situation, when the programmer refers to calc
Tuition(), C++ has to decide which calcTuition() is intended.
Obviously, if the two functions differed in the type of arguments, there's
no problem. Even if the arguments were the same, the class name should
be sufficient to resolve the call, and this example is no different. The call
s.calcTuition() refers to Student::calcTuition() because s is
declared locally as a Student, whereas gs.calcTuition() refers to
GraduateStudent::calcTuition().

But what if the exact class of the object can't be determined at compile time?
To demonstrate how this can occur, change the preceding program in a
seemingly trivial way:

```
//
//   OverloadOverride - demonstrate when a function is
//                      declare-time overloaded vs. runtime
//                      overridden
//
#include <cstdio>
#include <cstdlib>
#include <iostream>
using namespace std;

class Student
{
  public:
    void calcTuition()
    {
        cout << "We're in Student::calcTuition" << endl;
    }
};
```

```
class GraduateStudent : public Student
{
  public:
    void calcTuition()
    {
        cout << "We're in GraduateStudent::calcTuition"
             << endl;
    }
};

void fn(Student& x)
{
    x.calcTuition(); // to which calcTuition() does
                     // this refer?
}

int main(int nNumberofArgs, char* pszArgs[])
{
    // pass a base class object to function
    // (to match the declaration)
    Student s;
    fn(s);

    // pass a specialization of the base class instead
    GraduateStudent gs;
    fn(gs);

    // wait until user is ready before terminating program
    // to allow the user to see the program results
    system("PAUSE");
    return 0;
}
```

This program generates the following output:

```
We're in Student::calcTuition
We're in Student::calcTuition
Press any key to continue . . .
```

Instead of calling `calcTuition()` directly, the call is now made through an intermediate function, `fn()`. Depending on how `fn()` is called, x can be a `Student` or a `GraduateStudent`. A `GraduateStudent` IS_A `Student`.

Refer to Chapter 19 if you don't remember why a `GraduateStudent` IS_A `Student`.

The argument x passed to `fn()` is declared to be a reference to `Student`.

Passing an object by reference can be a lot more efficient than passing it by value. See Chapter 17 for a treatise on making copies of objects.

You might want `x.calcTuition()` to call `Student::calcTuition()` when `x` is a `Student` but to call `GraduateStudent::calcTuition()` when `x` is a `GraduateStudent`. It would be really cool if C++ were that smart.

The type that you've been accustomed to until now is called the *static,* or *compile-time,* type. The declared type of `x` is `Student` in both cases because that's what the declaration in `fn()` says. The other kind is the *dynamic,* or *runtime,* type. In the case of the example function `fn()`, the runtime type of `x` is `Student` when `fn()` is called with `s` and `GraduateStudent` when `fn()` is called with `gs`. Aren't we having fun?

The capability of deciding at runtime which of several overloaded member functions to call based on the runtime type is called *polymorphism,* or late binding. Deciding which overloaded to call at compile time is called *early binding* because that sounds like the opposite of late binding.

Overloading a base class function polymorphically is called *overriding the base class function.* This new name is used to differentiate this more complicated case from the normal overload case.

Why You Need Polymorphism

Polymorphism is key to the power of object-oriented programming. It's so important that languages that don't support polymorphism can't advertise themselves as OO languages. (I think it's a government regulation — you can't label a language that doesn't support OO unless you add a disclaimer from the Surgeon General, or something like that.)

Without polymorphism, inheritance has little meaning. Remember how I made nachos in the oven? In this sense, I was acting as the late binder. The recipe read: Heat the nachos in the oven. It didn't read: If the type of oven is microwave, do this; if the type of oven is conventional, do that; if the type of oven is convection, do this other thing. The recipe (the code) relied on me (the late binder) to decide what the action (member function) heat means when applied to the oven (the particular instance of class `Oven`) or any of its variations (subclasses), such as a microwave oven (`Microwave`). This is the way people think, and designing a language along the lines of the way people think allows the programming model to more accurately describe the real world.

How Polymorphism Works

Any given language can support either early or late binding based upon the whims of its developers. Older languages like C tend to support early binding alone. Recent languages like Java and C# support only late binding. As a fence straddler, C++ supports both early and late binding.

You may be surprised that the default for C++ is early binding. The reason is simple, if a little dated. First, C++ has to act as much like C as possible by default to retain upward compatibility with its predecessor. Second, poly-morphism adds a small amount of overhead to every function call both in terms of data storage and code needed to perform the call. The founders of C++ were concerned that any additional overhead would be used as a reason not to adopt C++ as the system's language of choice, so they made the more efficient early binding the default.

One final reason is that it can be useful as a programmer of a given class to decide whether you want a given member function to be overridden at some time in the future. This argument is strong enough that Microsoft's new C# language also allows the programmer to flag a function as not overridable (however, the default is overridable).

To make a member function polymorphic, the programmer must flag the function with the C++ keyword `virtual`, as shown in the following modification to the declaration in the OverloadOveride program:

```
class Student
{
  public:
    virtual void calcTuition()
    {
        cout << "We're in Student::calcTuition" << endl;
    }
};
```

The keyword `virtual` that tells C++ that `calcTuition()` is a polymorphic member function. That is to say, declaring `calcTuition()` virtual means that calls to it will be bound late if there is any doubt as to the runtime type of the object with which `calcTuition()` is called.

Executing the OverloadOveride program with `calcTuition()` declared vir-tual generates the following output:

```
We're in Student::calcTuition
We're in GraduateStudent::calcTuition
Press any key to continue . . .
```

If you're comfortable with the debugger that comes with your C++ environment, you really should single-step through this example. It's so cool to see the program single-step into `Student::calcTuition()` the first time that `fn()` is called but into `GraduateStudent::calcTuition()` on the second call. I don't think that you can truly appreciate polymorphism until you've tried it.

You need to declare the function virtual only in the base class. The "virtualness" is carried down to the subclass automatically. In this book, however, I follow the coding standard of declaring the function virtual everywhere (virtually).

When Is a Virtual Function Not?

Just because you think that a particular function call is bound late doesn't mean that it is. If not declared with the same arguments in the subclasses, the member functions are not overridden polymorphically, whether or not they are declared virtual.

One exception to the identical declaration rule is that if the member function in the base class returns a pointer or reference to a base class object, an overridden member function in a subclass may return a pointer or reference to an object of the subclass. In other words, the function `makeACopy()` is polymorphic, even though the return type of the two functions differ:

```
class Base
{
  public:
    // return a copy of the current object
    Base* makeACopy();
};

class SubClass : public Base
{
  public:
    // return a copy of the current object
    SubClass* makeACopy();
};

void fn(Base& bc)
{
    BaseClass* pCopy = bc.makeACopy();

    // proceed on...
}
```

In practice, this is quite natural. A `makeACopy()` function should return an object of type `SubClass`, even though it might override `BaseClass::makeACopy()`.

Considering Virtual Considerations

You need to keep in mind a few things when using virtual functions. First, static member functions cannot be declared virtual. Because static member functions are not called with an object, there is no runtime object upon which to base a binding decision.

Second, specifying the class name in the call forces a call to bind early, whether or not the function is virtual. For example, the following call is to `Base::fn()` because that's what the programmer indicated, even if `fn()` is declared virtual:

```
void test(Base& b)
{
   b.Base::fn();      // this call is not bound late
}
```

Finally, constructors cannot be virtual because there is no (completed) object to use to determine the type. At the time the constructor is called, the memory that the object occupies is just an amorphous mass. It's only after the constructor has finished that the object is a member of the class in good standing.

By comparison, the destructor should almost always be declared virtual. If not, you run the risk of improperly destructing the object, as in the following circumstance:

```
class Base
{
   public:
     ~Base();
};

class SubClass : public Base
{
   public:
     ~SubClass();
};

void finishWithObject(Base* pHeapObject)
{
    // ...work with object...
    // now return it to the heap
    delete pHeapObject; // this calls ~Base() no matter
}                       // the runtime type of
                        // pHeapObject
```

If the pointer passed to `finishWithObject()` really points to a `SubClass`, the `SubClass` destructor is not invoked properly — because the destructor has been not been declared virtual, it's always bound early. Declaring the destructor virtual solves the problem.

So when would you not want to declare the destructor virtual? There's only one case. Virtual functions introduce a "little" overhead. Let me be more specific. When the programmer defines the first virtual function in a class, C++ adds an additional, hidden pointer — not one pointer per virtual function, just one pointer if the class has any virtual functions. A class that has no virtual functions (and does not inherit any virtual functions from base classes) does not have this pointer.

Now, one pointer doesn't sound like much, and it isn't unless the following two conditions are true:

- ✔ The class doesn't have many data members (so that one pointer represents a lot compared to what's there already).

- ✔ You intend to create a lot of objects of this class (otherwise, the overhead doesn't make any difference).

If these two conditions are met and your class doesn't already have virtual member functions, you may not want to declare the destructor virtual.

Except for this one case, always declare destructors to be virtual, even if a class is not subclassed (yet) — you never know when someone will come along and use your class as the base class for her own. If you don't declare the destructor virtual, document it!

Chapter 21

Factoring Classes

● ●

In This Chapter

▶ Factoring common properties into a base class

▶ Using abstract classes to hold factored information

▶ Declaring abstract classes

▶ Inheriting from an abstract class

▶ Dividing a program into multiple modules using a project file

● ●

The concept of inheritance allows one class to inherit the properties of a base class. Inheritance has a number of purposes, including paying for my son's college. The main benefit of inheritance is the ability to point out the relationship between classes. This is the so-called IS_A relationship — a `MicrowaveOven IS_A Oven` and stuff like that.

Factoring is great stuff if you make the correct correlations. For example, the microwave versus conventional oven relationship seems natural. Claim that microwave is a special kind of toaster, and you're headed for trouble. True, they both make things hot, they both use electricity, and they're both found in the kitchen, but the similarity ends there — a microwave can't make toast.

Identifying the classes inherent in a problem and drawing the correct relationships among these classes is a process known as *factoring*. (The word is related to the arithmetic that you were forced to do in grade school: factoring out the least common denominators, for example, 12 is equal to 2 times 2 times 3.)

Factoring

This section describes how you can use inheritance to simplify your programs using a bank account example. Suppose that you were asked to a write a simple bank program that implemented the concept of a savings account and a checking account.

I can talk until I'm blue in the face about these classes; however, object-oriented programmers have come up with a concise way to describe the salient points of a class in a drawing. The Checking and Savings classes are shown in Figure 21-1. (This is only one of several ways to graphically express the same thing.)

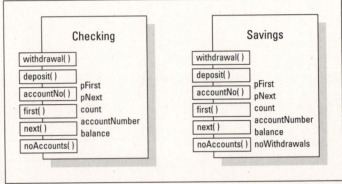

Figure 21-1:
Independent
classes
Checking
and
Savings.

To read this figure and the other figures, remember the following:

- The big box is the class, with the class name at the top.
- The names in boxes are member functions.
- The names not in boxes are data members.
- The names that extend partway out of the boxes are publicly accessible members; that is, these members can be accessed by functions that are not part of the class or any of its descendents. Those members that are completely within the box are not accessible from outside the class.
- A thick arrow (see Figure 21-2) represents the IS_A relationship.
- A thin arrow represents the HAS_A relationship.

A Car IS_A Vehicle, but a Car HAS_A Motor.

You can see in Figure 21-1 that the Checking and Savings classes have a lot in common. For example, both classes have a withdrawal() and deposit() member function. Because the two classes aren't identical, however, they must remain as separate classes. (In a real-life bank application, the two classes would be a good deal more different than in this example.) Still, there should be a way to avoid this repetition.

You could have one of these classes inherit from the other. Savings has more members than Checking, so you could let Savings inherit from Checking. This arrangement is shown in Figure 21-2. The Savings class inherits all the members. The class is completed with the addition of the data member `noWithdrawals` and by overriding the function `withdrawal()`. You have to override `withdrawal()` because the rules for withdrawing money from a savings account are different from those for withdrawing money from a checking account.

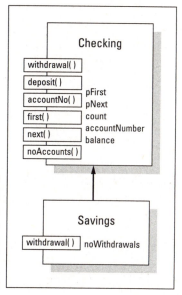

Figure 21-2:
`Savings` imple-mented as a subclass of `Checking`.

Although letting `Savings` inherit from `Checking` is laborsaving, it's not com-pletely satisfying. The main problem is that it, like the weight listed on my driver's license, misrepresents the truth. This inheritance relationship implies that a savings account is a special type of checking account, which it is not.

"So what?" you say. "Inheriting works, and it saves effort." True, but my res-ervations are more than stylistic trivialities — my reservations are at some of the best restaurants in town (at least that's what all the truckers say). Such misrepresentations are confusing to the programmer, both today's and tomorrow's. Someday, a programmer unfamiliar with our programming tricks will have to read and understand what our code does. Misleading representa-tions are difficult to reconcile and understand.

In addition, such misrepresentations can lead to problems down the road. Suppose, for example, that the bank changes its policies with respect to checking accounts. Say it decides to charge a service fee on checking accounts only if the minimum balance dips below a given value during the month.

A change like this can be easily handled with minimal changes to the class `Checking`. You'll have to add a new data member to the class `Checking` to keep track of the minimum balance during the month. Let's go out on a limb and call it `minimumBalance`.

But now you have a problem. Because Savings inherits from Checking, Savings gets this new data member as well. It has no use for this member because the minimum balance does not affect savings accounts, so it just sits there. Remember that every checking account object has this extra minimum Balance member. One extra data member may not be a big deal, but it adds further confusion.

Changes like this accumulate. Today it's an extra data member — tomorrow it's a changed member function. Eventually, the savings account class is carrying a lot of extra baggage that is applicable only to checking accounts.

Now the bank comes back and decides to change some savings account policy. This requires you to modify some function in Checking. Changes like this in the base class automatically propagate down to the subclass unless the function is already overridden in the subclass Savings. For example, suppose that the bank decides to give away toasters for every deposit into the checking account. (Hey — it could happen!) Without the bank (or its programmers) knowing it, deposits to checking accounts would automatically result in toaster donations. Unless you're very careful, changes to Checking may unexpectedly appear in Savings.

How can you avoid these problems? Claiming that Checking is a special case of Savings changes but doesn't solve our problem. What you need is a third class (call it Account, just for grins) that embodies the things that are common between Checking and Savings. This relationship is shown in Figure 21-3.

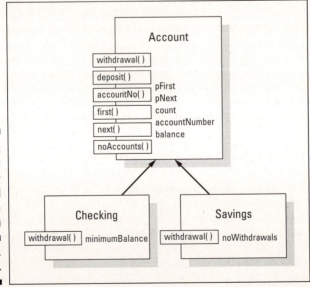

Figure 21-3:
Basing
Checking
and
Savings
on a
common
Account
class.

How does building a new account solve the problems? First, creating a new `Account` class is a more accurate description of the real world (whatever that is). In our concept of things (or at least in mine), there really is something known as an account. Savings accounts and checking accounts are special cases of this more fundamental concept.

In addition, the class `Savings` is insulated from changes to the class `Checking` (and vice versa). If the bank institutes a fundamental change to all accounts, you can modify `Account`, and all subclasses will automatically inherit the change. But if the bank changes its policy only for checking accounts, you can modify just the `Checking` account class without modifying `Savings`.

This process of culling common properties from similar classes is the essence of class factoring.

Factoring is legitimate only if the inheritance relationship corresponds to reality. Factoring together a class `Mouse` and `Joystick` because they're both hardware pointing devices is legitimate. Factoring together a class `Mouse` and `Display` because they both make low-level operating system calls is not.

Implementing Abstract Classes

As intellectually satisfying as factoring is, it introduces a problem of its own. Return one more time to the bank account classes, specifically the common base class `Account`. Think for a minute about how you might go about defining the different member functions defined in `Account`.

Most `Account` member functions are no problem because both account types implement them in the same way. Implementing those common functions with `Account::withdrawal()` is different, however. The rules for withdrawing from a savings account are different than those for withdrawing from a checking account. You'll have to implement `Savings::withdrawal()` differently than you do `Checking::withdrawal()`. But how are you supposed to implement `Account::withdrawal()`?

Let's ask the bank manager for help. I imagine the conversation going something like the following:

"What are the rules for making a withdrawal from an account?" you ask expectantly.

"What type of account? Savings or checking?" comes the reply.

"From an account," you say. "Just an account."

Blank look. (One might say a "blank bank look" . . . then again, maybe not.)

The problem is that the question doesn't make sense. There's no such thing as "just an account." All accounts (in this example) are either checking accounts or savings accounts. The concept of an account is an abstract one that factors out properties common to the two concrete classes. It is incomplete because it lacks the critical property `withdrawal()`. (After you get further into the details, you may find other properties that a simple account lacks.)

An *abstract class* is one that exists only in subclasses. A *concrete class* is a class that is not abstract. Hardly an abstract concept.

C++ supports a concept known as an abstract class to describe an incomplete concept such as an account.

Describing the abstract class concept

An abstract class is a class with one or more pure virtual functions. Oh, great! That helps a lot.

Okay, a *pure virtual* function is a virtual member function that is marked as having no implementation. Most likely it has no implementation because no implementation is possible with the information provided in the class, including any base classes. A conventional, run-of-the-mill non-pure virtual function is known as a *concrete function* (note that a concrete function may be virtual).

The syntax for declaring a function pure virtual is demonstrated in the following class `Account`:

```
// Account - this class is an abstract class
class Account
{
  public:
    Account(unsigned accNo, double initialBalance = 0.0);

    // access functions
    unsigned int accountNo( );
    double acntBalance( );
    static int noAccounts( );

    // transaction functions
    void deposit(double amount);

    // the following is a pure virtual function
    virtual void withdrawal(double amount) = 0;

  protected:
    // keep accounts in a linked list so there's no limit
    // to the number of accounts
```

```
    static int count;      // number of accounts
    unsigned   accountNumber;
    double     balance;
};
```

The = 0 after the declaration of withdrawal() indicates that the programmer does not intend to define this function. The declaration is a placeholder
for the subclasses. The subclasses of Account are expected to override this
function with a concrete function. The programmer must provide an implementation for each member function not declared pure virtual.

I think this notation is silly, and I don't like it any more than you do. But it's
here to stay, so you just have to learn to live with it. There is a reason, if not
exactly a justification, for this notation. Every virtual function must have an
entry in a special table. This entry contains the address of the function. The
entry for a pure virtual function is 0. Some other languages define an abstract
keyword — no, I mean a keyword abstract.

An abstract class cannot be instanced with an object; that is, you can't make
an object out of an abstract class. For example, the following declaration is
not legal:

```
void fn( )
{
    // declare an account with 100 dollars
    Account acnt(1234, 100.00);// this is not legal
    acnt.withdrawal(50);        // what would you expect
                                // this call to do?
}
```

If the declaration were allowed, the resulting object would be incomplete,
lacking in some capability. For example, what should the preceding call do?
Remember, there is no Account::withdrawal().

Abstract classes serve as base classes for other classes. An Account contains all the properties associated with a generic bank account. You can
create other types of bank accounts by inheriting from Account.

Making an honest class out of an abstract class

The subclass of an abstract class remains abstract until all pure virtual functions have been overridden. The class Savings is not abstract because it
overrides the pure virtual function withdrawal() with a perfectly good
definition. The class Savings knows how to perform withdrawal() when

called on to do so. So does the class `Checking` even if the answer is different. Neither class is virtual because the function `withdrawal()` overrides the pure virtual function in the base class.

Passing abstract classes

Because you can't instance an abstract class, it may sound odd that it's possible to declare a pointer or a reference to an abstract class. With polymorphism, however, this isn't as crazy as it sounds. Consider the following code snippet:

```
void fn(Account *pAccount);   // this is legal
void otherFn( )
{
    Savings s;
    Checking c;

    // this is legitimate because Savings IS_A Account
    fn(&s);
    // same here
    fn(&c);
}
```

Here, `pAccount` is declared as a pointer to an `Account`. However, it's understood that when the function is called, it will be passed the address of some nonabstract subclass object such as `Savings` or `Checking`.

All objects received by `fn()` will be of either class `Savings` or class `Checking` (or some future equally nonabstract subclass of `Account`). The function is assured that you will never pass an actual object of class `Account` because you could never create one to pass in the first place.

The enclosed CD-ROM includes a set of programs Budget1 through Budget5. Each program solves essentially the same problem. Each program allows the user to create and collect the balance of a series of checking and savings accounts. However, each program in the sequence is a bit more object-oriented than its predecessors. Budget1 is a completely functional implementation with no concept of classes. Budget2 implements separate `Savings` and `Checking` classes. The Budget3 program factors the similarities in these two classes into a common, abstract `Account` class using the techniques presented in this chapter. Budget4 and Budget5 go on to use features presented in the following chapters.

Part V
Optional Features

In this part . . .

The goal of this book is not to turn you into a C++ language lawyer; it's to give you a solid understanding of the fundamentals of C++ and object-oriented programming.

The earlier parts in this book cover the essential features you need to know to produce a well-written, object-oriented C++ program. C++, however, is a big language (it has a serious case of feature-itis, if you ask me), and I have yet to discuss many features such as file input/output and the Standard Template Library. Part V rights this wrong.

C++ programmers have increasingly come to exploit the features of this library in the past few years. The BUDGET4 and BUDGET5 programs on the enclosed CD-ROM demonstrate how.

Chapter 22

A New Assignment Operator, Should You Decide to Accept It

In This Chapter

▶ Introducing the assignment operator

▶ Knowing why and when the assignment operator is necessary

▶ Understanding similarities between the assignment operator and the copy constructor

The *intrinsic* data types are built into the language, such as `int`, `float`, and `double` and the various pointer types. Chapters 3 and 4 describe the operators that C++ defines for the intrinsic data types. C++ enables the programmer to define the operators for classes that the programmer has created in addition to these intrinsic operators. This is called *operator overloading*.

Normally, operator overloading is optional and not attempted by beginning C++ programmers. A lot of experienced C++ programmers (including me) don't think operator overloading is such a great idea either. However, you must figure out how to overload one operator: the assignment operator.

Comparing Operators with Functions

An operator is nothing more than a built-in function with a peculiar syntax. The following addition operation

```
a + b
```

could be understood as though it were written

```
operator+(a, b)
```

In fact, C++ gives each operator a function-style name. The functional name of an operator is the operator symbol preceded by the keyword `operator` and followed by the appropriate argument types. For example, the + operator that adds an `int` to an `int` generating an `int` is called `int operator+ (int, int)`.

Any existing operator can be defined for a user-defined class. Thus, I could create a `Complex operator*(Complex&, Complex&)` that would allow me to multiply two objects of type `Complex`. The new operator may have the same semantics as the operator it overloads, but it doesn't have to. The following rules apply when overloading operators:

- ✔ The programmer cannot overload the . (dot), :: (colon), .*, and ?: (ternary) operators.

- ✔ The programmer cannot invent new operators. For example, you cannot invent the operation x $ y.

- ✔ The format of the operators cannot be changed. Thus, you cannot define an operation %i because % is already defined as a binary operator.

- ✔ The operator precedence cannot change. A program cannot force `operator+` to be evaluated before `operator*`.

- ✔ The operators cannot be redefined when applied to intrinsic types — you can't change the meaning of 1 + 2. Existing operators can be overloaded only for newly defined types.

Overloading operators is one of those things that seems like a much better idea than it really is. In my experience, operator overloading introduces more problems than it solves, with three notable exceptions that are the subject of this chapter.

Inserting a New Operator

The insertion and extraction operators << and >> are nothing more than the left and right shift operators overloaded for a set of input/output classes. These definitions are found in the include file `iostream` (which is why every program includes that file). Thus, `cout << "some string"` becomes `operator<<(cout, "some string")`. Our old friends `cout` and `cin` are predefined objects that are tied to the console and keyboard, respectively. I discuss this in detail in Chapter 23.

Creating Shallow Copies Is a Deep Problem

No matter what anyone may think of operator overloading, you'll need to overload the assignment operator for many classes that you generate. C++ provides a default definition for `operator=()` for all classes. This default definition performs a member-by-member copy. This works great for an intrinsic type like an `int` where the only "member" is the integer itself.

```
int i;
i = 10;    // "member by member" copy
```

This same default definition is applied to user-defined classes. In the following example, each member of `source` is copied over the corresponding member in `destination`:

```
void fn()
{
    MyStruct source, destination;
    destination = source;
}
```

The default assignment operator works for most classes; however, it is not correct for classes that allocate resources, such as heap memory. The programmer must overload `operator=()` to handle the transfer of resources.

The assignment operator is much like the copy constructor (see Chapter 17). In use, the two look almost identical:

```
void fn(MyClass& mc)
{
    MyClass newMC(mc);     //of course, this uses the
                           //copy constructor
    MyClass newerMC = mc;  //less obvious, this also invokes
                           //the copy constructor
    MyClass newestMC;      //this creates a default object
    newestMC = mc;         //and then overwrites it with
                           //the argument passed
}
```

The creation of `newMC` follows the standard pattern of creating a new object as a mirror image of the original using the copy constructor `MyClass(MyClass&)`. Not so obvious is that `newerMC` is also created using the copy constructor. `MyClass a = b` is just another way of writing

`MyClass a(b)` — in particular, this declaration does *not* involve the assignment operator despite its appearance. However, `newestMC` is created using the default constructor and then overwritten with `mc` using the assignment operator.

The rule is this: The copy constructor is used when a new object is being created. The assignment operator is used if the left-hand object already exists.

Like the copy constructor, an assignment operator should be provided whenever a shallow copy is not appropriate. (Chapter 17 discusses shallow versus deep copy constructors.) A simple rule is to provide an assignment operator for classes that have a user-defined copy constructor.

Notice that the default copy constructor does work for classes that contain members that themselves have copy constructors, like in the following example:

```
class Student
{
  public:
    int nStudentID;
    string sName;
};
```

The C++ library class `string` does allocate memory off the heap, so the authors of that class include a copy constructor and an assignment operator that (one hopes) perform all the operations necessary to create a successful copy of a `string`. The default copy constructor for `Student` invokes the `string` copy constructor to copy `sName` from one student to the next. Similarly, the default assignment operator for `Student` does the same.

Overloading the Assignment Operator

The `DemoAssignmentOperator` program demonstrates how to provide an assignment operator. The program also includes a copy constructor to provide a comparison:

```
//DemoAssignmentOperator - demonstrate the assignment
//                         operator on a user defined class
#include <cstdio>
#include <cstdlib>
#include <iostream>
// the following is necessary if your compiler doesn't
// understand the C++ '09 keyword 'nullptr'
#define nullptr 0
```

```
using namespace std;

// DArray - a dynamically sized array class used to
//          demonstrate the assignment and copy constructor
//          operators
class DArray
{
  public:
    DArray(int nLengthOfArray = 0)
      : nLength(nLengthOfArray), pArray(nullptr)
    {
        cout << "Creating DArray of length = "
            << nLength << endl;
        if (nLength > 0)
        {
            pArray = new int[nLength];
        }
    }
    DArray(DArray& da)
    {
        cout << "Copying DArray of length = "
            << da.nLength << endl;
        copyDArray(da);
    }
    ~DArray()
    {
        deleteDArray();
    }

    //assignment operator
    DArray& operator=(const DArray& s)
    {
        cout << "Assigning source of length = "
            << s.nLength
            << " to target of length = "
            << this->nLength << endl;

        //delete existing stuff...
        deleteDArray();
        //...before replacing with new stuff
        copyDArray(s);
        //return reference to existing object
        return *this;
    }

    int& operator[](int index)
    {
        return pArray[index];
    }
```

```
    int size() { return nLength; }

    void out(const char* pszName)
    {
        cout << pszName << ": ";
        int i = 0;
        while (true)
        {
            cout << pArray[i];
            if (++i >= nLength)
            {
                break;
            }
            cout << ", ";
        }
        cout << endl;
    }

  protected:
    void copyDArray(const DArray& da);
    void deleteDArray();

    int nLength;
    int* pArray;
};

//copyDArray() - create a copy of a dynamic array of ints
void DArray::copyDArray(const DArray& source)
{
    nLength = source.nLength;
    pArray = nullptr;
    if (nLength > 0)
    {
        pArray = new int[nLength];
        for(int i = 0; i < nLength; i++)
        {
            pArray[i] = source.pArray[i];
        }
    }
}

//deleteDArray() - return heap memory
void DArray::deleteDArray()
{
    nLength = 0;
    delete pArray;
    pArray = nullptr;
}

int main(int nNumberofArgs, char* pszArgs[])
{
```

```
    // a dynamic array and assign it values
    DArray da1(5);
    for (int i = 0; i < da1.size(); i++)
    {
        // uses user defined index operator to access
        // members of the array
        da1[i] = i;
    }
    da1.out("da1");

    // now create a copy of this dynamic array using
    // copy constructor; this is same as da2(da1)
    DArray da2 = da1;
    da2[2] = 20;    // change a value in the copy
    da2.out("da2");

    // overwrite the existing da2 with the original da1
    da2 = da1;
    da2.out("da2");


    // wait until user is ready before terminating program
    // to allow the user to see the program results
    system("PAUSE");
    return 0;
}
```

The class DArray defines an integer array of variable length: You tell the class how big an array to create when you construct the object. It does this by wrapping the class around two data members: nLength, which contains the length of the array, and pArray, a pointer to an appropriately sized block of memory allocated off the heap.

The default constructor initializes nLength to the indicated length and then pArray to nullptr.

The nullptr keyword is new to the '09 standard. If your compiler doesn't recognize nullptr, you can add the following definition near the top of your program, as I have done here:

```
#define nullptr 0
```

If the length of the array is actually greater than 0, the constructor allocates an array of int's of the appropriate size off the heap.

The copy constructor creates an array of the same size as the source object and then copies the contents of the source array into the current array using the protected method copyDArray(). The destructor returns the memory allocated in the constructor to the heap using the `deleteDArray()` method. This method nulls out the pointer `pArray` once the memory has been deleted.

The assignment `operator=()` is a method of the class. It looks to all the world like a destructor immediately followed by a copy constructor. This is typical. Consider the assignment in the example `da2 = da1`. The object `da2` already has data associated with it. In the assignment, the original dynamic array must be returned to the heap by calling `deleteDArray()`, just like the `DArray` destructor. The assignment operator then invokes `copyDArray()` to copy the new information into the object, much like the copy constructor.

There are two more details about the assignment operator. First, the return type of `operator=()` is `DArray&`, and the returned value is always `*this`. Expressions involving the assignment operator have a value and a type, both of which are taken from the final value of the left-hand argument. In the following example, the value of `operator=()` is `2.0`, and the type is `double`.

```
double d1, d2;
void fn(double);
d1 = 2.0;          // the type of this expression is double
                   // and the value is 2.0
```

This is what enables the programmer to write the following:

```
d2 = d1 = 2.0
fn(d2 = 3.0);      // performs the assignment and passes the
                   // resulting value to fn()
```

The value of the assignment `d1 = 2.0` (2.0) and the type (`double`) are passed to the assignment to `d2`. In the second example, the value of the assignment `d2 = 3.0` is passed to the function `fn()`.

A user-created assignment operator should support the same semantics as the intrinsic version:

```
fn(DArray&);       // given this declaration...
fn(da2 = da1);     // ...this should be legal
```

The second detail is that `operator=()` was written as a member function. The left-hand argument is taken to be the current object (`this`). Unlike other operators, the assignment operator cannot be overloaded with a nonmember function.

You can delete the default assignment operator if you don't want to define your own:

```
class NonCopyable
{
  public:
    NonCopyable(const NonCopyable&) = delete;
    NonCopyable& operator=(const NonCopyable&) = delete;
};
```

An object of class `NonCopyable` cannot be copied via either construction or assignment:

```
void fn(NonCopyable& src)
{
    NonCopyable copy(src);   // not allowed
    copy = src;              // nor is this
}
```

If your compiler does not support this '09 extension, you can declare the assignment operator protected:

```
class NonCopyable
{
  protected:
    NonCopyable(const NonCopyable&) {};
    NonCopyable& operator=(const NonCopyable&)
        {return *this};
};
```

If your class allocates resources such as memory off the heap, you *must* make the default assignment operator and copy constructors inaccessible, ideally by replacing them with your own version.

Overloading the Subscript Operator

The earlier `DemoAssignmentOperator` example program actually slipped in a third operator that is often overloaded for container classes: the subscript operator.

The following definition allows an object of class to `DArray` to be manipulated like an intrinsic array:

```
int& operator[](int index)
{
    return pArray[index];
}
```

This makes an assignment like the following legal:

```
int n = da[0]; // becomes n = da.operator[](0);
```

Notice, however, that rather than return an integer value, the subscript operator returns a reference to the value within `pArray`. This allows the calling function to modify the value as demonstrated within the `DemoAssignmnentOperator` program:

```
da2[2] = 20;
```

You can see further examples of overloading the index operator for container classes in Chapter 27.

Chapter 23

Using Stream I/O

*P*rograms appearing before this chapter read from the `cin` input object and output through the `cout` output object. Perhaps you haven't really thought about it much, but this input/output technique is a subset of what is known as *stream I/O*.

In this chapter, I describe stream I/O in more detail. I must warn you that stream I/O is too large a topic to be covered completely in a single chapter — entire books are devoted to this one topic. Fortunately for both of us, there isn't all that much that you need to know about stream I/O to write the vast majority of programs.

How Stream I/O Works

Stream I/O is based on overloaded versions of `operator>>()` and `operator <<()`. The declaration of these overloaded operators is found in the include file `iostream`, which are included in all the programs beginning in Chapter 1. The code for these functions is included in the standard library, which your C++ program links with.

The following code shows just a few of the prototypes appearing in iostream:

```
//for input we have:
istream& operator>>(istream& source, char    *pDest);
istream& operator>>(istream& source, string &sDest);
istream& operator>>(istream& source, int    &dest);
istream& operator>>(istream& source, double &dest);
//...and so forth...

//for output we have:
ostream& operator<<(ostream& dest, char    *pSource);
ostream& operator<<(ostream& dest, string &sDest);
ostream& operator<<(ostream& dest, int      source);
ostream& operator<<(ostream& dest, double   source);
//...and so it goes...
```

When overloaded to perform I/O, operator>>() is called the *extractor* and operator<<() is called the *inserter*. The class istream is the basic class for input from a file or a device such as the keyboard. C++ opens the istream object cin when the program starts. Similarly, ostream is the basis for output.

Default stream objects

C++ adds a chunk of code to the front of your program that executes before main() gets control. Among other things, this code creates the default input/output objects shown in Table 23-1.

Table 23-1		Standard Stream I/O Objects
Object	**Class**	**Purpose**
cin	istream	Standard char input
wcin	wistream	Standard wchar_t "wide char" input.
cout	ostream	Standard char output
wcout	wostream	Standard wchar_t "wide char" output
cerr	ostream	Standard error output
wcerr	wostream	Standard error wchar_t "wide char" output
clog	ostream	Standard log.
wclog	ostream	Standard wchar_t "wide char" log

You've seen `cin` and `cout` as they read input from the keyboard and output to the display, respectively. The user can reroute standard input and standard output to a file when he executes a program as follows:

```
C:>MyProgram <InputFile.txt >DefaultOut.txt
```

Here the operator is saying "Execute `MyProgram` but read standard input from `InputFile.txt` instead of the keyboard and send what would otherwise go to the standard output to the file `DefaultOut.txt`."

Rerouting input and output works from the DOS prompt in Windows and under all versions of Unix and Linux. It's the easiest way to perform file input/output when you're trying to write something quick and dirty.

By default, the `cerr` object outputs to the display just like `cout`, except it is rerouted separately — rerouting `cout`-type default output to a file does not reroute `cerr` output. This allows a program to display error messages to the operator even if `cout` has been rerouted to a file.

Error messages should be sent to `cerr` rather than `cout` just in case the operator has rerouted standard output.

The `wcin`, `wcout`, and `wcerr` are wide version of standard input, output, and error, respectively. These are designed to handle Unicode symbols:

```
cout  << "This is narrow output" << endl;
wcout << L"This is wide output"  << endl;
```

Stream Input/Output

The classes `ifstream` and `ofstream` defined in the include file `fstream` are subclasses of `istream` and `ostream` designed to perform stream input and output to disk files. You can use the same extractors and inserters on `ifstream` and `ofstream` objects that you've been using on `cin` and `cout`.

The `ifstream` is actually an instantiation of the template class `basic_ifstream<T>` with `T` set to `char`. I discuss template classes in Chapter 26. The `basic_ifstream<T>` template class is instantiated with other types as well to provide different types of input classes. For example, the wide stream file class `wifstream` is based on the same `basic_ifstream<T>` with `T` set to `wchar_t`. The `ofstream` is based on `basic_ofstream<T>`.

The classes `ifstream` and `ofstream` provide constructors used to open a file for output:

```
ifstream::ifstream(const char *pszFileName,
  ios_base::openmode mode = ios_base::in);
ofstream::ofstream(const char *pszFileName,
  ios_base::openmode mode = ios_base::out|ios_base::trunc);
```

The first argument is a pointer to the name of the file to open. The second argument specifies the mode. The type openmode is an integer type defined in ios_base. Also defined within ios_base are the possible values for mode listed in Table 23-2. These are bit fields that get bitwise ORed together. (See Chapter 4 for an explanation of the ORing of bit fields.) The default mode for ifstream is to open the file for input (that's logical enough).

Table 23-2   Constants that Control How Files Are Opened

Flag	Meaning
ios_base::app	Seek to end-of-file before each write.
ios_base::ate	Seek to end-of-file immediately after opening the file, if it exists.
ios_base::binary	Open file in binary mode (alternative is text mode).
ios_base::in	Open file for input (implied for istream).
ios_base::out	Open file for output (implied for ostream).
ios_base::trunc	Truncate file, if it exists (default for ostream).

The default for ofstream is to open for output and to truncate the file if it exists already. The alternative to truncate is ios_base::app, which means append new output onto the end of the file if it exists already. Both options create a file if it doesn't already exist.

For example, the following StreamOutput program opens the file MyName.txt and then writes some important and absolutely true information to that file:

```
// StreamOutput - simple output to a file
#include <fstream>
using namespace std;

int main(int nNumberofArgs, char* pszArgs[])
{
    ofstream my("MyName.txt");
    my << "Stephen Davis is suave and handsome\n"
       << "and definitely not balding prematurely"
       << endl;
    system("PAUSE");
    return 0;
}
```

The destructor for the file stream classes automatically close the associated file. In my simple example, the MyName.txt file was closed when the my object went out of scope upon returning from main(). Global objects are closed as part of program termination.

Open modes

Table 23-2 shows the different modes that are possible when opening a file. However, you need to answer three basic questions every time you open a file:

- Do you want to read from the file or write to the file? Use ifstream to read and ofstream for writing. If you intend to both write to and read from the same file, use the fstream and set mode to in|out, but good luck — it's much better to write to a file completely and then close it and reopen it for reading as a separate object.

- If you are writing to the file and it already exists, do you want to add to the existing contents (in which case open with ate set) or truncate the file and start over (in which case use trunc)?

- Are you reading or writing text or binary data? Both ifstream and ofstream default to text mode. Use binary mode if you are reading or writing raw, nontext data.

The primary difference between binary and text mode lies in the way that newlines are handled. The Unix operating system was written in the days when typewriters were still fashionable (when it was called "typing" instead of "keyboarding"). Unix ended sentences with a linefeed followed by a carriage return.

Subsequent operating systems saw no reason to continue using two characters to end a sentence but they couldn't agree on which character to use. Some used the carriage return, others used the linefeed, now renamed newline. The C++ standard is the single newline.

When a file is opened in text mode, the C++ library converts the single newline character into what is appropriate for your operating system on output, whether it's a carriage return plus linefeed, a single carriage return, a linefeed, or something else entirely. It performs the opposite conversion while reading a file. The C++ library does no such conversions for a file opened in binary mode.

Always use binary mode when manipulating a file that's not in human-readable format. Otherwise, if a byte in the data stream just happens to be the same as a carriage return or a linefeed, the file I/O library will modify it.

Hey, file, what state are you in?

A constructed `fstream` object (including `ifstream` and `ofstream`) becomes a proxy for the file that it is associated with. For example, the stream object maintains state information about the I/O process. The member function `bad()` returns `true` if something "bad" happens. That nebulous term means that the file couldn't be opened, some internal object was messed up, or things are just generally hosed. A lesser error `fail()` indicates that either something `bad()` happened or the last read failed — for example, if you try to read an `int` and all the program can find is a character that rates a `fail()` but not a `bad()`. The member function `good()` returns `true` if both `bad()` and `fail()` are `false`.

Attempts to input from or output to a stream object that has an error set are ignored. The member function `clear()` zeros out the `fail` flag to give you another chance if the error is temporary — in general, `clear()` clears "failures" but not "bad" things. All attempts to output to an `ofstream` object that has an error have no effect if `my.good()` is not true.

This last paragraph is meant quite literally — no input or output is possible as long as the internal error state of the stream object you're using is nonzero. The program won't even try until you call `clear()` to clear the error flags if the error is temporary and you can clear it.

Can you show me an example?

The following example program demonstrates how to go about using the `ifstream` class to extract a series of integers:

```
// StreamInput - simple input from a file using fstream
#include <cstdio>
#include <cstdlib>
#include <fstream>
#include <iostream>
using namespace std;

ifstream& openFile()
{
    ifstream* pFileStream = 0;
    for(;;)
    {
        // open the file specified by the user
        string sFileName;
        cout << "Enter the name of a file with integers:";
        cin >> sFileName;
```

```
        //open file for reading
        const char* pszFileName = sFileName.c_str();
        pFileStream = new ifstream(pszFileName);
        if (pFileStream->good())
        {
            cerr << "Successfully opened "
                 << pszFileName << endl;
            break;
        }
        cerr << "Couldn't open " << pszFileName << endl;
        delete pFileStream;
    }
    return *pFileStream;
}

int main(int nNumberofArgs, char* pszArgs[])
{
    // get a file stream
    ifstream& fileStream = openFile();

    // stop when no more data in file
    while (!fileStream.eof())
    {
        // read a value
        int nValue = 0;
        fileStream >> nValue;

        // stop if the file read failed (probably because
        // we ran upon something that's not an int or
        // because we found a newline with nothing after
        // it)
        if (fileStream.fail())
        {
            break;
        }

        // output the value just read
        cout << nValue << endl;
    }

    system("PAUSE");
    return 0;
}
```

The function `openFile()` prompts the user for the name of a file to open. The function creates an `ifstream()` object with the specified name. Creating an `ifstream` object automatically opens the file for input. If the file is opened properly, the function returns a reference to the `ifstream` object to use for reading. Otherwise, the program deletes the object and tries again. The only way to get out of the loop is to enter a valid filename or abort the program.

Don't forget to delete the `pFileStream` object if the open fails. These are the sneaky ways that memory leaks creep in.

The program reads integer values from the object referenced by `fileStream` until either `fail()` or the program reaches the end-of-file as indicated by the member function `eof()`.

Don't overflow that buffer!

If you look closely at the `openfile()` method in the StreamInput example program you'll see yet another way to make sure that the operator doesn't overflow the character buffer. Let's review. I could have used something like the following:

```
char szFileName[80];   // any array size is possible
cin >> szFileName;     // input the name of the file to open
```

You can probably find code like this in the early chapters of this book (when you were still wearing your C++ training wheels). The problem with this approach is that nothing tells the extractor that the buffer is only 80 characters long — it will continue to read until it sees a newline, which might be thousands of characters later.

Well, 80 characters is a bit small. How about we increase the buffer size to 256 characters? That sort of misses the point; the implicit assumption you are making with this type of approach is that any buffer overflow is the result of an honest mistake (and a very long filename!). More and more this is not the case. Several major worms have been launched on the backs of buffer overflow attacks. (Wikipedia has an interesting article on the subject at http://en.wikipedia.org/wiki/Buffer_overflow.)

One approach to avoiding buffer overflow that you have seen in earlier chapters is to use the `getline()` method to limit to the size of the buffer the number of characters that the program will read:

```
char szFileName[80];
cin.getline(szFileName, 80); // read not more than 80 chars
```

This code segment says read a line of input (up to the next newline character) but not more than 80 characters since that's the size of the buffer. Any characters not read are left for the next call to `getline()`.

Another approach is to make the buffer size fit the number of available characters. The extractor for the `string` class is smart enough to dynamically resize the buffer to fit the available data:

```
string sFileName;
cin >> sFileName; // string sizes buffer to fit amount of data
   input
```

The call to `c_str()` returns a pointer to the character buffer inside `string`. This is necessary when you need a `char*` rather than a string object. However, don't modify the character string returned by `c_str()`. Also, be aware that the character buffer will get returned to the stack as soon as the `string` object is destructed.

TIP

Let me warn you one more time: Not only is nothing returned from reading an input stream that has an error, but also the buffer comes back unchanged. This program can easily come to the false conclusion that it has just read the same value it previously read. Furthermore, eof() will never return a true on an input stream that has an error.

The output from this program appears as follows (I added boldface to my input):

```
Enter the name of a file with integers:chicken
Couldn't open chicken
Enter the name of a file with integers:integers.txt
Successfully opened integers.txt
1
2
3
4
5
6
Press any key to continue . . .
```

Other Methods of the Stream Classes

The istream and ostream classes provide a number of methods as shown in Table 23-3 (this is not a complete list). The prototypes for these functions reside in the fstream include file. They are described in the remainder of this section.

Table 23-3   Major Methods of the I/O Stream Classes

Method	Meaning
bool bad()	Returns true if a serious error has occurred.
void clear(iostate flags = ios_base::goodbit)	Clears (or sets) the I/O state flags.
void close()	Closes the file associated with a stream object.
bool eof()	Returns true if no more characters are left in the file to be read.
iostate exception()	Returns the conditions that will cause an exception.

(continued)

Table 23-3 *(continued)*

Method	Meaning
`void exception(iostate)`	Sets the conditions that will cause an exception. Multiple conditions can be ORed together; e.g., `exception(ios_base::badbit|ios_base::failbit)`. See Chapter 24 for a discussion of exceptions.
`char fill()` `char fill(char newFill)`	Returns or sets the fill character.
`fmtflags flags()` `fmtflags flags(fmtflags f)`	Returns or sets format flags. (See the next section.)
`void flush()`	Flushes the output buffer to the disk.
`int gcount()`	Returns the number of bytes read during the last input.
`char get()`	Reads individual characters from the file.

`char getline(`
`    char* buffer,`
`    int count,`
`    char delimiter = '\n')`
	Reads multiple characters up until either the end-of-file, until a delimiter is encountered, or until `count - 1` characters read. Tack a null onto the end of the line read. Do not store the delimiter read into the buffer.

`bool good()`	Returns `true` if no error conditions are set.

`void open(`
`    const char* filename,`
`    openmode mode = default)`
	Same arguments as the constructor. Performs the same file open on an existing object that the constructor performs when creating a new object.

`streamsize precision()`
`streamsize precision(`
`    streamsize s)`
	Reads or sets the number of digits displayed for floating-point variables.

`ostream& put(char ch)`	Writes a single character to the stream.

`istream& read(`
`    char* buffer,`
`    streamsize num)`
	Reads a block of data. Reads either `num` bytes or until an end-of-file is encountered, whichever occurs first.

Method	Meaning

`istream& seekg(`
`    pos_type position)`
`istream& seekg(`
`    off_type offset,`
`    ios_base::seekdir)`
	Positions the read pointer either `position` bytes from the beginning of the file or `offset` bytes from the current position. (See this section for details.)

`istream& seekp(`
`    pos_type position)`
`istream& seekp(`
`    off_type offset,`
`    ios_base::seekdir)`
	Positions the write pointer.

`fmtflags setf(fmtflags)`	Sets specific format flags. Returns old value.
`pos_type tellg()`	Returns the position of the read pointer.
`pos_type tellp()`	Returns the position of the write pointer.
`fmtflags unsetf(fmtflags)`	Clears specific format flags. Returns old value.
`int width()` `int width(int w)`	Reads or sets the number of characters to be displayed by the next formatted output statement.

`ostream& write(`
`    const char* buffer,`
`    streamsize num)`
	Writes a block of data to the output file.

Reading and writing streams directly

The inserter and extractor operators provide a convenient mechanism for reading formatted input. However, sometimes you just want to say, "Give it to me; I don't care what the format is." Several methods are useful in this context.

The simplest function, `get()`, just returns the next character in the input file. It's output equivalent is `put()`. The function `getline()` returns a string of characters up until some terminator — the default is a newline. `getline()` strips off the terminator but makes no other attempt to reformat or otherwise interpret the input.

The member function `read()` is even more basic. This function reads the number of characters that you specify, or less if the program encounters an end-of-file. The function `gcount()` always returns the actual number of characters read. The output equivalent is `write()`.

The following example program uses the read() and write() functions to create a backup of any file you give it by making a copy with the string ".backup" appended to the name:

```cpp
// FileCopy - make backup copies of the files passed
//            to the program
#include <cstdio>
#include <cstdlib>
#include <fstream>
#include <iostream>
using namespace std;

int main(int nNumberofArgs, char* pszArgs[])
{
    // repeat the process for every file passed
    for (int n = 1; n < nNumberofArgs; n++)
    {
        // create a filename and a ".backup" name
        const char* pszSource = pszArgs[n];
        string target = string(pszSource) + ".backup";
        const char* pszTarget = target.c_str();

        // now open the source for reading and the
        // target for writing
        ifstream input(pszSource,
                       ios_base::in|ios_base::binary);
        ofstream output(pszTarget,
          ios_base::out|ios_base::binary|ios_base::trunc);
        if (input.good() && output.good())
        {
            cout << "Copying " << pszSource << "...";

            // read and write blocks until either an error
            // occurs or the read file reaches EOF
            while(!input.eof() && input.good())
            {
                char buffer[4096];
                input.read(buffer, 4096);
                output.write(buffer, input.gcount());
            }
            cout << "finished" << endl;
        }
        else
        {
            cerr << "Couldn't copy " << pszSource << endl;
        }
    }

    system("PAUSE");
    return 0;
}
```

The program iterates through the arguments passed to it, remembering that pszArgs[0] points to the name of the program itself. For every source file passed as an argument, the program creates the target filename by tacking ".backup" onto the end. It then opens the source file for binary input and the target for binary output, specifying to truncate the target file if it already exists.

If either the input or output object has an error set, the program outputs a "Couldn't copy" message without attempting to figure out what went wrong. If both objects are good(), however, the program enters a loop in which it reads 4K blocks from the input and writes them out to the output.

Notice that in the call to write(), the program uses the value returned from gcount() rather than hardcoding 4096. This is because, unless the source file just happens to be an integer multiple of 4096 bytes in length, the last call to read() will fetch less than the requested number of bytes before encountering end-of-file.

Controlling format

The flags(), setf(), and unsetf() methods are all used to set or retrieve a set of format flags maintained within the istream or ostream object. These format flags get set when the object is created to a default value that represents the most common format options. The options are shown in Table 23-4.

Table 23-4	The I/O Stream Format Flags
Flag	*If flag is true then...*
boolalpha	Displays bool as either true or false rather than 1 or 0.
dec	Reads or writes integers in decimal format (default).
fixed	Displays floating point in fixed point as opposed to scientific (default).
hex	Reads or writes integers in hexadecimal.
left	Displays output left justified (i.e., pads on the right).
oct	Reads or writes integers in octal.
right	Displays output right justified (i.e., pads on the left).
scientific	Displays floating point in scientific format.
showbase	Displays a leading 0 for octal output and leading 0x for hexadecimal output.
showpoint	Displays a decimal point for floating-point output even if the fractional portion is 0.

(continued)

Table 23-4 *(continued)*

Flag	If flag is true then...
skipws	Skips over whitespace when reading using the extractor.
unitbuf	Flushes output after each output operation.
uppercase	Replaces lowercase letters with their uppercase equivalents on output.

The following code segment has been used in the past to display numbers in hexadecimal format (see the BitTest program in Chapter 4):

```cpp
// read the current format flags
// (this is important when you need to restore the output
// format at a later time)
ios_base::fmtflags prevValue = cout.flags();

// clear the decimal flag
cout.unsetf(cout.dec);

// now set the hexadecimal flag
cout.setf(cout.hex);

// ...do stuff..

// call flags() to restore the format flags to their
// previous value
cout.flags(prevValue);
```

In this example, the program must both set the hexadecimal flags using setf() and unset (that is, clear) the decimal flag using unsetf() because the decimal, octal, and hexadecimal flags are mutually exclusive.

The final call to flags() restores the format flags to their previously read value. This is not necessary if the program is about to terminate anyway.

Further format control is provided by the width() method that sets the minimum width of the next output operation. In the event that the field does not take up the full width specified, the inserter adds the requisite number of fill characters. The default fill character is a space, but you can change this by calling fill(). Whether C++ adds the fill characters on the left or right is determined by whether the left or right format flag is set.

For example, the following segment:

```
int i = 123;
cout.setf(cout.right);
cout.unsetf(cout.left);
cout.fill('+');
cout << "i = [";
cout.width(10);
cout << i;
cout << "]" << endl;
```

generates the following output:

```
i = [+++++++123]
```

Notice that the width() method applies only to the very next output statement. Unlike the other formatting flags, the width() must be reset after every value that you output.

What's up with endl?

Most programs in this book terminate an output stream by inserting the object endl. However, some programs include \n within the text to output a newline. What's the deal?

The \n is, in fact, the newline character. The expression cout << "First line\nSecond line; outputs two lines. The endl object outputs a newline, but continues one step further.

Disks are slow devices. Writing to disk more often than necessary will slow down your program considerably. To avoid this, the fstream class collects output into an internal buffer. The class writes the contents to disk when the buffer is full (this is known as *flushing the buffer*). The endl object outputs a newline and then flushes the output buffer. The member function flush() flushes the output buffer without tacking a newline onto the end.

Note that the standard error object cerr does not buffer output.

Positioning the pointer within a file

The istream class maintains a read pointer that is the location within the file of the next byte to read. You can retrieve this using the tellg() method.

(Similarly, the `tellp()` returns a pointer to the next location to write in an `ostream` object.) Having saved off the location, you can later return to the same location by passing the value read by `tellg()` to `seekg()`.

An overloaded version of `seekg()` takes not an absolute position but an offset and a seek direction. The legal value for the seek direction is one of the following three constants:

- ✔ `ios_base::beg` (beg for *beginning of file*): The offset must be positive and is taken to be the number of bytes from the beginning of the file,

- ✔ `ios_base::end` (end for *end of file*): The offset must be negative and is taken to be the number of bytes from the end of the file.

- ✔ `ios_base::cur` (cur for *current position*): The offset can be either positive or negative and is the number of bytes to move the pointer (either forward or backward) from its current position.

Moving the read (or write) pointer around in a file can be very slow (in computer terms), so be judicious in the use of this feature.

Using the stringstream Subclasses

The stream classes give the programmer mechanisms for easily breaking input among `int`, `float`, and `char` array variables (among others). A set of so-called `stringstream` classes allow the program to read from an array of characters in memory as if it were reading from a file. The classes `istringstream` and `ostringstream` are defined in the include file `sstream`.

The older versions of these classes are `istrstream` and `ostrstream` defined in the include file `strstream`.

The `stringstream` classes have the same semantics as the corresponding file-based classes. This is demonstrated in the following StringStream program, which parses account information from a file:

```
// StringStream - read and parse the contents of a file
#include <cstdio>
#include <cstdlib>
#include <fstream>
#include <sstream>
#include <iostream>
using namespace std;

// parseAccountInfo - read a passed buffer as if it were
```

```
//              an actual file - read the following
//              format:
//               name, account balance
//              return true if all worked well
bool parseString(const char* pString,
                 char* pName, int arraySize,
                 long& accountNum, double& balance)
{
    // associate an istrstream object with the input
    // character string
    istringstream inp(pString);

    // read up to the comma separator
    inp.getline(pName, arraySize, ',');

    // now the account number
    inp >> accountNum;

    // and the balance
    inp >> balance;

    // return the error status
    return !inp.fail();
}

int main(int nNumberofArgs, char* pszArgs[])
{
    // must provide filename
    char szFileName[128];
    cout << "Input name of file to parse:";
    cin.getline(szFileName, 128);

    // get a file stream
    ifstream* pFileStream = new ifstream(szFileName);
    if (!pFileStream->good())
    {
        cerr << "Can't open " << pszArgs[1] << endl;
        return 0;
    }

    // read a line out of file, parse it and display
    // results
    for(int nLineNum = 1;;nLineNum++)
    {
        // read a buffer
        char buffer[256];
        pFileStream->getline(buffer, 256);
        if (pFileStream->fail())
        {
            break;
```

```
        }
        cout << nLineNum << ":" << buffer << endl;

        // parse the individual fields
        char name[80];
        long accountNum;
        double balance;
        bool result = parseString(buffer, name, 80,
                                    accountNum, balance);
        if (result == false)
        {
            cerr << "Error parsing string\n" << endl;
            continue;
        }

        // output the fields we parsed out
        cout << "Read the following fields:" << endl;
        cout << "   name = " << name << "\n"
             << "   account = " << accountNum << "\n"
             << "   balance = " << balance << endl;

        // put the fields back together in a different
        // order (inserting the 'ends' makes sure the
        // buffer is null terminated
        ostringstream out;
        out << name << ", "
            << balance << " "
            << accountNum << ends;

        string oString = out.str();
        cout << "Reordered fields: " << oString << endl;
    }

    system("PAUSE");
    return 0;
}
```

This program begins by opening a file called Accounts.txt containing account information in the format of: *name, accountNumber, balance, \n*. Assuming that the file was opened successfully, the program enters a loop, reading lines until the contents of the file are exhausted. The call to get line() reads up to the default newline terminator. The program passes the line just read to the function parseString().

parseString() associates an istringstream object with the character string. The program reads characters up to the ',' (or the end of the string buffer) using the getline() member function. The program then uses the conventional extractors to read accountNum and balance. The reads from inp have worked if inp.fail() returns false.

After the call to `parseString()`, `main()` outputs the buffer read from the file followed by the parsed values. It then uses the `ostringstream` class to reconstruct a `string` object with the same data but a different format (just for the fun of it).

The result from a sample execution appears as follows:

```
Input name of file to parse:Accounts.txt
1:Chester, 12345 56.60
Read the following fields:
   name = Chester
   account = 12345
   balance = 56.6
Reordered fields: Chester, 56.6 12345
2:Arthur,  34567 67.50
Read the following fields:
   name = Arthur
   account = 34567
   balance = 67.5
Reordered fields: Arthur, 67.5 34567
3:Trudie,  56x78 78.90
Error parsing string

4:Valerie, 78901 89.10
Read the following fields:
   name = Valerie
   account = 78901
   balance = 89.1
Reordered fields: Valerie, 89.1 78901
Press any key to continue . . .
```

Reflect a second before continuing. Notice how the program was able to resync itself after the error in the input file. Notice, also, the simplicity of the heart of the program, the `parseString()` function. Consider what this function would look like without the benefit of the `istringstream` class.

Manipulating Manipulators

You can use stream I/O to output numbers and character strings by using default formats. Usually the defaults are fine, but sometimes they don't cut it.

For example, I was less than tickled when the total from the result of a financial calculation from a recent program appeared as 249.600006 rather than 249.6 (or, better yet, 249.60). There must be a way to bend the defaults to my desires. True to form, C++ provides not one but two ways to control the format of output.

Depending on the default settings of your compiler, you may get 249.6 as your output. Nevertheless, you really want 249.60.

First, you can control the format by invoking a series of member functions on the stream object. For example, the number of significant digits to display is set by using the function `precision()` as follows (see Table 23-3):

```
#include <iostream>
void fn(double interest, double dollarAmount)
{
    cout << "Dollar amount = ";
    cout.precision(2);
    cout << dollarAmount;
    cout.precision(4);
    cout << interest
         << endl;
}
```

In this example, the function `precision()` sets the precision to 2 immediately before outputting the value `dollarAmount`. This gives you a number such as 249.60, the type of result you want. It then sets the precision to 4 before outputting the interest.

A second approach uses what are called manipulators. (Sounds like someone behind the scenes of the New York Stock Exchange, doesn't it?) *Manipulators* are objects defined in the include file `iomanip` to have the same effect as the member function calls. (You must include `iomanip` to have access to the manipulators.) The only advantage to manipulators is that the program can insert them directly into the stream rather than resort to a separate function call.

The most common manipulators and their corresponding meanings are shown in Table 23-5.

Table 23-5   Common Manipulators and Stream Format Control Functions

Manipulator	Member Function	Description
dec	setf(dec)	Sets radix to 10
hex	setf(hex)	Sets radix to 16
oct	setf(oct)	Sets radix to 8
setfill(c)	fill(c)	Sets the fill character to c
setprecision(n)	precision(n)	Sets display precision to n
setw(n)	width(n)	Sets width of field to n characters*

*This returns to its default value after the next field is output.

If you rewrite the preceding example to use manipulators, the program appears as follows:

```
#include <iostream>
#include <iomanip>
void fn(double interest, double dollarAmount)
{
    cout << "Dollar amount = "
         << setprecision(2) << dollarAmount
         << setprecision(4) << interest
         << endl;
}
```

Chapter 24

Handling Errors — Exceptions

● ●

In This Chapter

▶ Introducing an exceptional way of handling program errors

▶ Finding what's wrong with good ol' error returns

▶ Examining throwing and catching exceptions

▶ Packing more heat into that throw

● ●

1 know that it's hard to accept, but occasionally functions don't work properly — not even mine. The traditional means of reporting failure is to return some indication to the caller. C++ includes a new, improved mechanism for capturing and handling errors called *exceptions*. An exception is defined as "a case in which a rule or principle does not apply." Exception is also defined as an objection to something. Either definition works: An exception is an unexpected (and presumably objectionable) condition that occurs during the execution of the program.

The exception mechanism is based on the keywords try, catch, and throw (that's right, more variable names that you can't use). In outline, it works like this: A function *try*s to get through a piece of code. If the code detects a problem, it *throw*s an error indication that the calling function must *catch*.

The following code snippet demonstrates how that works in 1s and 0s:

```
//
//  FactorialException - demonstrate exceptions using
//                       a factorial function
//
#include <cstdio>
#include <cstdlib>
#include <iostream>
using namespace std;

// factorial - compute factorial
int factorial(int n) throw (string)
{
```

```cpp
    // you can't handle negative values of n;
    // better check for that condition first
    if (n < 0)
    {
        throw string("Argument for factorial negative");
    }

    // go ahead and calculate factorial
    int accum = 1;
    while(n > 0)
    {
        accum *= n;
        n--;
    }
    return accum;
}

int main(int nNumberofArgs, char* pszArgs[])
{
    try
    {
        // this will work
        cout << "Factorial of 3 is "
             << factorial(3) << endl;

        // this will generate an exception
        cout << "Factorial of -1 is "
             << factorial(-1) << endl;

        // control will never get here
        cout << "Factorial of 5 is "
             << factorial(5) << endl;
    }
    // control passes here
    catch(string error)
    {
        cout << "Error occurred: " << error << endl;
    }
    catch(...)
    {
        cout << "Default catch " << endl;
    }

    // wait until user is ready before terminating program
    // to allow the user to see the program results
    system("PAUSE");
    return 0;
}
```

`main()` starts out by creating a block outfitted with the `try` keyword. Within this block, it can proceed the way it would if the block were not present. In this case, `main()` attempts to calculate the factorial of a negative number. Not to be hoodwinked, the clever `factorial()` function detects the bogus request and throws an error indication using the `throw` keyword. Control passes to the `catch` phrase, which immediately follows the closing brace of the `try` block. The second call to `factorial()` is not performed.

The declaration for `factorial()` also announces to the compiler that it may throw a `string` object somewhere under the right conditions. This is a relatively new, and so far optional, feature. If absent, the function may throw any object that it wants. If present, the function can throw only one of the types of objects included in the declaration.

Justifying a New Error Mechanism?

What's wrong with error returns like FORTRAN used to make? Factorials cannot be negative, so I could have said something like "Okay, if `factorial()` detects an error, it returns a negative number. The actual value indicates the source of the problem." What's wrong with that? That's how it's been done for ages.

Unfortunately, several problems arise. First, although it's true that the result of a factorial can't be negative, other functions aren't so lucky. For example, you can't take the log of a negative number either, but the negative return value trick won't work here — logarithms can be either negative or positive.

Second, there's just so much information that you can store in an integer. Maybe you can have –1 for "argument is negative" and –2 for "argument is too large." But, if the argument is too large, you want to know what the argument is, because that information might help you debug the problem. There's no place to store that type of information.

Third, the processing of error returns is optional. Suppose someone writes `factorial()` so that it dutifully checks the argument and returns a negative number if the argument is out of range. If a function that calls `factorial()` doesn't check the error return, returning an error value doesn't do any good. Sure, you can make all kinds of menacing threats, such as "You will check your error returns or else," and the programmer may have the best of intentions, but you all know that people get lazy and return to their old, non-error-checking ways.

Even if you do check the error return from `factorial()` or any other function, what can the function do with the error? It can probably do nothing more than output an error message of your own and return another error indication to the caller, which probably does the same. Pretty soon, there's more error detection code than "real" code.

The exception mechanism addresses these problems by removing the error path from the normal code path. Furthermore, exceptions make error handling obligatory. If your function doesn't handle the thrown exception, control passes up the chain of called functions until C++ finds a function to handle the error. This also gives you the flexibility to ignore errors that you can't do anything about anyway. Only the functions that can actually correct the problem need to catch the exception.

Examining the Exception Mechanism

Take a closer look at the steps that the code goes through to handle an exception. When the throw occurs, C++ first copies the thrown object to some neutral place. It then begins looking for the end of the current `try` block.

If a `try` block is not found in the current function, control passes to the calling function. A search is then made of that function. If no `try` block is found there, control passes to the function that called it, and so on up the stack of calling functions. This process is called *unwinding the stack*.

An important feature of stack unwinding is that as each stack is unwound, objects that go out of scope are destructed just as though the function had executed a `return` statement. This keeps the program from losing assets or leaving objects dangling.

When the encasing `try` block is found, the code searches the first `catch` phrase immediately following the closing brace of the `catch` block. If the object thrown matches the type of argument specified in the `catch` statement, control passes to that `catch` phrase. If not, a check is made of the next `catch` phrase. If no matching `catch` phrases are found, the code searches for the next higher level try block in an ever-outward spiral until an appropriate `catch` can be found. If no `catch` phrase is found, the program is terminated.

Consider the following example:

```
// CascadingException - the following program demonstrates
//              an example of stack unwinding; it also
//              shows how the throw() clause is used in
//              the function declaration
#include <cstdio>
```

```cpp
#include <cstdlib>
#include <iostream>
using namespace std;

// prototypes of some functions that we will need later
void f1() throw();
void f2();
void f3() throw(int);

class Obj
{
  public:
    Obj(char c) : label(c)
    { cout << "Constructing object " << label << endl;}
    ~Obj()
    { cout << "Destructing object " << label << endl; }

  protected:
    char label;
};

int main(int nNumberofArgs, char* pszArgs[])
{
    f1();

    // wait until user is ready before terminating program
    // to allow the user to see the program results
    system("PAUSE");
    return 0;
}

// f1 -an empty throw() clause in the declaration of this
//     function means that it does not throw an exception
void f1() throw()
{
    Obj a('a');
    try
    {
        Obj b('b');
        f2();
    }
    catch(float f)
    {
        cout << "Float catch" << endl;
    }
    catch(int i)
    {
        cout << "Int catch" << endl;
    }
    catch(...)
    {
        cout << string("Generic catch") << endl;
    }
```

```
}

// f2 - the absence of a throw() clause in the
//      declaration of this function means that it may
//      throw any kind of object
void f2()
{
    try
    {
        Obj c('c');
        f3();
    }
    catch(string msg)
    {
        cout << "String catch" << endl;
    }
}

// f3 - this function may throw an int object
void f3() throw(int)
{
    Obj d('d');
    throw 10;
}
```

The output from executing this program appears as follows:

```
Constructing object a
Constructing object b
Constructing object c
Constructing object d
Destructing object d
Destructing object c
Destructing object b
Int catch
Destructing object a
Press any key to continue . . .
```

First, you see the four objects a, b, c, and d being constructed as main()
calls f1() which calls f2() which calls f3(). Rather than return, however,
f3() throws the integer 10. Because no try block is defined in f3(), C++
unwinds f3()'s stack, causing object d to be destructed. The next function up the chain, f2() defines a try block, but its only catch phrase is
designed to handle string, which doesn't match the int thrown. Therefore,
C++ continues looking. This unwinds f2()'s stack, resulting in object c being
destructed.

Back in f1(), C++ finds another try block. Exiting that block causes object
b to go out of scope. C++ skips the first catch phrase for a float. The next
catch phrase matches the int exactly, so C++ passes control to this phrase.

Control passes from the catch(int) phrase to the closing brace of the final catch phrase and from there back to main(). The final catch(...) phrase, which would catch any object thrown, is skipped because a matching catch phrase was already found.

Notice that f2() does not declare the types of objects it might throw but the functions f1() and f3() do. Why is this descriptor optional? The throw specification in the declaration was added to the definition of the language long after the exception mechanism itself. First, the new standard wants to remain compatible with the existing C++ code that doesn't declare the types of objects thrown. In addition, it's not clear that forcing the user to declare the type of object thrown is a good idea.

If I wanted to include the type of objects thrown by f2(), I would have to declare it as follows:

```
void f2() throw(int);
```

Even though f2() doesn't throw an int directly, it does so indirectly by calling f3() and not catching the int thrown there. In a real-world program, it can get complicated trying to keep track of all the objects that a function could possibly throw.

What Kinds of Things Can 1 Throw?

The thing following the throw keyword is actually an expression that creates an object of some kind. In the examples so far, I've thrown an int and a string object, but throw can handle any type of object. This means you can throw almost as much information as you want. Consider the following update to the factorial program, CustomExceptionClass:

```
//
//   CustomExceptionClass - demonstrate the flexibility
//             of the exception mechanism by creating
//             a custom exception class
//
#include <cstdio>
#include <cstdlib>
#include <iostream>
#include <sstream>
using namespace std;

// MyException - generic exception handling class
class MyException
{
  public:
    MyException(const char* pMsg, int n,
               const char* pFunc,
```

```
                         const char* pFile, int nLine)
        : msg(pMsg), errorValue(n),
          funcName(pFunc), file(pFile), lineNum(nLine)
    {}

    virtual string display()
    {
        ostringstream out;
        out << "Error <" << msg << ">"
            << " - value is " << errorValue << "\n"
            << "in function " << funcName << "()\n"
            << "in file " << file
            << " line #" << lineNum << ends;
        return out.str();
    }
  protected:
    // error message
    string msg;
    int    errorValue;

    // function name, file name and line number
    // where error occurred
    string funcName;
    string file;
    int lineNum;
};

// factorial - compute factorial
int factorial(int n) throw(MyException)
{
    // you can't handle negative values of n;
    // better check for that condition first
    if (n < 0)
    {
        throw MyException("Negative argument not allowed",
                    n, __func__, __FILE__, __LINE__);
    }

    // go ahead and calculate factorial
    int accum = 1;
    while(n > 0)
    {
        accum *= n;
        n--;
    }
    return accum;
}

int main(int nNumberofArgs, char* pszArgs[])
{
    try
```

```
{
    // this will work
    cout << "Factorial of 3 is "
         << factorial(3) << endl;

    // this will generate an exception
    cout << "Factorial of -1 is "
         << factorial(-1) << endl;

    // control will never get here
    cout << "Factorial of 5 is "
         << factorial(5) << endl;
}
// control passes here
catch(MyException e)
{
    cout << e.display() << endl;
}
catch(...)
{
    cout << "Default catch " << endl;
}

// wait until user is ready before terminating program
// to allow the user to see the program results
system("PAUSE");
return 0;
}
```

This program appears much the same as the factorial program at the beginning of this chapter. The difference is the use of a user-defined MyException class that contains more information concerning the nature of the error than a simple string contains. The factorial program is able to throw the error message, the illegal value, and the exact location where the error occurred.

__FILE__ , __LINE__ and __func__ are intrinsic #defines that are set to the name of the source file, the current line number in that file, and the name of the current function, respectively.

The catch snags the MyException object and then uses the built-in display() member function to display the error message. (See Chapter 23 for a review of how to use the ostringstream class to format an internal string.) The output from this program appears as follows:

```
Factorial of 3 is 6
Error <Negative argument not allowed> - value is -1
in function factorial()
in file C:\CPP_Programs\Chap25\CustomExceptionClass\main.cpp line #53
Press any key to continue . . .
```

Just Passing Through

A function that allocates resources locally may need to catch an exception, do some processing and then rethrow it up the stack chain. Consider the following example:

```
void fileFunc()
{
    ofstream* pOut = new ofstream("File.txt");
    otherFunction();
    delete pOut;
}
```

As anyone who's read Chapter 8 knows, the memory allocated by new isn't returned to the heap automatically. If otherFunction() were to throw an exception, control would exit the program without invoking delete, and the memory allocated at the beginning of fileFunc() would be lost.

To avoid this problem, fileFunc() can include a catch(...) to catch any exception thrown:

```
void fileFunc()
{
    ofstream* pOut = new ofstream("File.txt");
    try
    {
        otherFunction();

        delete pOut;
    }
    catch(...)
    {
        delete pOut;
        throw;
    }
}
```

Within this phrase, fileFunc() returns the memory it allocated earlier to the heap. However, it is not in a position to process the remainder of the exception because it has no idea what could have gone wrong. It doesn't even know what type of object it just caught.

The throw keyword without any arguments rethrows the current exception object back up the chain to some function that can properly process the error.

Chapter 25

Inheriting Multiple Inheritance

. . . .

In This Chapter

▶ Introducing multiple inheritance

▶ Avoiding ambiguities with multiple inheritance

▶ Avoiding ambiguities with virtual inheritance

▶ Figuring out the ordering rules for multiple constructors

▶ Getting a handle on problems with multiple inheritance

. . . .

*I*n the class hierarchies discussed in other chapters, each class inherits from a single parent. Such single inheritance is sufficient to describe most real-world relationships. Some classes, however, represent the blending of two classes into one. (Sounds sort of romantic, doesn't it?)

An example of such a class is the sleeper sofa that integrates a harsh bed into an uncomfortable sofa. To adequately describe a sleeper sofa in C++, the sleeper sofa should be able to inherit both bed- and sofa-like properties. This is called *multiple inheritance*.

Describing the Multiple Inheritance Mechanism

Figure 25-1 shows the inheritance graph for class `SleeperSofa` that inherits both from class `Sofa` and from class `Bed`.

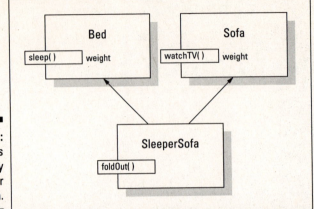

Figure 25-1:
Class
hierarchy
of a sleeper
sofa.

The code to implement class `SleeperSofa` looks like the following:

```
//
//   MultipleInheritance - a single class can inherit from
//                         more than one base class
//
#include <cstdio>
#include <cstdlib>
#include <iostream>
using namespace std;

class Bed
{
  public:
    Bed(){}
    void sleep(){ cout << "Sleep" << endl; }
    int weight;
};

class Sofa
{
  public:
    Sofa(){}
    void watchTV(){ cout << "Watch TV" << endl; }
    int weight;
};

// SleeperSofa - is both a Bed and a Sofa
class SleeperSofa : public Bed, public Sofa
{
  public:
    SleeperSofa(){}
    void foldOut(){ cout << "Fold out" << endl; }
```

```
};

int main(int nNumberofArgs, char* pszArgs[])
{
    SleeperSofa ss;

    // you can watch TV on a sleeper sofa like a sofa...
    ss.watchTV();      // calls Sofa::watchTV()

    //...and then you can fold it out...
    ss.foldOut();      // calls SleeperSofa::foldOut()

    // ...and sleep on it
    ss.sleep();        // calls Bed::sleep()

    // wait until user is ready before terminating program
    // to allow the user to see the program results
    system("PAUSE");
    return 0;
}
```

Here the classes Bed and Sofa appear as conventional classes. Unlike in earlier examples, however, the class SleeperSofa inherits from both Bed and Sofa. This is apparent from the appearance of both classes in the class declaration. SleeperSofa inherits all the members of both base classes. Thus, both of the calls ss.sleep() and ss.watchTV() are legal. You can use a SleeperSofa as a Bed or a Sofa. Plus the class SleeperSofa can have members of its own, such as foldOut(). The output of this program appears as follows:

```
Watch TV
Fold out
Sleep
Press any key to continue . . .
```

Is this a great country or what?

Straightening Out Inheritance Ambiguities

Although multiple inheritance is a powerful feature, it introduces several possible problems. One is apparent in the preceding example. Notice that both Bed and Sofa contain a member weight. This is logical because both have a measurable weight. The question is, "Which weight does SleeperSofa inherit?"

The answer is "both." `SleeperSofa` inherits a member `Bed::weight` and a separate member `Sofa::weight`. Because they have the same name, unqualified references to `weight` are now ambiguous. This is demonstrated in the following snippet, which generates a compile-time error:

```
#include <iostream>

void fn()
{
    SleeperSofa ss;
    cout << "weight = "
         << ss.weight    // illegal - which weight?
         << "\n";
}
```

The program must now indicate one of the two weights by specifying the desired base class. The following code snippet is correct:

```
#include <iostream>
void fn()
{
    SleeperSofa ss;
    cout << "sofa weight = "
         << ss.Sofa::weight  // specify which weight
         << "\n";
}
```

Although this solution corrects the problem, specifying the base class in the application function isn't desirable because it forces class information to leak outside the class into application code. In this case, `fn()` has to know that `SleeperSofa` inherits from `Sofa`. These types of so-called name collisions weren't possible with single inheritance but are a constant danger with multiple inheritance.

Adding Virtual Inheritance

In the case of `SleeperSofa`, the name collision on `weight` was more than a mere accident. A `SleeperSofa` doesn't have a bed weight separate from its sofa weight. The collision occurred because this class hierarchy doesn't completely describe the real world. Specifically, the classes have not been completely factored.

Thinking about it a little more, it becomes clear that both beds and sofas are special cases of a more fundamental concept: furniture. (I suppose I could get even more fundamental and use something like object with mass, but furniture is fundamental enough.) Weight is a property of all furniture. This relationship is shown in Figure 25-2.

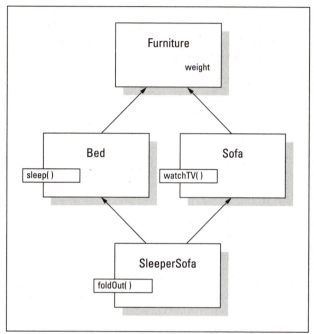

Figure 25-2:
Further
factoring of
beds and
sofas (by
weight).

Factoring out the class Furniture should relieve the name collision. With
much relief and great anticipation of success, I generate the C++ class hierarchy shown in the following program, MultipleInheritanceFactoring:

```
//
//   MultipleInheritanceFactoring - a single class can
//                   inherit from more than one base class
//
#include <cstdio>
#include <cstdlib>
#include <iostream>
using namespace std;

// Furniture - more fundamental concept; this class
//             has "weight" as a property
class Furniture
{
  public:
    Furniture(int w) : weight(w) {}
    int weight;
};

class Bed : public Furniture
{
  public:
```

```
        Bed(int weight) : Furniture(weight) {}
        void sleep(){ cout << "Sleep" << endl; }
};

class Sofa : public Furniture
{
  public:
    Sofa(int weight) : Furniture(weight) {}
    void watchTV(){ cout << "Watch TV" << endl; }
};

// SleeperSofa - is both a Bed and a Sofa
class SleeperSofa : public Bed, public Sofa
{
  public:
    SleeperSofa(int weight) : Bed(weight), Sofa(weight) {}
    void foldOut(){ cout << "Fold out" << endl; }
};

int main(int nNumberofArgs, char* pszArgs[])
{
    SleeperSofa ss(10);

    // Section 1 -
    // the following is ambiguous; is this a
    // Furniture::Sofa or a Furniture::Bed?
    /*
    cout << "Weight = "
         << ss.weight
         << endl;
     */

    // Section 2 -
    // the following specifies the inheritance path
    // unambiguously - sort of ruins the effect
    SleeperSofa* pSS = &ss;
    Sofa* pSofa = (Sofa*)pSS;
    Furniture* pFurniture = (Furniture*)pSofa;
    cout << "Weight = "
         << pFurniture->weight
         << endl;

    // wait until user is ready before terminating program
    // to allow the user to see the program results
    system("PAUSE");
    return 0;
}
```

Imagine my dismay when I find that this doesn't help at all — the reference to `weight` in Section 1 of `main()` is still ambiguous. "Okay," I say (not really understanding why weight is still ambiguous), "I'll try casting ss to a Furniture."

```
#include <iostream.h>

void fn()
{
  SleeperSofa ss;
  Furniture* pF;
  pF = (Furniture*)&ss; // use a Furniture pointer...
  cout << "weight = "   // ...to get at the weight
       << pF->weight
       << "\n";
};
```

Casting ss to a Furniture doesn't work either. Now, I get some strange message that the cast of SleeperSofa* to Furniture* is ambiguous. What's going on?

The explanation is straightforward. SleeperSofa doesn't inherit from Furniture directly. Both Bed and Sofa inherit from Furniture and then SleeperSofa inherits from them. In memory, a SleeperSofa looks like Figure 25-3.

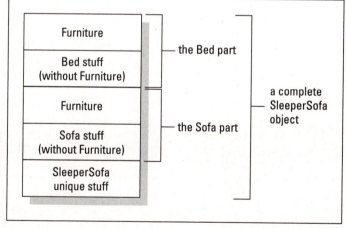

Figure 25-3:
Memory
layout of a
SleeperSofa.

You can see that a SleeperSofa consists of a complete Bed followed by a complete Sofa followed by some SleeperSofa unique stuff. Each of these subobjects in SleeperSofa has its own Furniture part, because each inherits from Furniture. Thus, a SleeperSofa contains two Furniture objects!

I haven't created the hierarchy shown in Figure 25-2 after all. The inheritance hierarchy I've actually created is the one shown in Figure 25-4.

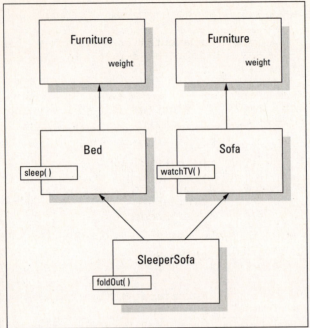

Figure 25-4:
Actual
result of my
first attempt.

The MultipleInheritanceFactoring program demonstrates this duplication of the base class. Section 2 specifies exactly which `weight` object by recasting the pointer `SleeperSofa` first to a `Sofa*` and then to a `Furniture*`.

But `SleeperSofa` containing two `Furniture` objects is nonsense. `SleeperSofa` needs only one copy of `Furniture`. I want `SleeperSofa` to inherit only one copy of `Furniture`, and I want `Bed` and `Sofa` to share that one copy. C++ calls this *virtual inheritance* because it uses the virtual keyword.

Armed with this new knowledge, I return to class `SleeperSofa` and implement it as follows:

```
//
//   VirtualInheritance - using virtual inheritance the
//              Bed and Sofa classes can share a common base
//
#include <cstdio>
#include <cstdlib>
#include <iostream>
```

```
using namespace std;

// Furniture - more fundamental concept; this class
//             has "weight" as a property
class Furniture
{
  public:
    Furniture(int w) : weight(w) {}
    int weight;
};

class Bed : virtual public Furniture
{
  public:
    Bed(int w = 0) : Furniture(w) {}
    void sleep(){ cout << "Sleep" << endl; }
};

class Sofa : virtual public Furniture
{
  public:
    Sofa(int w = 0) : Furniture(w) {}
    void watchTV(){ cout << "Watch TV" << endl; }
};

// SleeperSofa - is both a Bed and a Sofa
class SleeperSofa : public Bed, public Sofa
{
  public:
    SleeperSofa(int w) : Furniture(w) {}
    void foldOut(){ cout << "Fold out" << endl; }
};

int main(int nNumberofArgs, char* pszArgs[])
{
    SleeperSofa ss(10);

    // the following is no longer ambiguous;
    // there's only one weight shared between Sofa and Bed
    // Furniture::Sofa or a Furniture::Bed?
    cout << "Weight = "
         << ss.weight
         << endl;

    // wait until user is ready before terminating program
    // to allow the user to see the program results
    system("PAUSE");
    return 0;
}
```

Notice the addition of the keyword `virtual` in the inheritance of `Furniture` in `Bed` and `Sofa`. This says, "Give me a copy of `Furniture` unless you already have one somehow, in which case I'll just use that one." A `SleeperSofa` ends up looking like Figure 25-5 in memory.

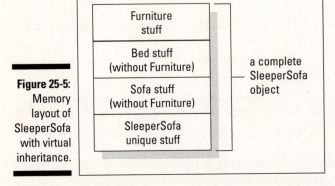

Figure 25-5: Memory layout of SleeperSofa with virtual inheritance.

Here you can see that a `SleeperSofa` inherits `Furniture`, and then `Bed` minus the `Furniture` part, followed by `Sofa` minus the `Furniture` part. Bringing up the rear are the members unique to `SleeperSofa`. (Note that this may not be the order of the elements in memory, but that's not important for the purpose of this discussion.)

Now the reference in `fn()` to `weight` is not ambiguous because a `SleeperSofa` contains only one copy of `Furniture`. By inheriting `Furniture` virtually, you get the desired inheritance relationship as expressed in Figure 25-2.

If virtual inheritance solves this problem so nicely, why isn't it the norm? The first reason is that virtually inherited base classes are handled internally much differently than normally inherited base classes, and these differences involve extra overhead. The second reason is that sometimes you want two copies of the base class.

As an example of the latter, consider a `TeacherAssistant` who is both a `Student` and a `Teacher`, both of which are subclasses of `Academician`. If the university gives its teaching assistants two IDs — a student ID and a separate teacher ID — the class `TeacherAssistant` will need to contain two copies of class `Academician`.

Constructing the Objects of Multiple Inheritance

The rules for constructing objects need to be expanded to handle multiple inheritance. The constructors are invoked in the following order:

1. First, the constructor for any virtual base classes is called in the order in which the classes are inherited.

2. Then the constructor for all nonvirtual base classes is called in the order in which the classes are inherited.

3. Next, the constructor for all member objects is called in the order in which the member objects appear in the class.

4. Finally, the constructor for the class itself is called.

Notice that base classes are constructed in the order in which they are inherited and not in the order in which they appear on the constructor line.

Voicing a Contrary Opinion

I should point out that not all object-oriented practitioners think that multiple inheritance is a good idea. In addition, many object-oriented languages don't support multiple inheritance.

Multiple inheritance is not an easy thing for the language to implement. This is mostly the compiler's problem (or the compiler writer's problem). But multiple inheritance adds overhead to the code when compared to single inheritance, and this overhead can become the programmer's problem.

More importantly, multiple inheritance opens the door to additional errors. First, ambiguities such as those mentioned in "Straightening Out Inheritance Ambiguities" pop up. Second, in the presence of multiple inheritance, casting a pointer from a subclass to a base class often involves changing the value of the pointer in sophisticated and mysterious ways. Let me leave the details to the language lawyers and compiler writers.

Third, the way in which constructors are invoked can be a little mysterious. Notice in the VirtualInheritance example that SleeperSofa must invoke the Furniture constructor directly. The SleeperSofa cannot initialize weight through either the Bed or the Sofa constructors.

I suggest that you avoid using multiple inheritance until you're comfortable with C++. Single inheritance provides enough expressive power to get used to. Later, you can study the manuals until you're sure that you understand exactly what's going on when you use multiple inheritance. One exception is the use of commercial libraries such as Microsoft's Foundation Classes (MFC), which use multiple inheritance quite a bit. These classes have been checked out and are safe.

Don't get me wrong. I'm not out and out against multiple inheritance. The fact that Microsoft and others use multiple inheritance effectively in their class libraries proves that it can be done. However, multiple inheritance is a feature that you want to hold off on using until you're ready for it.

Chapter 26

Tempting C++ Templates

● ●

In This Chapter

▶ Examining how templates can be applied to functions

▶ Combining common functions into a single template definition

▶ Defining a template or class

▶ Reviewing the advantages of a template over the more generic "void" approach

● ●

*T*he standard C++ library provides a complete set of math, time, input/
output, and DOS operations, to name just a few. Many of the earlier programs in this book use the so-called character string functions defined in the
include file `strings`. The argument types for many of these functions are
fixed. For example, both arguments to `strcpy(char*, char*)` must be a
pointer to a null-terminated character string — nothing else makes sense.

There are functions that are applicable to multiple types. Consider the example of the lowly `maximum()` function, which returns the maximum of two
arguments. All of the following variations make sense:

```
int maximum(int n1, int n2); // return max of two integers
unsigned maximum (unsigned u1, unsigned u2);
double   maximum (double d1, double d2);
char     maximum (char c1, char c2);
```

I would like to implement `maximum()` for all four cases.

Of course, I could overload `maximum()` with all the possible versions:

```
double maximum(double d1, double d2)
{
    if (d1 > d2)
    {
        return d1;
    }
    return d2;
}
```

```
int maximum(int n1, int n2)
{
    if (n1 > n2)
    {
        return n1;
    }
    return n2;
}
char maximum(char c1, char c2)
{
    if (c1 > c2)
    {
        return c1;
    }
    return c2;
}

// ...repeat for all other numeric types...
```

This approach works. Now C++ selects the best match, maximum(int, int), for a reference such as maximum(1, 2). However, creating the same function for each type of variable is a gross waste of time.

The source code for all the maximum(T, T) functions follows the same pattern, where T is one of the numeric types. It would be so convenient if you could write the function once and let C++ supply the type T as needed when the function is used. In fact, C++ lets you do exactly this. These so-called *template definitions* are the subject of this chapter.

Generalizing a Function into a Template

A template function enables you to write something that looks like a function but uses one or more type holders that C++ converts into a true type at compile time.

The following MaxTemplate program defines a template for a generic maximum() function:

```
// MaxTemplate - create a template max() function
//               that returns the greater of two types
#include <cstdio>
#include <cstdlib>
#include <iostream>
#include <typeinfo>

using namespace std;

// simplistic exception class for this example only
```

```
template <class T> T maximum(T t1, T t2)
{
    if (t1 > t2)
    {
        return t1;
    }
    return t2;
};

int main(int argc, char* pArgs[])
{
    // find the maximum of two int's;
    // here C++ creates maximum(int, int)
    cout << "The maximum of -1 and 2 is "
         << maximum(-1, 2)
         << endl;

    // repeat for two doubles;
    // in this case, we have to provide T explicitly since
    // the types of the arguments is different
    cout << "The maximum of 1 and 2.5 is "
         << maximum<double>(1, 2.5)
         << endl;

    system("PAUSE");
    return 0;
}
```

The keyword template is followed by angle brackets containing one or more type holders known as template parameters, each preceded by the keyword class, a constant, or both. In this case, the definition of maximum<T>(T, T) will call the "unknown type" T. Following the angle brackets is what looks like a normal function definition. In this case, the template function T maximum<T>(T t1, T t2) returns the larger of two objects t1 and t2, each of which is of type T, where T is a class to be defined later.

A template function is useless until it is converted into a real function. C++ replaces T with an actual type known as a template argument. The main() function first invokes the template definition, passing two arguments of type int. In this case, C++ can instantiate the template providing int as the definition for T.

Creating a function from a template is called *instantiating* the template.

The second call is a problem — no single type can be provided for T in the template definition that matches both the int first argument and double second argument. Here the explicit reference instantiates the function maximum(double, double). C++ promotes the int argument 1 to the double 1.0 before making the call.

The output from this program appears as follows:

```
The maximum of -1 and 2 is 2
The maximum of 1 and 2.5 is 2.5
Press any key to continue . . .
```

Be careful about terminology. For example, I'm a hip, bad bicyclist, which is not the same thing as a bad hip bicyclist. Here's another example: A template function is not a function. The prototype for a template function is maximum<T>(T, T). The function that this template creates when T is int is the function (not template function) maximum(int, int). Your life will be easier if you remember to keep the terms straight.

Template Classes

C++ also allows the programmer to define template classes. A *template class* follows the same principle of using a conventional class definition with a placeholder for some unknown support classes. For example, the following TemplateVector program creates a vector for any class that the user provides. (A *vector* is a type of container in which the objects are stored in a row; an *array* is the classic vector example.)

```cpp
// TemplateVector - implement a vector that uses a
//                  template type
#include <cstdlib>
#include <cstdio>
#include <iostream>
using namespace std;

// TemplateVector - a simple templatized array
template <class T>
class TemplateVector
{
  public:
    TemplateVector(int nArraySize)
    {
        // store off the number of elements
        nSize = nArraySize;
        array = new T[nArraySize];
        reset();
    }
    int size() { return nWriteIndex; }
    void reset() { nWriteIndex = 0; nReadIndex = 0; }
    void add(const T& object)
    {
        if (nWriteIndex < nSize)
        {
            array[nWriteIndex++] = object;
        }
```

```
        }
        T& get()
        {
            return array[nReadIndex++];
        }

    protected:
        int nSize;
        int nWriteIndex;
        int nReadIndex;
        T* array;
};

// create and display two vectors:
//         one of integers and another of names
void intFn();
void nameFn();

int main(int argc, char* pArgs[])
{
    intFn();
    nameFn();

    system("PAUSE");
    return 0;
}

// intFn() - manipulate a collection of integers
void intFn()
{
    // create a vector of integers
    TemplateVector<int> integers(10);

    // add values to the vector
    cout << "Enter integer values to add to a vector\n"
         << "(Enter a negative number to terminate):"
         << endl;
    for(;;)
    {
        int n;
        cin  >> n;

        if (n < 0) { break; }
        integers.add(n);
    }

    cout << "\nHere are the numbers you entered:" << endl;
    for(int i = 0; i < integers.size(); i++)
    {
        cout << i << ":" << integers.get() << endl;
    }
}

// Names - create and manipulate a vector of names
```

```
class Name
{
  public:
    Name() = default;
    Name(string s) : name(s) {}
    const string& display() { return name; }
  protected:
    string name;
};

void nameFn()
{
    // create a vector of Name objects
    TemplateVector<Name> names(20);

    // add values to the vector
    cout << "Enter names to add to a second vector\n"
         << "(Enter an 'x' to quit):" << endl;
    for(;;)
    {
        string s;
        cin >> s;
        if (s == "x" || s == "X") { break; }
        names.add(Name(s));
    }

    cout << "\nHere are the names you entered" << endl;
    for(int i = 0; i < names.size(); i++)
    {
        Name& name = names.get();
        cout << i << ":" << name.display() << endl;
    }
}
```

The template class `TemplateVector<T>` contains an array of objects of class `T`. The template class presents two member functions: `add()` and `get()`. The `add()` function adds an object of class `T` into the next empty spot in the array. The corresponding function `get()` returns the next object in the array. The `nWriteIndex` and `nReadIndex` members keep track of the next empty entry and the next entry to read, respectively.

The `intFn()` function creates a vector of integers with room for 10 with the declaration:

```
TemplateVector<int> integers(10);
```

The program reads integer values from the keyboard, saves them off, and then spits the values back out using the functions provided by `TemplateVector`.

The second function, `nameFn()`, creates a vector of `Name` objects. Again, the function reads in names and then displays them back to the user.

Notice that the `TemplateVector` handles both `int` values and `Name` objects with equal ease. Notice also the similarity between the `nameFn()` and `intFn()` functions, even though integers and names have nothing to do with each other.

A sample session appears as follows (I've bolded input from the keyboard):

```
Enter integer values to add to a vector
(Enter a negative number to terminate):
5
10
15
-1

Here are the numbers you entered:
0:5
1:10
2:15
Enter names to add to a second vector
(Enter an 'x' to quit):
Chester
Trude
Lollie
Bodie
x

Here are the names you entered
0:Chester
1:Trude
2:Lollie
3:Bodie
Press any key to continue . . .
```

Tips for Using Templates

You should remember a few things when using templates. First, no code is generated for a template. (Code is generated after the template is converted into a concrete class or function.) This implies that a `.cpp` source file is almost never associated with a template class. The entire template class definition, including all the member functions, is contained in the `include` file so that it can be available for the compiler to expand.

Second, a template class does not consume memory. Therefore, there is no penalty for creating template classes if they are never instanced. On the other hand, a template class uses memory every time it is instanced. Thus, the code for `Array<Student>` consumes memory even if `Array<int>` already exists.

Finally, a template class cannot be compiled and checked for errors until it is converted into a real class. Thus, a program that references the template class `Array<T>` might compile even though `Array<T>` contains obvious syntax errors. The errors won't appear until a class such as `Array<int>` or `Array<Student>` is created.

Chapter 27

Standardizing on the Standard Template Library

Some programs can deal with data as it arrives and dispense with it. Most programs, however, must store data for later processing. A structure that is used to store data is known generically as a *container* or a *collection*. (I use the terms interchangeably.) This book has relied heavily on the array for data storage so far. The array container has a couple of nice properties: It stores and retrieves things quickly. In addition, the array can be declared to hold any type of object in a type-safe way. Weighed against these advantages, however, are two large negatives.

First, you must know the size of the array at the time it is created. This requirement is generally not achievable, although you will sometimes know that the number of elements cannot exceed some "large value." Viruses, however, commonly exploit this type of "it can't be larger than this" assumption, which turns out to be incorrect. There is no real way to "grow" an array except to declare a new array and copy the contents of the old array into the newer, larger version.

Second, inserting elements anywhere within the array involves copying elements within the array. This is costly in terms of both memory and computing time. Sorting the elements within an array is even more expensive.

C++ now comes with the Standard Template Library, or STL, which includes many different types of containers, each with its own set of advantages (and disadvantages).

> The C++ Standard Template Library is a very large library of sometimes-complex containers. This session is considered just an overview of the power of the STL.

The string Container

The most common form of array is the null-terminated character string used to display text, which clearly shows both the advantages and disadvantages of the array. Consider how easy the following appears:

```
cout << "This is a string";
```

But things go sour quickly when you try to perform an operation even as simple as concatenating two of these null-terminated strings:

```
char* concatCharString(const char* s1, const char* s2)
{
    int length = strlen(s1) + strlen(s2) + 1;
    char* s = new char[length];
    strcpy(s, s1);
    strcat(s, s2);
    return s;
}
```

The STL provides a `string` container to handle display strings. The `string` class provides a number of operations (including overloaded operators) to simplify the manipulation of character strings (see Table 27-1). The same `concat()` operation can be performed as follows using `string` objects:

```
string concat(const string& s1, const string& s2)
{
    return s1 + s2;
}
```

Table 27-1	Major Methods of the `string` Class
Method	**Meaning**
`string()`	Creates an empty string object.
`string(const char*)`	Creates a string object from a null-terminated character array.
`string(const string& s)`	Creates a new `string` object as a copy of an existing `string` object s.
`~string()`	Destructor returns internal memory to the heap.

Method	Meaning
`string& operator=(const string& s)`	Overwrites the current object with a copy of the string s.
`istream& operator>>()`	Extracts a string from the input file. Stops when after `istream::width()` characters read, error occurs, EOF encountered, or white space encountered. Guaranteed to not overflow the internal buffer.
`ostream& operator<<()`	Inserts string to the output file.
`string operator+(const string& s1,` `const string& s2)` `string operator+(const sring& s1,` `const char* pszS2)`	Creates a new string that is the concatenation of two existing strings.
`string& operator+=(` `const string& s);` `string& Operator+=(` `const char* pszS)`	Appends a string to the end of the current string.
`char& operator[](size_type index)`	Returns the index'th character of the current string.
`bool operator==(const string& s1,` `const string& s2)`	Returns true if the two strings are lexographically equivalent.
`bool operator<(const string& s1,` `const string& s2)`	Returns true if s1 is lexicographically less than s2 (i.e., if s1 occurs before s2 in the dictionary).
`bool operator>(const string& s1,` `const string& s2)`	Returns true if s1 is lexicographically greater than s2 (i.e., if s1 occurs after s2 in the dictionary).
`string& append(const string& s)` `string& append(const char* pszS)`	Appends a string to the end of the current string.
`char at(size_type index)`	Returns a reference to the index'th character in the current string.
`size_t capacity()`	Returns the number of characters the current string object can accommodate without allocating more space from the heap.

(continued)

Table 27-1 *(continued)*

Method	Meaning
`int compare(const string& s)`	Returns < 0 if the current object is lexicographically less than s, 0 if the current object is equal to s, and > 0 if the current object is greater than s.[*]
`const char* c_str()` `const char* data()`	Returns a pointer to the null-terminated character array string within the current object.
`bool empty()`	Returns true if the current object is empty.
`size_t find(const string& s,` `    size_t index = 0);`	Searches for the substring s within the current string starting at the index'th character. Returns the index of the substring. Return string::npos if the substring is not found.

`string& insert(size_t index,`
`    const string& s)`
`string& insert(size_t index,`
`    const char* pszS)`
	Inserts a string into the current string starting at offset index.

`size_t max_size()`	Returns the maximum number of objects that a string object can hold, ever.

`string& replace(size_t index,`
`    size_t num,`
`    const string& s)`
`string& replace(size_t index,`
`    size_t num,`
`    const char* pszS)`
	Replaces num characters in the current string starting at offset index. Enlarges the size of the current string if necessary.

`void resize(size_t size)`	Resizes the internal buffer to the specified length.
`size_t size()` `size_t length()`	Returns the length of the current string.
`string substr(size_t index,` `    size_t length)`	Returns a string consisting of the current string starting at offset index and continuing for length characters.

The C++ '09 standard says that functions such as `max_size()` return a number of type `size_type`. I have listed the argument types in Table 27-1 as `size_t` because that's the way they are declared in the gcc compiler that comes with this book. Currently they are both synonyms for `unsigned long int`. Be forewarned that at some future date these two types might diverge and the argument types in Table 27-1 might change from `size_t` to `size_type`.

The following STLString program demonstrates just a few of the capabilities of the `string` class:

```cpp
// STLString - demonstrates just a few of the features
//             of the string class which is part of the
//             Standard Template Library
#include <cstdlib>
#include <cstdio>
#include <iostream>
using namespace std;

// removeSpaces - remove any spaces within a string
string removeSpaces(const string& source)
{
    // make a copy of the source string so that we don't
    // modify it
    string s = source;

    // find the offset of the first space;
    // search the string until no more spaces found
    size_t offset;
    while((offset = s.find(" ")) != string::npos)
    {
        // remove the space just discovered
        s.erase(offset, 1);
    }
    return s;
}

// insertPhrase - insert a phrase in the position of
//                <ip> for insertion point
string insertPhrase(const string& source)
{
    string s = source;
    size_t offset = s.find("<ip>");
    if (offset != string::npos)
    {
        s.erase(offset, 4);
        s.insert(offset, "Randall");
    }
    return s;
```

```
    }

int main(int argc, char* pArgs[])
{
    // create a string that is the sum of two strings
    cout << "string1 + string2 = "
         << (string("string 1") + string("string 2"))
         << endl;

    // create a test string and then remove all spaces
    // from it using simple string methods
    string s2("This is a test string");
    cout << "<" << s2 << "> minus spaces = <"
         << removeSpaces(s2) << ">" << endl;

    // insert a phrase within the middle of an existing
    // sentence (at the location of "<ip>")
    string s3 = "Stephen <ip> Davis";
    cout << s3 + " -> " + insertPhrase(s3) << endl;

    system("PAUSE");
    return 0;
}
```

The `main()` function begins by using `operator+()` to append two strings
together. `main()` then calls the `removeSpaces()` method to remove any
spaces found in the string provided. It does this by using the `string.`
`find()` operation to return the offset of the first " " that it finds. Once found,
`removeSpaces()` uses the `erase()` method to remove the space. The function picks up where it left off, searching for spaces and erasing them until
`find()` returns `npos`, indicating that it didn't find what it was looking for.

The constant `npos` is a constant of type `size_t` that is the largest unsigned
value possible. It is numerically equal to –1.

The `insertPhrase()` method uses the `find()` method to find the insertion point flagged by the substring `"<ip>"`. The function then calls `erase`
to remove the `"<ip>"` flag and `string.insert()` to insert a new string in the
middle of an existing string.

The resulting output is as follows:

```
string1 + string2 = string1string2
<this is a test string> minus spaces = <thisisateststring>
Stephen <ip> Davis -> Stephen Randall Davis
Press any key to continue . . .
```

The `string` class is actually an instantiation of the template class `basic_class<T>` with `T` set to `char`. The `wstring` class is another name for `basic_class<wchar_t>`. This class provides the same character manipulations shown here for wide strings. The C++ '09 definition adds `u16string` and `u32string`, which extends the string manipulation methods to UTF-16 and UTF-32 character strings. All comparisons between two string objects are performed lexicographically — that is, which of the two strings would appear first in the dictionary of the current language.

Iterating through Lists

The Standard Template Library provides a large number of containers — many more than I can describe in a single session. However, I provide here a description of one of the more useful families of containers.

The STL `list` container retains objects by linking them like Lego blocks. (Chapter 13 shows a simplistic implementation of a linked list.) Objects can be snapped apart and snapped back together in any order. This makes the `list` ideal for inserting objects, sorting, merging, and otherwise rearranging objects. Table 27-2 shows some of the methods of the `list` containers.

Table 27-2	Major Methods of the `list` Template Class
Method	**Meaning**
`list<T>()`	Creates an empty list of objects of class `T`.
`~list<T>()`	Destructs the list, including invoking the destructor on any `T` objects remaining in the list.
`list operator=(const list<T>& l)`	Replaces the contents of the current list with copies of the objects in list `l`.
`bool operator==(const list<T>& l1, const list<T>& l2)`	Performs a lexicographic comparison between each element in the two lists.
`list<T>::iterator begin()`	Returns an iterator that points to the first element in the current list.
`void clear()`	Removes and destructs every object in the current list.
`bool empty()`	Returns true if the current list is empty.

(continued)

Table 27-2 *(continued)*

Method	Meaning
`list<T>::iterator end()`	Returns an iterator that points to the next entry beyond the end of the current list.

`list<T>::iterator insert(`
`   list<T>::iterator loc,`
`   const T& object)`
	Adds `object` to the list at the position pointed at by the iterator `loc`. Returns an iterator that points to the added object.

`void pop_back()` `void pop_front()`	Removes the last or first object from the current list.

`void push_back(const T&`
`object)`
`void push_front(const T&`
`object)`
	Adds an object to the end or front of the current list.

`list<T>::reverse_iterator` `rbegin()`	Returns an iterator that points to the last entry in the list (useful when iterating backward through the list, starting at the end and working toward the beginning).
`list<T>::reverse_iterator` `rend()`	Returns an iterator that points to the entry before the first entry in the list (useful when iterating backwards through the list).
`void remove(const T&` `object)`	Removes all objects from the current list that are the same as `object` (as determined by `operator==(T&, T&)`).
`size_t size()`	Returns the number of entries in the current list.
`void sort()`	Sorts the current list such that each object in the list is less than the next object as determined by `operator<(T&, T&)`.

`void`
`splice(list<T>::iterator`
`pos,`
`   list<T>& source)`
	Removes the objects from the `source` list and adds them to the current list in front of the object referenced by `pos`.

`void unique()`	Removes any subsequent equal objects (as determined by `operator==(T&, T&)`).

The constructor for list<T> creates an empty list. Objects can be added either to the front or end of the list using the push_front() or push_back(). For example, the following code snippet creates an empty list of Student objects and adds two to the list:

```
list<Student> students;
students.push_back(Student("Dewie Cheatum"));
students.push_back(Student("Marion Haste"));
```

Making your way through a list

The programmer iterates through an array by providing the index of each element. However, this technique doesn't work for containers like list that don't allow for random access. One could imagine a solution based in methods such as getFirst() and getNext(); however, the designers of the Standard Template Library wanted to provide a common method for traversing any type of container. For this, the Standard Template Library defines the iterator.

An *iterator* is an object that points to the members of a container. In general, every iterator supports the following functions:

✔ A class can return an iterator that points to the first member of the collection.

✔ The iterator can be moved from one member to the next.

✔ The program can retrieve the element pointed to by the iterator.

The Standard Template Library also provides reverse iterators for moving backward through lists. Everything I say about iterators applies equally for reverse iterators.

The code necessary to iterate through a list is different from that necessary to traverse a vector (to name just two examples). However, the iterator hides these details.

The method begin() returns an iterator that points to the first element in the list. The indirection operator*() retrieves a reference to the object pointed at by the iterator. The ++ operator moves the iterator to the next element in the list. A program continues to increment its way through the list until the iterator is equal to the value returned by end(). The following code snippet starts at the beginning of a list of students and displays each of their names:

```
void displayStudents(list<Student>& students)
{
    // allocate an iterator that points to the first
    // element in the list
    list<Student>::iterator iter = students.begin();

    // continue to loop through the list until the
    // iterator hits the end of the list
    while(iter != students.end())
    {
        // retrieve the Student the iterator points at
        Student& s = *iter;
        cout << s.sName << endl;

        // now move the iterator over to the next element
        // in the list
        iter++;
    }
}
```

Declarations for iterators can get very complex. This is probably the best justification for the `auto` declaration introduced with the '09 standard:

```
for(auto iter = students.end(); iter != students.end(); iter++)
{
    cout << iter->sName << endl;
}
```

This declares `iter` to be an iterator of whatever type is returned by the method `list<Student>::end()`, avoiding the tortured declarations shown in the earlier code snippet. How cool is that!

Operations on an entire list

The STL library defines certain operations on the entire list. For example, the `list<T>::sort()` method says "I'll sort the list for you if you'll just tell me which objects go first." You do this by defining `operator<(T&, T&)`. This operator is already defined for the intrinsic types and many library classes such as `string`. For example, you don't have to do anything to sort a list of integers:

```
list<int> scores;
scores.push_back(10);
scores.push_back(1);
scores.push_back(5);
scores.sort();
```

The programmer must define her own comparison operator for her own classes if she wants C++ to sort them. For example, the following comparison sorts `Student` objects by their student ID:

```
bool operator<(const Student& s1, const Student& s2)
{
    return s1.ssID < s2.ssID;
}
```

Can you show me an example?

The following STLListStudents program demonstrates several functions
you've seen in this section. It creates a list of user-defined Student objects,
iterates the list, and sorts the list.

The program appears as follows:

```
// STLListStudents - use a list to contain and sort a
//                   user defined class
#include <cstdio>
#include <cstdlib>
#include <iostream>
#include <list>

using namespace std;

// Student - some example user defined class
class Student
{
  public:
    Student(const char* pszS, int id)
      : sName(pszS), ssID(id) {}
    string sName;
    int ssID;
};

// the following function is required to support the
// sort operation
bool operator<(const Student& s1, const Student& s2)
{
    return s1.ssID < s2.ssID;
}

// displayStudents - iterate through the list displaying
//                   each element
void displayStudents(list<Student>& students)
{
    // allocate an iterator that points to the first
    // element in the list
    list<Student>::iterator iter = students.begin();

    // continue to loop through the list until the
    // iterator hits the end of the list
    while(iter != students.end())
    {
```

```
            // retrieve the Student the iterator points at
            Student& s = *iter;
            cout << s.ssID << " - " << s.sName << endl;

            // now move the iterator over to the next element
            // in the list
            iter++;
        }
    }

    int main(int argc, char* pArgs[])
    {
        // define a collection of students
        list<Student> students;

        // add three student objects to the list
        students.push_back(Student("Marion Haste", 10));
        students.push_back(Student("Dewie Cheatum", 5));
        students.push_back(Student("Stew Dent", 15));

        // display the list
        cout << "The original list:" << endl;
        displayStudents(students);

        // now sort the list and redisplay
        students.sort();
        cout << "\nThe sorted list:" << endl;
        displayStudents(students);

        system("PAUSE");
        return 0;
    }
```

This program defines a list of user-defined `Student` objects. Three calls to `push_back()` add elements to the list (hard-coding these calls keeps the program smaller). The program then calls `displayStudents()` to display the contents of the list both before and after the list has been sorted using the template library `sort()` function.

The output of this program appears as follows:

```
The original list:
10 - Marion Haste
5 - Dewie Cheatum
15 - Stew Dent

The sorted list:
5 - Dewie Cheatum
10 - Marion Haste
15 - Stew Dent
Press any key to continue . . .
```

Part VI
The Part of Tens

The 5th Wave   By Rich Tennant

"We're here to clean the code."

In this part . . .

What *For Dummies* book would be complete without a Part of Tens? In Chapter 28, I cover ten ways to avoid adding bugs to your C++ program. (Most of these suggestions work for C programs too, at no extra charge.)

Chapter 29 lists ten major additions to the language in recent years. Each of these extensions seems to be dragging the language in a different direction. Once you feel comfortable with the topics covered in this book, you may want to use this section as a guide in your further studies of the language.

Chapter 28

Ten Ways to Avoid Adding Bugs to Your Program

. . . .

In This Chapter

▶ Enabling all warnings and error messages

▶ Using a clear and consistent coding style

▶ Limiting the visibility

▶ Adding comments to your code while you write it

▶ Single-stepping every path at least once

▶ Avoiding overloaded operators

▶ Heap handling

▶ Using exceptions to handle errors

▶ Use static assertions

▶ Avoiding multiple inheritance

. . . .

In this chapter, I look at several ways to minimize errors, as well as ways to make debugging the errors that are introduced easier.

Enable All Warnings and Error Messages

The syntax of C++ allows for a lot of error checking. When the compiler encounters a construct that it can't decipher, it has no choice but to generate an error message. Although the compiler attempts to sync back up with the next statement, it does not attempt to generate an executable program.

Disabling warning and error messages is a bit like unplugging the Check Engine light on your car dashboard because it bothers you: Ignoring the problem doesn't make it go away. If your compiler has a Syntax Check from Hell mode, enable it.

Don't start debugging your code until you remove or at least understand all warnings generated during compilation. Enabling all warning messages if you then ignore them does you no good. If you don't understand the warning, look it up. What you don't know *will* hurt you.

Adopt a Clear and Consistent Coding Style

Coding in a clear and consistent style not only enhances the readability of your program but also results in fewer coding mistakes. Remember, the less brain power you have to spend deciphering C++ syntax, the more you have left over for thinking about the logic of the program at hand. A good coding style enables you to do the following with ease:

- Differentiate class names, object names, and function names
- Know something about the object based on its name
- Differentiate preprocessor symbols from C++ symbols (that is, #defined objects should stand out)
- Identify blocks of C++ code at the same level (this is the result of consistent indentation)

In addition, you need to establish a standard module header that provides information about the functions or classes in the module, the author (presumably, that's you), the date, the version of the compiler you're using, and a modification history.

Finally, all programmers involved in a single project should use the same style. Trying to decipher a program with a patchwork of different coding styles is confusing.

Limit the Visibility

Limiting the visibility of class internals to the outside world is a cornerstone of object-oriented programming. The class is responsible for its own internals; the application is responsible for using the class to solve the problem at hand.

Specifically, limited visibility means that data members should not be accessible outside the class — that is, they should be marked as protected. (Another storage class, private, is not discussed in this book.) In addition, member functions that the application software does not need to know about should also be marked protected. Don't expose any more of the class internals than necessary.

A related rule is that public member functions should trust application code as little as possible. Any argument passed to a public member function should be treated as though it might cause bugs until it has been proven safe. A function such as the following is an accident waiting to happen:

```cpp
class Array
{
  public:
    explicit Array(int s)
    {
        size = 0;
        // new throws exception if memory not available
        pData = new int[s];
        size = s;
    }
    ~Array()
    {
        delete pData;
        size = 0;
        pData = 0;
    }
    //either return or set the array data
    int data(int index)
    {
        return pData[index];
    }
    int data(int index, int newValue)
    {
        int oldValue = pData[index];
        pData[index] = newValue;
        return oldValue;
    }
  protected:
    int size;
    int *pData;
};
```

The function data(int) allows the application software to read data out of Array. This function is too trusting; it assumes that the index provided is within the data range. What if the index is not? The function data(int, int) is even worse because it overwrites an unknown location.

What's needed is a check to make sure that the index is in range. In the following, only the data(int) function is shown for brevity:

```
int data(unsigned int index)
{
    if (index >= size)
    {
        throw Exception("Array index out of range");
    }
    return pData[index];
}
```

Now an out-of-range index will be caught by the check. (Making index unsigned precludes the necessity of adding a check for negative index values.)

Comment Your Code While You Write It

You can avoid errors if you comment your code while you write it rather than wait until everything works and then go back and add comments. I can understand not taking the time to write voluminous headers and function descriptions until later, but you always have time to add short comments while writing the code.

Short comments should be enlightening. If they're not, they aren't worth much. You need all the enlightenment you can get while you're trying to make your program work. When you look at a piece of code you wrote a few days ago, comments that are short, descriptive, and to the point can make a dramatic contribution to helping you figure out exactly what it was you were trying to do.

In addition, consistent code indentation and naming conventions make the code easier to understand. It's all very nice when the code is easy to read after you're finished with it, but it's just as important that the code be easy to read while you're writing it. That's when you need the help.

Single-Step Every Path at Least Once

It may seem like an obvious statement, but I'll say it anyway: As a programmer, it's important for you to understand what your program is doing. Nothing gives you a better feel for what's going on under the hood than single-stepping the program with a good debugger. (Code::Blocks contains an integrated debugger.)

Beyond that, as you write a program, you sometimes need raw material to figure out some bizarre behavior. Nothing gives you that material better than single-stepping new functions as they come into service.

Finally, when a function is finished and ready to be added to the program, every logical path needs to be traveled at least once. Bugs are much easier to find when the function is examined by itself rather than after it has been thrown into the pot with the rest of the functions — and your attention has gone on to new programming challenges.

Avoid Overloading Operators

Other than using the assignment operator `operator=()`, you should hold off overloading operators until you feel comfortable with C++. Overloading operators other than assignment is almost never necessary and can significantly add to your debugging woes as a new programmer. You can get the same effect by defining and using the proper public member functions instead.

After you've been C-plus-plussing for a few months, feel free to return and start overloading operators to your heart's content.

Manage the Heap Systematically

As a general rule, programmers should allocate and release heap memory at the same "level." If a member function `MyClass::create()` allocates a block of heap memory and returns it to the caller, there should be a member function `MyClass::release()` that returns the memory to the heap. Specifically, `MyClass::create()` should not require the parent function to release the memory. This certainly doesn't avoid all memory problems — the parent function may forget to call `MyClass::release()` — but it does reduce the possibility somewhat.

Use Exceptions to Handle Errors

The exception mechanism in C++ is designed to handle errors conveniently and efficiently. In general, you should throw an error indicator rather than return an error flag. The resulting code is easier to write, read, and maintain. Besides, other programmers have come to expect it — you wouldn't want to disappoint them, would you?

It is not necessary to throw an exception from a function that returns a "didn't work" indicator if this is a part of everyday life for that function. Consider a function lcd() that returns the least common denominators of a number passed to it as an argument. That function will not return any values when presented a prime number (a prime number cannot be evenly divided by any other number). This is not an error — the lcd() function has nothing to say when given a prime.

Declare Destructors Virtual

Don't forget to create a destructor for your class if the constructor allocates resources (such as heap memory) that need to be returned when the object reaches its demise. Having created a destructor, don't forget to declare it virtual (almost) every time especially if you know that your class is likely to be inherited and extended by subclasses. The problem is demonstrated in the following code snippet:

```
class Person
{
  public:
    Person(char* pszName) { psName = new string(pszName); }
    ~Person() { delete psName; psName = 0; }

  protected:
    string* psName;
};
class Student : public Person
{
  public:
    Student(char* pszName, unsigned ID)
        : Person(pszName), mID(ID) {}

  protected:
    unsigned mID;
};

void fn()
{
    Student student("Stewart Dent", 1234);
}
```

The function fn() creates a student object. The Student class extends a class Person that allocates heap memory to hold the person's name in the constructor and returns it in the destructor. The Person constructor is dutifully invoked by fn() when the student object is created. Unfortunately, the ~Person() destructor is not invoked when the student goes out of scope because it has not been declared virtual.

Making the following change to the class solves the problem:

```
class Person
{
  public:
    Person(char* pszName) { psName = new string(pszName);}
    virtual ~Person() { delete psName; psName = 0; }

  protected:
    string* psName;
};
```

Okay, so when should I not declare the destructor virtual? Declaring any member in a class virtual means that C++ must add an extra pointer or two to each object of that class to keep track of its virtual members. Thus, if you were to declare a lot of `Person` objects, an extra few pointers per object might be a big deal.

As a general rule, if you expect to have your destructor invoked, declare it virtual. And if you are about to inherit from an existing base class, make sure that its destructor is declared virtual.

Avoid Multiple Inheritance

Multiple inheritance, like operator overloading, adds another level of complexity that you don't need to deal with when you're just starting out. Fortunately, most real-world relationships can be described with single inheritance.

Feel free to use multiple-inherited classes from commercial libraries. For example, the Microsoft MFC classes that are key to Visual Studio 6 make heavy use of multiple inheritance. Microsoft has spent a considerable amount of time setting up its classes, and it knows what it's doing.

After you feel comfortable with your level of understanding of C++, experiment with setting up some multiple inheritance hierarchies. That way, you'll be ready when the unusual situation that requires multiple inheritance to describe it accurately arises.

Chapter 29

Ten Major Recent Additions to C++

In This Chapter

▶ Using smart pointers

▶ Initializing objects with a variable-length list

▶ Initializing data members inline

▶ Instantiating an extern template

▶ Implementing thread local storage

▶ Using r-value references to avoid creating copies of objects

▶ Implementing concepts

▶ Defining lamda expressions

▶ Defining variadic templates

▶ Using typeid

In this chapter, I look at ten major additions to the C++ language. Most (but not all) of these additions weren't made formal until the release of the C++ 2009 standard. All of these topics are beyond the range of an introductory book; I merely touch on these topics to give you an idea of where you might want to study next.

Use Smart Pointers

Loss of memory due to forgetting to return memory to the heap is one of the biggest sources of error in C++ programs. Both Java and C#, two followers to the C++ language, instituted a process known as *garbage collection* that collects unreferenced memory and returns it to the heap for you. Garbage collection has been discussed for C++ as well but has been rejected for several reasons, including the overhead it levies on your program.

The problem could be "solved" if dynamically allocated memory were tied to an object rather than a pointer. The destructor of an object is invoked when it goes out of scope. This destructor could keep track of when it was appropriate to return the memory to the heap.

The standard library includes a `shared_ptr<T>` template class, which allocates memory off the heap and returns it to the heap when necessary. This template class also overloads the necessary operators to give it the look and feel of an actual pointer, as demonstrated in the following code snippet:

```
struct MyClass
{
    int value;
};
void fn()
{
    // allocate a pointer and allocate it to an object
    shared_ptr<MyClass> ptrObj(new MyClass);

    // use the ptrObj like a real pointer to a MyClass
    // object
    ptrObj->value = 5;

    // destructor invoked when ptrObj goes out of scope
    // to return the memory to the heap
}
```

A `MyClass` object is allocated off the heap and its address assigned to a `ptrObj` for safekeeping. This `ptrObj` can be used exactly like a pointer. The `shared_ptr<MyClass>` class keeps track of the number of objects that reference that particular piece of memory,and when that count drops to 0 the destructor returns the memory to the heap.

Initialize Variables with a Variable-Length List

You have seen one case in which an initializer list can have a variable number of objects:

```
int array[] = {1, 2, 3};
```

In this case, the number of elements in the array is determined by simply counting the number of objects in the list. The C++ '09 definition extends this ability to other container classes through the introduction of the `initializer_list<T>` template class.

C++ tries to interpret any sequence of objects of the same type as an instance of `initialize_list<T>`. Thus, I might declare a container class as follows:

```
#include <initializer_list>
#include <list>
class MyContainer
{
  public:
    MyContainer(initializer_list<int> l)
    {
        nSize = l.size();

        // add each element in the initializer list to
        // our container elems
        for(auto ptr = l.begin(); ptr != l.end; ptr++)
        {
            elems.push_back(*ptr);
        }
    }

    int size() { return nSize;}

  protected:
    int nSize;
    list<int> elems;
};

// declare a MyContainer object
MyContainer myContainer1 = {1, 2, 3, 4, 5};
```

Notice that the constructor accepts an `initializer_list` object. This very simple list class provides a `size()` method to return the number of elements in the list along with a `begin()` and `end()` methods that return iterators just like those demonstrated in Chapter 27.

The `initializer_list` class extends to flexible initialization syntax available to arrays to more complex container types.

Initialize Data Members Inline

The programmer can initialize a variable when it is declared, as in the following:

```
int value = 10;
```

However, this ability did not extend to data members of classes. These could only be initialized in the constructor prior to '09:

```
// Version A
class MyClass
{
  public:
    MyClass() : value(10) {}

    int value;
};
```

The '09 definition extends initialization to data members as follows:

```
// Version B
class MyClass
{
  public:
    MyClass(){}

    int value = 10;
};
```

The compiler treats Version A and Version B exactly alike.

Instantiate an Extern Template

A template class does not generate code until it has been instantiated with a class. Once instantiated, however, it is difficult for a compiler to not repeat the process separately for every module that uses the template. Consider the following definition contained within an include file:

```
template <typename T>
  T max(T t1, T t2)
  {
      if (t1 > t2)
          return t1;
      return t2;
  }
```

Suppose that two source files, ModuleA and ModuleB, both invoke max(int, int). It should be possible for C++ to instantiate the template once and reference both modules to the same definition. This turns out to be very difficult to do.

It has always been possible to instantiate a template explicitly, for example including the following within ModuleA:

```
template int max<int>;
```

From within ModuleB (and every other module that uses `max<int>`) I can say:

```
extern template int max<int>;
```

This is equivalent to a prototype declaration. It tells the compiler that the `max()` function has been defined, but it also says that `max<T>` has been expanded somewhere else, in another module.

This use of `extern` may avoid the generation of a lot of duplicate source code caused by instantiating the same templates numerous times.

Implement Thread Local Storage

More and more computers are being offered with multicore options in which more than one CPU is included on the same piece of silicon. To get maximum advantage from a multicore processor, however, the programmer needs to divide her program to be able to execute in separate threads. Each thread can be assigned to its own processor and run independent of the other threads that make up the program.

Multithreading libraries have been available for C++ for years, but C++ '09 has taken the initial steps towards implementing multithreading within the language itself through the introduction of `thread_local` storage.

Variables that have global scope or static scope (see Chapter 6) are shared between all threads. Each thread gets its own copy of variables declared `thread_local` storage. A `thread_local` variable is constructed when the thread starts and its destructor is invoked when the thread exits.

The thread support library accessible through the include file `thread` contains functions for starting, stopping, and communicating with separate threads.

Use Rvalue References

Expressions can be divided into two types: lvalues and rvalues. An lvalue is a value that can appear on the left side of an assignment operator; an rvalue can appear only on the right. Some operators generate lvalues (the assignment operator itself, for example, returns an lvalue). Other operators, such as addition, return only rvalues. Thus, the following is not legal:

```
int a, b;
(a + b) = 3;  // error: a + b is an rvalue
```

Generally the values returned by a function are rvalues. The one big exception is that functions that return a reference to an object can appear on the left side of an assignment:

```
MyObject& fn1();
fn1() = MyObject();
```

Such assignments are performed by first creating the MyObject() and then copying it into the object referenced by fn1(). Copying the MyObject means reallocating and duplicating any resources created by the class. However, this is fairly ridiculous because we know that the MyObject created here is just a temporary anyway and will get destructed as soon as the assignment has been completed.

Rather than copy the temporary MyObject(), why not use move semantics and just "steal" any resources created by the constructor and hand them over to the object referenced by fn1()? The programmer can write much more efficient classes when she can differentiate between references to rvalues and lvalues being passed to a function.

The 2009 standard allows the programmer to express this difference as follows:

```
void fn(MyObject&  lhr); // argument is an lvalue
void fn(MyObject&& rhr); // argument is an rvalue
```

The details are beyond the scope of this book, but with judicious use of rvalue declarations, the programmer can greatly reduce the number of temporary objects created and destructed.

Implement Concepts

Multiple inheritance is often used by the programmer to tell the C++ compiler that a class has some capability, as shown in the following snippet:

```
class Assignable
{
  public:
    virtual Assignable& operator=(Assignable const&) = 0;
};
class MyClass : public BaseClass, public Assignable {...};
```

Any class that inherits from the abstract class `Assignable` must implement the assignment operator before it can be used to create an object. This is particularly useful in the implementation of template classes.

C++ '09 formalizes this promissory class in the form of a `concept`, defined as follows:

```
auto concept LessThanComparable<typename T>
{
    bool operator<(T, T);
}
```

A subsequent template definition can then rely upon this promise to implement the comparison operator:

```
template<typename T> requires LessThanComparable<T>
const T& min(const T& t1, const T& t2)
{
    if (t1 < t2)
        return t1;
    else
        return t2;
}
```

A sometimes more convenient construct allows the concept name to be used instead of the `typename` in the template definition as follows:

```
template <LessThanComparable T> class MyContainer
{
    // the following sort method uses the operator<()
    // comparison operator from class T to perform the
    // sort
    void sort();
    // ...class definition continues...
};
```

The concept approach generates considerably less code than using multiple inheritance for the same purpose. If you are familiar with Java or C#, you will recognize a lot of similarities between the role played by concepts in C++ and interfaces in those languages.

Define Lamda Expressions

Lambda expressions are a way to define function objects that are intended to be used locally in a concise way that does not interfere with the overall logic flow. Consider the following code snippet taken from the C++ '09 proposal.

```
double dUpperLimit = 1.1 * dMinSalary;
std::find_if(employees.begin(),employees.end(),
    [&](const employee& e)
             { return e.salary() >= dMinSalary && e.salary() < dUpperLimit; });
```

Here `employees` is a collection of `Employee` objects. The `find_if()` function takes as its arguments an iterator that points to where in the list to start (in this case, the beginning of the list), an iterator that points to where in the list to stop (in this case, the end of the list) and an object that implements some selection criteria.

Define Variadic Templates

Variadic templates allow the programmer to define a template with a variable number of classes:

```
template<typename... Attributes> class TableRow;
```

Now the class `TableRow` can be instantiated with any number of attributes.

```
class TableRow<int, string, std:list<Grades>> Student;
```

Note: C and C++ have always allowed variadic functions, functions with an unspecified number of arguments (`printf()` is an example of such a function). This extends the concept to class definitions.

Use typeid()

Normally the programmer should differentiate the difference between the declared type and the runtime type through virtual member functions:

```
class Base
{
  public:
    virtual aMethod();
};
class Derived : public Base
{
  public:
    virtual aMethod();
};

void fn(Base* pB)
{
    // which of the above functions is invoked is
```

```
    // determined at runtime based upon the runtime
    // type
    pB->aMethod();
}
```

However, it is possible to ask an object for its runtime type using the keyword `typeid`, which returns a reference to a constant of type `type_info`. Thus, the programmer could differentiate between subclasses of `Base` by comparing the value returned from `typeid` as follows:

```
void fn(Base* pB)
{
    // differentiate between type of Base object
    // using the typeid
    const type_info& ti = typeid(*pB);
    if (ti == typeid(Base))
    {
        // it's a Base object
    }
    else if (ti == typeid(Derived))
    {
        // it's actually a Derived object
    }
}
```

I stress *could* make the determination using `typeid` only because it's generally not a good idea; however, it is possible. This technique is especially useful when you are creating debug code and you don't want to modify either the `Base` or `Derived` classes because they are in separate modules that you don't control and can't modify.

Appendix

About the CD

*T*he CD-ROM accompanying *C++ For Dummies,* 6th Edition contains several features. All readers, no matter what system they're using, will appreciate the source code to the programs that appear in the book.

In addition, 32-bit Windows users will welcome the inclusion of the Code::Blocks development environment coupled with the GNU gcc compiler ready to be installed.

System Requirements

Make sure that your computer meets the minimum system requirements shown in the following list. If your computer doesn't match up to most of these requirements, you may have problems using the software and files on the CD. For the latest and greatest information, please refer to the ReadMe file located at the root of the CD-ROM:

✔ A PC running Microsoft Windows or Linux with kernel 2.4 or later or a Macintosh running Apple OS X or later

✔ An Internet connection

✔ A CD-ROM drive

If you need more information on the basics, check out these books published by Wiley Publishing, Inc.: *PCs For Dummies,* 11th Edition, by Dan Gookin; *Macs For Dummies,* 10th Edition, by Edward C. Baig; *iMacs For Dummies,* 5th Edition, by Mark L. Chambers; *Windows XP For Dummies,* 2nd Edition, and *Windows Vista For Dummies,* both by Andy Rathbone.

Using the CD

To install the items from the CD to your hard drive, follow these steps.

1. **Insert the CD into your computer's CD-ROM drive.**

   The license agreement appears.

   Note to Windows users: The interface won't launch if you have autorun disabled. In that case, choose Start➪Run. (For Windows Vista, choose Start➪All Programs➪Accessories➪Run.) In the dialog box that appears, type *D:\Start.exe*. (Replace *D* with the proper letter if your CD drive uses a different letter. If you don't know the letter, see how your CD drive is listed under My Computer.) Click OK.

   Note for Mac Users: When the CD icon appears on your desktop, double-click the icon to open the CD and double-click the Start icon.

   Note for Linux Users: The specifics of mounting and using CDs vary greatly between different versions of Linux. Please see the manual or help information for your specific system if you experience trouble using this CD.

2. **Read through the license agreement and then click the Accept button if you want to use the CD.**

   The CD interface appears. The interface allows you to browse the contents and install the programs with just a click of a button (or two).

What You'll Find on the CD

The following sections are arranged by category and provide a summary of the software and other goodies you'll find on the CD. If you need help with installing the items provided on the CD, refer to the installation instructions in the preceding section.

For each program listed, I provide the program platform (Windows or Mac) plus the type of software. The programs fall into one of the following categories:

✔ *Shareware programs* are fully functional, free, trial versions of copy-righted programs. If you like particular programs, register with their authors for a nominal fee and receive licenses, enhanced versions, and technical support.

✔ *Freeware programs* are free, copyrighted games, applications, and utili-ties. You can copy them to as many computers as you like — for free — but they offer no technical support.

✔ *GNU software* is governed by its own license, which is included inside the folder of the GNU software. There are no restrictions on distribu-tion of GNU software. See the GNU license at the root of the CD for more details.

✔ *Trial, demo,* or *evaluation* versions of software are usually limited either by time or functionality (such as not letting you save a project after you create it).

CPP programs

For all environments. All the examples provided in this book are located in the CPP_Programs directory on the CD and work with Macintosh, Linux, Unix, and Windows and later computers. These files contain the sample code from the book. Each example program is in its own folder. For example, the Conversion program from Chapter1 is in:

```
CPP_Programs/Chap01/Conversion
```

For Windows. I have built a set of workspace and set of project files for Code::Blocks that allows you to recompile all the programs in the book with a single mouse click. The AllPrograms.workspace file is located in the CPP_ Programs folder. (See Chapter 1 for an explanation of Code::Blocks Project files.)

Code::Blocks development environment

For Windows. Code::Blocks is a freeware environment designed to work with a number of different compilers. The version included on the CD-ROM is bundled with the GNU gcc C++ compiler (version 4.4).

Troubleshooting

I tried my best to compile programs that work on most computers with the minimum system requirements. Alas, your computer may differ, and some programs may not work properly for some reason.

Remember that most C++ compilers don't support the 2009 C++ standard as of this writing. Some of the programs included in the book may require some slight modification to compile on compilers other than GNU gcc version 4.4 or later. Specifically, not every feature used in the example programs are available in Visual Studio as of this writing. (Advanced features are flagged with the '09 icon in the book.)

Fortunately, the good people at GNU provide a gcc for almost every platform you can think of. You can download a version for your machine at `www.gnu.org`. A copy of gcc for 32-bit Windows is included with Code::Blocks on the enclosed CD-ROM.

Even gcc doesn't enable C++ '09 features by default. Be sure to follow the instructions in Chapter 1 to enable '09 features.

I include Code::Blocks workspace and project files for the included C++ source. This allows you to recompile all the program with literally a single click. However, these project files assume that the programs are installed in the directory C:\\CPP_Programs. You'll have to set up your own project files if you decide to install the source code in a different directory.

Other possible problems you might run into are not enough memory (RAM) for the programs you want to use, or having other programs running that are affecting installation or running of a program. If you get an error message such as `Not enough memory` or `Setup cannot continue`, try one or more of the following suggestions and then try using the software again:

- ✔ **Turn off any antivirus software running on your computer.** Installation programs sometimes mimic virus activity and may make your computer incorrectly believe that it's being infected by a virus.

- ✔ **Close all running programs.** The more programs you have running, the less memory is available to other programs. Installation programs typically update files and programs; so if you keep other programs running, installation may not work properly.

- ✔ **Have your local computer store add more RAM to your computer.** This is, admittedly, a drastic and somewhat expensive step. However, adding more memory can really help the speed of your computer and allow more programs to run at the same time.

Customer Care

If you have trouble with the CD-ROM, please call Wiley Product Technical Support at 800-762-2974. Outside the United States, call 317-572-3993. You can also contact Wiley Product Technical Support at `http://support.wiley.com`. Wiley Publishing will provide technical support only for installation and other general quality control items. For technical support on the applications themselves, consult the program's vendor or author at `www.stephendavis.com`.

To place additional orders or to request information about other Wiley products, please call 877-762-2974.

Index

• N •

INESS, CAREERS & PERSONAL FINANCE

nting For Dummies, 4th Edition*
470-24600-9

keeping Workbook For Dummies†
470-16983-4

nodities For Dummies
470-04928-0

Business in China For Dummies
470-04929-7

E-Mail Marketing For Dummies
978-0-470-19087-6

Job Interviews For Dummies, 3rd Edition*†
978-0-470-17748-8

Personal Finance Workbook For Dummies*†
978-0-470-09933-9

Real Estate License Exams For Dummies
978-0-7645-7623-2

Six Sigma For Dummies
978-0-7645-6798-8

Small Business Kit For Dummies,
2nd Edition*†
978-0-7645-5984-6

Telephone Sales For Dummies
978-0-470-16836-3

INESS PRODUCTIVITY & MICROSOFT OFFICE

s 2007 For Dummies
470-03649-5

2007 For Dummies
470-03737-9

2007 For Dummies
470-00923-9

ok 2007 For Dummies
470-03830-7

PowerPoint 2007 For Dummies
978-0-470-04059-1

Project 2007 For Dummies
978-0-470-03651-8

QuickBooks 2008 For Dummies
978-0-470-18470-7

Quicken 2008 For Dummies
978-0-470-17473-9

Salesforce.com For Dummies,
2nd Edition
978-0-470-04893-1

Word 2007 For Dummies
978-0-470-03658-7

CATION, HISTORY, REFERENCE & TEST PREPARATION

n American History For Dummies
7645-5469-8

ra For Dummies
7645-5325-7

ra Workbook For Dummies
7645-8467-1

story For Dummies
470-09910-0

ASVAB For Dummies, 2nd Edition
978-0-470-10671-6

British Military History For Dummies
978-0-470-03213-8

Calculus For Dummies
978-0-7645-2498-1

Canadian History For Dummies, 2nd Edition
978-0-470-83656-9

Geometry Workbook For Dummies
978-0-471-79940-5

The SAT I For Dummies, 6th Edition
978-0-7645-7193-0

Series 7 Exam For Dummies
978-0-470-09932-2

World History For Dummies
978-0-7645-5242-7

D, GARDEN, HOBBIES & HOME

For Dummies, 2nd Edition
71-92426-5

ollecting For Dummies, 2nd Edition
470-22275-1

g Basics For Dummies, 3rd Edition
645-7206-7

Drawing For Dummies
978-0-7645-5476-6

Etiquette For Dummies, 2nd Edition
978-0-470-10672-3

Gardening Basics For Dummies*†
978-0-470-03749-2

Knitting Patterns For Dummies
978-0-470-04556-5

Living Gluten-Free For Dummies†
978-0-471-77383-2

Painting Do-It-Yourself For Dummies
978-0-470-17533-0

TH, SELF HELP, PARENTING & PETS

Management For Dummies
70-03715-7

y & Depression Workbook
mmies
645-9793-0

For Dummies, 2nd Edition
645-4149-0

aining For Dummies, 2nd Edition
645-8418-3

Horseback Riding For Dummies
978-0-470-09719-9

Infertility For Dummies†
978-0-470-11518-3

Meditation For Dummies with CD-ROM,
2nd Edition
978-0-471-77774-8

Post-Traumatic Stress Disorder For Dummies
978-0-470-04922-8

Puppies For Dummies, 2nd Edition
978-0-470-03717-1

Thyroid For Dummies, 2nd Edition†
978-0-471-78755-6

Type 1 Diabetes For Dummies*†
978-0-470-17811-9

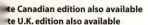
te Canadian edition also available
te U.K. edition also available

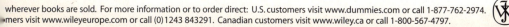
wherever books are sold. For more information or to order direct: U.S. customers visit www.dummies.com or call 1-877-762-2974.
mers visit www.wileyeurope.com or call (0)1243 843291. Canadian customers visit www.wiley.ca or call 1-800-567-4797.

WILEY

INTERNET & DIGITAL MEDIA

AdWords For Dummies
978-0-470-15252-2

Blogging For Dummies, 2nd Edition
978-0-470-23017-6

Digital Photography All-in-One Desk Reference For Dummies, 3rd Edition
978-0-470-03743-0

Digital Photography For Dummies, 5th Edition
978-0-7645-9802-9

Digital SLR Cameras & Photography For Dummies, 2nd Edition
978-0-470-14927-0

eBay Business All-in-One Desk Reference For Dummies
978-0-7645-8438-1

eBay For Dummies, 5th Edition*
978-0-470-04529-9

eBay Listings That Sell For Dummies
978-0-471-78912-3

Facebook For Dummies
978-0-470-26273-3

The Internet For Dummies, 11th Edition
978-0-470-12174-0

Investing Online For Dummies, 5th Edition
978-0-7645-8456-5

iPod & iTunes For Dummies, 5th E
978-0-470-17474-6

MySpace For Dummies
978-0-470-09529-4

Podcasting For Dummies
978-0-471-74898-4

Search Engine Optimization For Dummies, 2nd Edition
978-0-471-97998-2

Second Life For Dummies
978-0-470-18025-9

Starting an eBay Business For Du
3rd Edition†
978-0-470-14924-9

GRAPHICS, DESIGN & WEB DEVELOPMENT

Adobe Creative Suite 3 Design Premium All-in-One Desk Reference For Dummies
978-0-470-11724-8

Adobe Web Suite CS3 All-in-One Desk Reference For Dummies
978-0-470-12099-6

AutoCAD 2008 For Dummies
978-0-470-11650-0

Building a Web Site For Dummies, 3rd Edition
978-0-470-14928-7

Creating Web Pages All-in-One Desk Reference For Dummies, 3rd Edition
978-0-470-09629-1

Creating Web Pages For Dummies, 8th Edition
978-0-470-08030-6

Dreamweaver CS3 For Dummies
978-0-470-11490-2

Flash CS3 For Dummies
978-0-470-12100-9

Google SketchUp For Dummies
978-0-470-13744-4

InDesign CS3 For Dummies
978-0-470-11865-8

Photoshop CS3 All-in-One Desk Reference For Dummies
978-0-470-11195-6

Photoshop CS3 For Dummies
978-0-470-11193-2

Photoshop Elements 5 For Dum
978-0-470-09810-3

SolidWorks For Dummies
978-0-7645-9555-4

Visio 2007 For Dummies
978-0-470-08983-5

Web Design For Dummies, 2nd
978-0-471-78117-2

Web Sites Do-It-Yourself For Du
978-0-470-16903-2

Web Stores Do-It-Yourself For Du
978-0-470-17443-2

LANGUAGES, RELIGION & SPIRITUALITY

Arabic For Dummies
978-0-471-77270-5

Chinese For Dummies, Audio Set
978-0-470-12766-7

French For Dummies
978-0-7645-5193-2

German For Dummies
978-0-7645-5195-6

Hebrew For Dummies
978-0-7645-5489-6

Ingles Para Dummies
978-0-7645-5427-8

Italian For Dummies, Audio Set
978-0-470-09586-7

Italian Verbs For Dummies
978-0-471-77389-4

Japanese For Dummies
978-0-7645-5429-2

Latin For Dummies
978-0-7645-5431-5

Portuguese For Dummies
978-0-471-78738-9

Russian For Dummies
978-0-471-78001-4

Spanish Phrases For Dummies
978-0-7645-7204-3

Spanish For Dummies
978-0-7645-5194-9

Spanish For Dummies, Audio S
978-0-470-09585-0

The Bible For Dummies
978-0-7645-5296-0

Catholicism For Dummies
978-0-7645-5391-2

The Historical Jesus For Dumm
978-0-470-16785-4

Islam For Dummies
978-0-7645-5503-9

Spirituality For Dummies, 2nd Edition
978-0-470-19142-2

NETWORKING AND PROGRAMMING

ASP.NET 3.5 For Dummies
978-0-470-19592-5

C# 2008 For Dummies
978-0-470-19109-5

Hacking For Dummies, 2nd Edition
978-0-470-05235-8

Home Networking For Dummies, 4th Edition
978-0-470-11806-1

Java For Dummies, 4th Edition
978-0-470-08716-9

Microsoft® SQL Server™ 2008 All-in-One Desk Reference For Dummies
978-0-470-17954-3

Networking All-in-One Desk Reference For Dummies, 2nd Edition
978-0-7645-9939-2

Networking For Dummies, 8th Edition
978-0-470-05620-2

SharePoint 2007 For Dummies
978-0-470-09941-4

Wireless Home Networking For Dummies, 2nd Edition
978-0-471-74940-0

Wiley Publishing, Inc.
End-User License Agreement

GNU General Public License

Version 3, 29 June 2007

Copyright © 2007 Free Software Foundation, Inc. <http://fsf.org/>

Everyone is permitted to copy and distribute verbatim copies of this license document, but changing it is not allowed.

Preamble

The GNU General Public License is a free, copyleft license for software and other kinds of works.

The licenses for most software and other practical works are designed to take away your freedom to share and change the works. By contrast, the GNU General Public License is intended to guarantee your freedom to share and change all versions of a program–to make sure it remains free software for all its users. We, the Free Software Foundation, use the GNU General Public License for most of our software; it applies also to any other work released this way by its authors. You can apply it to your programs, too.

When we speak of free software, we are referring to freedom, not price. Our General Public Licenses are designed to make sure that you have the freedom to distribute copies of free software (and charge for them if you wish), that you receive source code or can get it if you want it, that you can change the software or use pieces of it in new free programs, and that you know you can do these things.

To protect your rights, we need to prevent others from denying you these rights or asking you to surrender the rights. Therefore, you have certain responsibilities if you distribute copies of the software, or if you modify it: responsibilities to respect the freedom of others.

For example, if you distribute copies of such a program, whether gratis or for a fee, you must pass on to the recipients the same freedoms that you received. You must make sure that they, too, receive or can get the source code. And you must show them these terms so they know their rights.

Developers that use the GNU GPL protect your rights with two steps: (1) assert copyright on the software, and (2) offer you this License giving you legal permission to copy, distribute and/or modify it.

For the developers' and authors' protection, the GPL clearly explains that there is no warranty for this free software. For both users' and authors' sake, the GPL requires that modified versions be marked as changed, so that their problems will not be attributed erroneously to authors of previous versions.

Some devices are designed to deny users access to install or run modified versions of the software inside them, although the manufacturer can do so. This is fundamentally incompatible with the aim of protecting users' freedom to change the software. The systematic pattern of such abuse occurs in the area of products for individuals to use, which is precisely where it is most unacceptable. Therefore, we have designed this version of the GPL to prohibit the practice for those products. If such problems arise substantially in other domains, we stand ready to extend this provision to those domains in future versions of the GPL, as needed to protect the freedom of users.

Finally, every program is threatened constantly by software patents. States should not allow patents to restrict development and use of software on general-purpose computers, but in those that do, we wish to avoid the special danger that patents applied to a free program could make it effectively proprietary. To prevent this, the GPL assures that patents cannot be used to render the program non-free.

The precise terms and conditions for copying, distribution and modification follow.

Terms and Conditions

0. **Definitions.** "This License" refers to version 3 of the GNU General Public License. "Copyright" also means copyright-like laws that apply to other kinds of works, such as semiconductor masks. "The Program" refers to any copyrightable work licensed under this License. Each licensee is addressed as "you". "Licensees" and "recipients" may be individuals or organizations. To "modify" a work means to copy from or adapt all or part of the work in a fashion requiring copyright permission, other than the making of an exact copy. The resulting work is called a "modified version" of the earlier work or a work "based on" the earlier work. A "covered work" means either the unmodified Program or a work based on the Program.

    To "propagate" a work means to do anything with it that, without permission, would make you directly or secondarily liable for infringement under applicable copyright law, except executing it on a computer or modifying a private copy. Propagation includes copying, distribution (with or without modification), making available to the public, and in some countries other activities as well.

    To "convey" a work means any kind of propagation that enables other parties to make or receive copies. Mere interaction with a user through a computer network, with no transfer of a copy, is not conveying.

    An interactive user interface displays "Appropriate Legal Notices" to the extent that it includes a convenient and prominently visible feature that (1) displays an appropriate copyright notice, and (2) tells the user that there is no warranty for the work (except to the extent that warranties are provided), that licensees may convey the work under this License, and how to view a copy of this License. If the interface presents a list of user commands or options, such as a menu, a prominent item in the list meets this criterion.

1. **Source Code.** T he "source code" for a work means the preferred form of the work for making modifications to it. "Object code" means any non-source form of a work. A "Standard Interface" means an interface that either is an official standard defined by a recognized standards body, or, in the case of interfaces specified for a particular programming language, one that is widely used among developers working in that language.

    The "System Libraries" of an executable work include anything, other than the work as a whole, that (a) is included in the normal form of packaging a Major Component, but which is not part of that Major Component, and (b) serves only to enable use of the work with that Major Component, or to implement a Standard Interface for which an implementation is available to the public in source code form. A "Major Component", in this context, means a major essential component (kernel, window system, and so on) of the specific operating system (if any) on which the executable work runs, or a compiler used to produce the work, or an object code interpreter used to run it.

    The "Corresponding Source" for a work in object code form means all the source code needed to generate, install, and (for an executable work) run the object code and to modify the work, including scripts to control those activities. However, it does not include the work's System Libraries, or general-purpose tools or generally available free programs which are used unmodified in performing those activities but which are not part of the work. For example, Corresponding Source includes interface definition files associated with source files for the work, and the source code for shared libraries and dynamically linked subprograms that the work is specifically designed to require, such as by intimate data communication or control flow between those subprograms and other parts of the work.

The Corresponding Source need not include anything that users can regenerate automatically from other parts of the Corresponding Source.

The Corresponding Source for a work in source code form is that same work.

2. **Basic Permissions.** All rights granted under this License are granted for the term of copyright on the Program, and are irrevocable provided the stated conditions are met. This License explicitly affirms your unlimited permission to run the unmodified Program. The output from running a covered work is covered by this License only if the output, given its content, constitutes a covered work. This License acknowledges your rights of fair use or other equivalent, as provided by copyright law.

You may make, run and propagate covered works that you do not convey, without conditions so long as your license otherwise remains in force. You may convey covered works to others for the sole purpose of having them make modifications exclusively for you, or provide you with facilities for running those works, provided that you comply with the terms of this License in conveying all material for which you do not control copyright. Those thus making or running the covered works for you must do so exclusively on your behalf, under your direction and control, on terms that prohibit them from making any copies of your copyrighted material outside their relationship with you.

Conveying under any other circumstances is permitted solely under the conditions stated below. Sublicensing is not allowed; section 10 makes it unnecessary.

3. **Protecting Users' Legal Rights From Anti-Circumvention Law.** No covered work shall be deemed part of an effective technological measure under any applicable law fulfilling obligations under article 11 of the WIPO copyright treaty adopted on 20 December 1996, or similar laws prohibiting or restricting circumvention of such measures.

When you convey a covered work, you waive any legal power to forbid circumvention of technological measures to the extent such circumvention is effected by exercising rights under this License with respect to the covered work, and you disclaim any intention to limit operation or modification of the work as a means of enforcing, against the work's users, your or third parties' legal rights to forbid circumvention of technological measures.

4. **Conveying Verbatim Copies.** You may convey verbatim copies of the Program's source code as you receive it, in any medium, provided that you conspicuously and appropriately publish on each copy an appropriate copyright notice; keep intact all notices stating that this License and any non-permissive terms added in accord with section 7 apply to the code; keep intact all notices of the absence of any warranty; and give all recipients a copy of this License along with the Program.

You may charge any price or no price for each copy that you convey, and you may offer support or warranty protection for a fee.

5. **Conveying Modified Source Versions.** You may convey a work based on the Program, or the modifications to produce it from the Program, in the form of source code under the terms of section 4, provided that you also meet all of these conditions:

a) The work must carry prominent notices stating that you modified it, and giving a relevant date.

b) The work must carry prominent notices stating that it is released under this License and any conditions added under section 7. This requirement modifies the requirement in section 4 to "keep intact all notices".

c) You must license the entire work, as a whole, under this License to anyone who comes into possession of a copy. This License will therefore apply, along with any applicable section 7 additional terms, to the whole of the work, and all its parts, regardless of how they are packaged. This License gives no permission to license the work in any other way, but it does not invalidate such permission if you have separately received it.

d) If the work has interactive user interfaces, each must display Appropriate Legal Notices; however, if the Program has interactive interfaces that do not display Appropriate Legal Notices, your work need not make them do so.

A compilation of a covered work with other separate and independent works, which are not by their nature extensions of the covered work, and which are not combined with it such as to form a larger program, in or on a volume of a storage or distribution medium, is called an "aggregate" if the compilation and its resulting copyright are not used to limit the access or legal rights of the compilation's users beyond what the individual works permit. Inclusion of a covered work in an aggregate does not cause this License to apply to the other parts of the aggregate.

6. **Conveying Non-Source Forms.** You may convey a covered work in object code form under the terms of sections 4 and 5, provided that you also convey the machine-readable Corresponding Source under the terms of this License, in one of these ways:

    a) Convey the object code in, or embodied in, a physical product (including a physical distribution medium), accompanied by the Corresponding Source fixed on a durable physical medium customarily used for software interchange.

    b) Convey the object code in, or embodied in, a physical product (including a physical distribution medium), accompanied by a written offer, valid for at least three years and valid for as long as you offer spare parts or customer support for that product model, to give anyone who possesses the object code either (1) a copy of the Corresponding Source for all the software in the product that is covered by this License, on a durable physical medium customarily used for software interchange, for a price no more than your reasonable cost of physically performing this conveying of source, or (2) access to copy the Corresponding Source from a network server at no charge.

    c) Convey individual copies of the object code with a copy of the written offer to provide the Corresponding Source. This alternative is allowed only occasionally and noncommercially, and only if you received the object code with such an offer, in accord with subsection 6b.

    d) Convey the object code by offering access from a designated place (gratis or for a charge), and offer equivalent access to the Corresponding Source in the same way through the same place at no further charge. You need not require recipients to copy the Corresponding Source along with the object code. If the place to copy the object code is a network server, the Corresponding Source may be on a different server (operated by you or a third party) that supports equivalent copying facilities, provided you maintain clear directions next to the object code saying where to find the Corresponding Source. Regardless of what server hosts the Corresponding Source, you remain obligated to ensure that it is available for as long as needed to satisfy these requirements.

    e) Convey the object code using peer-to-peer transmission, provided you inform other peers where the object code and Corresponding Source of the work are being offered to the general public at no charge under subsection 6d.

A separable portion of the object code, whose source code is excluded from the Corresponding Source as a System Library, need not be included in conveying the object code work.

A "User Product" is either (1) a "consumer product", which means any tangible personal property which is normally used for personal, family, or household purposes, or (2) anything designed or sold for incorporation into a dwelling. In determining whether a product is a consumer product, doubtful cases shall be resolved in favor of coverage. For a particular product received by a particular user, "normally used" refers to a typical or common use of that class of product, regardless of the status of the particular user or of the way in which the particular user actually uses, or expects or is expected to use, the product. A product is a consumer product regardless of whether the product has substantial commercial, industrial or non-consumer uses, unless such uses represent the only significant mode of use of the product.

"Installation Information" for a User Product means any methods, procedures, authorization keys, or other information required to install and execute modified versions of a covered work in that User Product from a modified version of its Corresponding Source. The information must suffice to ensure that the continued functioning of the modified object code is in no case prevented or interfered with solely because modification has been made.

If you convey an object code work under this section in, or with, or specifically for use in, a User Product, and the conveying occurs as part of a transaction in which the right of possession and use of the User Product is transferred to the recipient in perpetuity or for a fixed term (regardless of how the transaction is characterized), the Corresponding Source conveyed under this section must be accompanied by the Installation Information. But this requirement does not apply if neither you nor any third party retains the ability to install modified object code on the User Product (for example, the work has been installed in ROM).

The requirement to provide Installation Information does not include a requirement to continue to provide support service, warranty, or updates for a work that has been modified or installed by the recipient, or for the User Product in which it has been modified or installed. Access to a network may be denied when the modification itself materially and adversely affects the operation of the network or violates the rules and protocols for communication across the network.

Corresponding Source conveyed, and Installation Information provided, in accord with this section must be in a format that is publicly documented (and with an implementation available to the public in source code form), and must require no special password or key for unpacking, reading or copying.

7. **Additional Terms.** "Additional permissions" are terms that supplement the terms of this License by making exceptions from one or more of its conditions. Additional permissions that are applicable to the entire Program shall be treated as though they were included in this License, to the extent that they are valid under applicable law. If additional permissions apply only to part of the Program, that part may be used separately under those permissions, but the entire Program remains governed by this License without regard to the additional permissions.

When you convey a copy of a covered work, you may at your option remove any additional permissions from that copy, or from any part of it. (Additional permissions may be written to require their own removal in certain cases when you modify the work.) You may place additional permissions on material, added by you to a covered work, for which you have or can give appropriate copyright permission.

Notwithstanding any other provision of this License, for material you add to a covered work, you may (if authorized by the copyright holders of that material) supplement the terms of this License with terms:

a) Disclaiming warranty or limiting liability differently from the terms of sections 15 and 16 of this License; or

b) Requiring preservation of specified reasonable legal notices or author attributions in that material or in the Appropriate Legal Notices displayed by works containing it; or

c) Prohibiting misrepresentation of the origin of that material, or requiring that modified versions of such material be marked in reasonable ways as different from the original version; or

d) Limiting the use for publicity purposes of names of licensors or authors of the material; or

e) Declining to grant rights under trademark law for use of some trade names, trademarks, or service marks; or

f) Requiring indemnification of licensors and authors of that material by anyone who conveys the material (or modified versions of it) with contractual assumptions of liability to the recipient, for any liability that these contractual assumptions directly impose on those licensors and authors.

All other non-permissive additional terms are considered "further restrictions" within the meaning of section 10. If the Program as you received it, or any part of it, contains a notice stating that it is governed by this License along with a term that is a further restriction, you may remove that term. If a license document contains a further restriction but permits relicensing or conveying under this License, you may add to a covered work material governed by the terms of that license document, provided that the further restriction does not survive such relicensing or conveying.

If you add terms to a covered work in accord with this section, you must place, in the relevant source files, a statement of the additional terms that apply to those files, or a notice indicating where to find the applicable terms.

Additional terms, permissive or non-permissive, may be stated in the form of a separately written license, or stated as exceptions; the above requirements apply either way.

8. **Termination.** You may not propagate or modify a covered work except as expressly provided under this License. Any attempt otherwise to propagate or modify it is void, and will automatically terminate your rights under this License (including any patent licenses granted under the third paragraph of section 11).

However, if you cease all violation of this License, then your license from a particular copyright holder is reinstated (a) provisionally, unless and until the copyright holder explicitly and finally terminates your license, and (b) permanently, if the copyright holder fails to notify you of the violation by some reasonable means prior to 60 days after the cessation.

Moreover, your license from a particular copyright holder is reinstated permanently if the copyright holder notifies you of the violation by some reasonable means, this is the first time you have received notice of violation of this License (for any work) from that copyright holder, and you cure the violation prior to 30 days after your receipt of the notice.

Termination of your rights under this section does not terminate the licenses of parties who have received copies or rights from you under this License. If your rights have been terminated and not permanently reinstated, you do not qualify to receive new licenses for the same material under section 10.

9. **Acceptance Not Required for Having Copies.** You are not required to accept this License in order to receive or run a copy of the Program. Ancillary propagation of a covered work occurring solely as a consequence of using peer-to-peer transmission to receive a copy likewise does not require acceptance. However, nothing other than this License grants you permission to propagate or modify any covered work. These actions infringe copyright if you do not accept this License. Therefore, by modifying or propagating a covered work, you indicate your acceptance of this License to do so.

10. **Automatic Licensing of Downstream Recipients.** Each time you convey a covered work, the recipient automatically receives a license from the original licensors, to run, modify and propagate that work, subject to this License. You are not responsible for enforcing compliance by third parties with this License.

An "entity transaction" is a transaction transferring control of an organization, or substantially all assets of one, or subdividing an organization, or merging organizations. If propagation of a covered work results from an entity transaction, each party to that transaction who receives a copy of the work also receives whatever licenses to the work the party's predecessor in interest had or could give under the previous paragraph, plus a right to possession of the Corresponding Source of the work from the predecessor in interest, if the predecessor has it or can get it with reasonable efforts.

You may not impose any further restrictions on the exercise of the rights granted or affirmed under this License. For example, you may not impose a license fee, royalty, or other charge for exercise of rights granted under this License, and you may not initiate litigation (including a cross-claim or counterclaim in a lawsuit) alleging that any patent claim is infringed by making, using, selling, offering for sale, or importing the Program or any portion of it.

11. **Patents.** A "contributor" is a copyright holder who authorizes use under this License of the Program or a work on which the Program is based. The work thus licensed is called the contributor's "contributor version".

A contributor's "essential patent claims" are all patent claims owned or controlled by the contributor, whether already acquired or hereafter acquired, that would be infringed by some manner, permitted by this License, of making, using, or selling its contributor version, but do not include claims that would be infringed only as a consequence of further modification of the contributor version. For purposes of this definition, "control" includes the right to grant patent sublicenses in a manner consistent with the requirements of this License.

Each contributor grants you a non-exclusive, worldwide, royalty-free patent license under the contributor's essential patent claims, to make, use, sell, offer for sale, import and otherwise run, modify and propagate the contents of its contributor version.

In the following three paragraphs, a "patent license" is any express agreement or commitment, however denominated, not to enforce a patent (such as an express permission to practice a patent or covenant not to sue for patent infringement). To "grant" such a patent license to a party means to make such an agreement or commitment not to enforce a patent against the party.

If you convey a covered work, knowingly relying on a patent license, and the Corresponding Source of the work is not available for anyone to copy, free of charge and under the terms of this License, through a publicly available network server or other readily accessible means, then you must either (1) cause the Corresponding Source to be so available, or (2) arrange to deprive yourself of the benefit of the patent license for this particular work, or (3) arrange, in a manner consistent with the requirements of this License, to extend the patent license to downstream recipients. "Knowingly relying" means you have actual knowledge that, but for the patent license, your conveying the covered work in a country, or your recipient's use of the covered work in a country, would infringe one or more identifiable patents in that country that you have reason to believe are valid.

If, pursuant to or in connection with a single transaction or arrangement, you convey, or propagate by procuring conveyance of, a covered work, and grant a patent license to some of the parties receiving the covered work authorizing them to use, propagate, modify or convey a specific copy of the covered work, then the patent license you grant is automatically extended to all recipients of the covered work and works based on it.

A patent license is "discriminatory" if it does not include within the scope of its coverage, prohibits the exercise of, or is conditioned on the non-exercise of one or more of the rights that are specifically granted under this License. You may not convey a covered work if you are a party to an arrangement with a third party that is in the business of distributing software, under which you make payment to the third party based on the extent of your activity of conveying the work, and under which the third party grants, to any of the parties who would receive the covered work from you, a discriminatory patent license (a) in connection with copies of the covered work conveyed by you (or copies made from those copies), or (b) primarily for and in connection with specific products or compilations that contain the covered work, unless you entered into that arrangement, or that patent license was granted, prior to 28 March 2007.

Nothing in this License shall be construed as excluding or limiting any implied license or other defenses to infringement that may otherwise be available to you under applicable patent law.

12. **No Surrender of Others' Freedom.** If conditions are imposed on you (whether by court order, agreement or otherwise) that contradict the conditions of this License, they do not excuse you from the conditions of this License. If you cannot convey a covered work so as to satisfy simultaneously your obligations under this License and any other pertinent obligations, then as a consequence you may not convey it at all. For example, if you agree to terms that obligate you to collect a royalty for further conveying from those to whom you convey the Program, the only way you could satisfy both those terms and this License would be to refrain entirely from conveying the Program.

13. **Use with the GNU Affero General Public License.** Notwithstanding any other provision of this License, you have permission to link or combine any covered work with a work licensed under version 3 of the GNU Affero General Public License into a single combined work, and to convey the resulting work. The terms of this License will continue to apply to the part which is the covered work, but the special requirements of the GNU Affero General Public License, section 13, concerning interaction through a network will apply to the combination as such.

14. **Revised Versions of this License.** The Free Software Foundation may publish revised and/or new versions of the GNU General Public License from time to time. Such new versions will be similar in spirit to the present version, but may differ in detail to address new problems or concerns.

    Each version is given a distinguishing version number. If the Program specifies that a certain numbered version of the GNU General Public License "or any later version" applies to it, you have the option of following the terms and conditions either of that numbered version or of any later version published by the Free Software Foundation. If the Program does not specify a version number of the GNU General Public License, you may choose any version ever published by the Free Software Foundation.

    If the Program specifies that a proxy can decide which future versions of the GNU General Public License can be used, that proxy's public statement of acceptance of a version permanently authorizes you to choose that version for the Program.

    Later license versions may give you additional or different permissions. However, no additional obligations are imposed on any author or copyright holder as a result of your choosing to follow a later version.

15. **Disclaimer of Warranty.** THERE IS NO WARRANTY FOR THE PROGRAM, TO THE EXTENT PERMITTED BY APPLICABLE LAW. EXCEPT WHEN OTHERWISE STATED IN WRITING THE COPYRIGHT HOLDERS AND/OR OTHER PARTIES PROVIDE THE PROGRAM "AS IS" WITHOUT WARRANTY OF ANY KIND, EITHER EXPRESSED OR IMPLIED, INCLUDING, BUT NOT LIMITED TO, THE IMPLIED WARRANTIES OF MERCHANTABILITY AND FITNESS FOR A PARTICULAR PURPOSE. THE ENTIRE RISK AS TO THE QUALITY AND PERFORMANCE OF THE PROGRAM IS WITH YOU. SHOULD THE PROGRAM PROVE DEFECTIVE, YOU ASSUME THE COST OF ALL NECESSARY SERVICING, REPAIR OR CORRECTION.

16. **Limitation of Liability.** IN NO EVENT UNLESS REQUIRED BY APPLICABLE LAW OR AGREED TO IN WRITING WILL ANY COPYRIGHT HOLDER, OR ANY OTHER PARTY WHO MODIFIES AND/OR CONVEYS THE PROGRAM AS PERMITTED ABOVE, BE LIABLE TO YOU FOR DAMAGES, INCLUDING ANY GENERAL, SPECIAL, INCIDENTAL OR CONSEQUENTIAL DAMAGES ARISING OUT OF THE USE OR INABILITY TO USE THE PROGRAM (INCLUDING BUT NOT LIMITED TO LOSS OF DATA OR DATA BEING RENDERED INACCURATE OR LOSSES SUSTAINED BY YOU OR THIRD PARTIES OR A FAILURE OF THE PROGRAM TO OPERATE WITH ANY OTHER PROGRAMS), EVEN IF SUCH HOLDER OR OTHER PARTY HAS BEEN ADVISED OF THE POSSIBILITY OF SUCH DAMAGES.

17. **Interpretation of Sections 15 and 16.** If the disclaimer of warranty and limitation of liability provided above cannot be given local legal effect according to their terms, reviewing courts shall apply local law that most closely approximates an absolute waiver of all civil liability in connection with the Program, unless a warranty or assumption of liability accompanies a copy of the Program in return for a fee.

END OF TERMS AND CONDITIONS